A PEOPLE APART

SUNY Series in Jewish Philosophy
Kenneth Seeskin, Editor

A PEOPLE APART

Chosenness and Ritual in Jewish Philosophical Thought

edited by

Daniel H. Frank

State University
of New York
Press

Published by
State University of New York Press, Albany

Production by Susan Geraghty
Marketing by Fran Keneston

Printed in the United States of America

For information, address State University of New York
Press, State University Plaza, Albany, N.Y., 12246

Library of Congress Cataloging in Publication Data

Library of Congress Cataloging-in-Publication Data

A People apart : chosenness and ritual in Jewish philosophical thought
/ edited by Daniel H. Frank.
    p. cm. — (SUNY series in Jewish philosophy)
  Includes bibliographical references and index.
  ISBN 0-7914-1631-3 (hardcover). ISBN 0-7914-1632-1 (pbk.)
  1. Jews—Election, Doctrine of—History of doctrines. 2. Jewish
law—Philosophy. 3. Judaism—Customs and practices—Philosophy.
4. Philosophy, Jewish. I. Frank, Daniel H., 1950–   . II. Series.
296.3'11—dc20   92-35706
                                                            CIP

10 9 8 7 6 5 4 3 2 1

Contents

INTRODUCTION

This volume of essays twins philosophical speculation on chosenness and ritual in Judaism. The justification for such twinning is historical, for historically Jews have set themselves apart, or have been set apart, on account of their particular rituals. Indeed, the very *idea* of 'chosenness' or 'election' entails some material content for its realization—and historically such content is in large measure ritual, the ritual law.

The Jews are "a people apart," chosen (choosing) to obey a divine law in its entirety, including a belief in their own chosenness. It is unarguable that the doctrine of chosenness (or election) is the most difficult for modern Jews to accept. It smacks of elitism or, at least, an antiassimilationist ideology. But for the last two hundred years our political life in the West has been driven by an antielitist, egalitarian, and assimilationist sensibility on both the individual and the cultural level. "Chosenness," "apartness," seems to resist the modern age. But perhaps not. Perhaps assimilation is compatible with ethnic diversity, if one demarcates assimilation at the political level as a corporate pro-attitude towards *supra*tribal ideals of justice and peace. Diverse cultural units, then, will naturally find their own way to the *common* goal. But such a construal, pleasing (American?) as it may be, will not exhaust the Jewish doctrine of election. Jews are not merely one people among others; they are traditionally taken to be (and take themselves to be) *first* among equals, God's chosen people. It is then the egalitarian side of the modern political sensibility that most fights against chosenness. The question then is: Is it possible for the modern Jew, *ex hypothesi* dwelling in a democratic society, a society that accords equal legal and political rights to all of its members on the basis of a natural equality, to defend the traditional Jewish doctrine of chosenness? Again, how can chosenness be rendered meaningful and viable for the modern Jew, all of whose social and political affiliations are permeated by an egalitarian outlook? To this it should immediately be added that by "modern" Jew I do not mean simply nontraditional, nonobservant Jews.

1

Traditional Jews as well must face the same problem. In fact, perhaps it is they who face it most directly, inasmuch as nontraditional Jews have tended to dismiss chosenness as historically irrelevant. For traditional Jews, chosenness is a real problem, for only they live in two worlds.

With such issues before us, we may turn to the first group of essays. The first three chapters address themselves, historically and systematically, to the problematics of election in Judaism. David Novak, in "The Election of Israel: Outline of a Philosophical Analysis," argues against both detractors and some notable defenders of chosenness. He argues against Spinoza and the kabbalists, on the one hand, and against Michael Wyschogrod and Hermann Cohen, on the other, in presenting his own defense of chosenness. Whereas the former make the election of Israel philosophically indefensible, the latter two, in defending the election of Israel, make it a doctrine abetting either a form of chauvinism (Wyschogrod), or, alternatively, a rather benign form of (nonchauvinistic) nationalism, one that entails the (merely) temporary, albeit necessary, separation of Israel (Jews) from the nations of the world (Cohen). Novak finds both of these latter two views unsatisfactory and, for his part, understands the election of Israel as not necessarily temporary (contra Cohen) but not thereby entailing some form of chauvinism (contra Wyschogrod). For Novak, the Torah, in its entirety, is given to Israel alone, but such an election does not negate the fact that *all* the nations are to live according to the Noahide laws and, as a result, have a share in the messianic era. Jews and non-Jews alike *share* common moral ground, and such obligations as Jews have by virtue of their election at Sinai carry no weight about the eventual reward for all moral agents.

Paralleling Novak's essay, Menachem Kellner, in "Chosenness, Not Chauvinism: Maimonides on the Chosen People," considers the possibility of articulating a Jewishly legitimate version of the doctrine of chosenness that does not entail chauvinism. His inquiry leads him to an examination of Maimonides' writings on the nature of Jews in general and on the notion of chosenness in particular. Kellner finds that Maimonides presents a genuinely Jewish way of affirming chosenness without thereby affirming ethnic superiority. In distinguishing between Jews and Israel, between the ethnic group (the children of Abraham) *and* the faith community, and understanding the latter as an *elective*, Maimonides, according to Kellner, is able to offer a version of election that is at root open ended (nonchauvinistic) and available to *all* who would follow Torah.

In his critique of Kellner's essay, Norbert Samuelson expresses his agreement with the basic thrust of Kellner's project, namely, the desire to develop a nonchauvinistic interpretation of chosenness. But Samuelson believes that Kellner has not succeeded, and cannot succeed, on the basis of Maimonidean materials; Maimonides cannot be rehabilitated to be used for the purposes Kellner wishes. For Samuelson, Kellner's radical distinction on behalf of Maimonides between Jews and Israel, between ethnic group and faith community, is too strong, abets the very position against which he (Kellner) argues, and, finally, is best eliminated to allow for the messianic, futuristic notion of chosenness offered by Hermann Cohen and the late Steven Schwarzschild. For his part, Kellner replies to Samuelson's critique, and all readers will want to follow the twists and turns of the debate closely, determining whether, historically, Maimonides did indeed distinguish between ethnic group and faith community and, if he did, whether such a distinction entails a nonchauvinistic view of chosenness.

The final chapter in this section, Ze'ev Levy's "Judaism and Chosenness: On Some Controversial Aspects from Spinoza to Contemporary Jewish Thought," lays out the role that the doctrine of chosenness has fulfilled in Jewish history, noting that the idea became more pronounced in proportion to oppression, as it furnished a certain ideological self-compensation for the suffering in the diaspora. For Levy, the bubble of such ideological self-compensation, a species of wish fulfillment, was burst by Spinoza, the first Jewish philosopher to come to grips with the doctrine of chosenness and to call it into question. Levy's historical overview next presents a number of post-Spinozistic approaches to chosenness, noting that since the nineteenth century there has been a growing tendency to replace the concept of chosenness by that of 'mission' or 'vocation.' But for Levy, a secular Zionist, such substitutions do not adequately answer the modern critique of the doctrine as historically irrelevant and philosophically illegitimate, inasmuch as it presupposes an indefensible ethnocentrism and is at odds with the Enlightenment ideal of the universal equality of all human beings and the essential equivalence of all human cultures. Levy's essay will force believers in the doctrine of Jewish election on the defensive. Perhaps they will want to enlist Novak and Kellner on their side.

As noted at the outset, the ritual law is paradigmatically expressive of Jewish chosenness. It is through ritual, not dogma, that Judaism has tended to define itself through the ages. But what exactly is the nature of the ritual law? Traditionally a distinction has been made between the *mishpatim* and the *chuqqim,* between the so-called rational laws and ritual laws. This distinction is taken as unproblematic, inasmuch as there seems to be a clear difference between the utility (and rationality) of laws against murder and theft and the apparent lack of utility (and rationality) of laws such as eating meat with milk and wearing cloth of mixed fabric. The latter are the *chuqqim,* the ritual laws, and it is these that are taken to be particularly expressive, even definatory, of Judaism. But as Lenn Goodman, in "Rational Law/Ritual Law," demonstrates, *all* laws have a ritual aspect. Goodman is not out to deny the traditional distinction between the *mishpatim* and the *chuqqim,* any more than was Maimonides in his magnificent discussion of *ta'amei ha-mitzvot* in the third part of the *Guide.* In a sense, Goodman completes Maimonides' project of explicating the law's rationality; where Maimonides is at pains to point out the reason(s) for *all* the laws, even the "ritual" laws, Goodman makes clear that *all* the laws, even the "rational" laws, have a ritual aspect, an aspect that completes their (rational) purpose by symbolically signifying and prescribing the *values* for which they stand. *All* the laws have, and must have, a ritual aspect, for, as Goodman puts it, "the broad moral purposes of law as law underdetermine the precise behavioral prescriptions needed if law is ever to prescribe or proscribe concrete particular actions." Trials and modes of punishment are (clothed in) rituals, and only because they are do the laws that they define have the force they do.

Goodman's essay, presented here in barest outline, repays close study, for if he is right to point to the interconnectedness of reason and ritual, if ritual is not *ipso facto* irrational, then the "idiosyncrasy" of the doctrine of election is diminished. Jews are now to be seen, not as engaged in "strange" rituals, divorced from universal moral values, but rather as involved in presenting, in their own way, those very values. Rituals are now to be understood as means to moral ends, not as (amoral) ends in themselves. I might just add that in following the conceptual thread of his argument, the reader will want to attend to the way in which Goodman develops his own position from historical sources, namely, Saadiah and Maimonides, and engages them in a way that is both historically sensitive and conceptually fruitful.

From law as ritual symbol to law as metaphor, Moshe Sokol, in "*Mitzvah* as Metaphor," develops a theory of ritual *mitzvot* which is grounded in the phenomenon of metaphor. Sokol suggests that the metaphorical function, namely, the restructuring of the reader's or listener's experience of the subject of the metaphor, and the interactive mechanism whereby the metaphor achieves its goal, by causing the reader to experience common features of the metaphor's subjects, may usefully be applied to an understanding of ritual *mitzvot*. Illustrating his thesis by reference to *teki'at shofar* (the blowing of the shofar), Sokol argues that one may best understand the nature of ritual *mitzvot* as aiming at a restructuring of the ritualist's experience of God, the Jewish people, or humanity, and doing so by means of an interaction of the ritualist's experience of the ritual with any or all of these subjects.

Sokol, in offering his metaphorical theory of ritual *mitzvot,* is taking part in the traditional discussion of *ta'amei ha-mitzvot,* the reason(s) or explanation(s) for the *mitzvot*. This project he shares with Goodman, and though the reader will note that Goodman and Sokol disagree about the nature of ritual, the former interpreting it as symbolic, the latter as metaphorical, they both agree that ritual has explanatory power and must be understood teleologically. And for the same reasons as Goodman's essay, Sokol's too seems to carry with it an implicit argument that goes some way toward demystifying the doctrine of divine election in Judaism. If Jewish ritual acts as a metaphor for restructuring the ritualist's experience of God and world, then those very rituals that are definatory of Jewish chosenness must be seen as no different *in kind* from those of other peoples. Given the *general* need of mankind to restructure reality so as to make it more explicable, Jews are now to be seen as differing from other peoples neither in the goals they strive to achieve nor in the use of ritual per se but, rather, in the *particular* rituals they have adopted.

Jewish particularism, the connecting thread between chosenness and ritual, is fully apparent in Joshua Golding's "Jewish Ritual and the Experience of 'Rootedness.'" In his essay, he focuses upon a universal experience, the sense of belonging or 'rootedness,' and discusses this phenomenon with specific reference to traditional participants in Jewish rituals. Such an experience of rootedness in the ritual, of finding one's place in and by means of the ritual, is to be accounted for in terms of what Golding calls "the doctrine of Jewish teleology." This doctrine suggests that the rituals and the commandments of the Torah befit the Jew's nature and that the phenomenon of rootedness, of 'fittingness,' is a sign of this. Nontraditional Jews, Jews who either participate in the rituals non-halakhically or do not participate in them at all, will I think find the essay exclusionary. But at the same time such readers, like those detractors of the doctrine of divine election, will be forced to ask where *they* belong and are rooted.

Norbert Samuelson, in "The Concept of Worship in Judaism" provides a structural overview of the history of different conceptions of worship in Judaism. At least three different notions of worship, that is, interpretations of love of God, emerge in different periods in Jewish intellectual history. For the Judaism of the Hebrew Bible, obedience to communal/ritual law is the highest form of worship. For medieval Jewish philosophy, it is the pursuit of scientific/philosophical truth. Finally, for modern Jewish philosophy, it is the struggle for the social/political good that is the highest form of worship. Although Judaism generally recognizes all three as proper modes of Jewish activity, Samuelson resists the temptation to view them as compatible with each other. The conditions of human finitude, the shortness of human life, require that we prioritize these activities, and here there is no agreement. For Samuelson, the source of the incompatibility of Judaism's multiple views of worship is the incoherence of its different (and incompatible) theologies.

But in a sense the source of such incompatibility is not intrinsic to Judaism itself as much as it is to the indiscriminate borrowing by Jews of (incompatible) *non*-Jewish models of the human good. What, after all, is the source of Judaism's different theologies, theologies that entail, say, philosophy or politics as the *summum bonum?* Again, what is the source of the medieval view that the highest form of worship is the pursuit of philosophical truth? And what is the source of the modern (Cohenian) view that the highest form of worship is the struggle for political and social justice? At first glance, the source would seem to be *extraneous* to Judaism itself; indeed, Aristotle and Kant (or maybe Marx) would seem to be the sources for, respectively, the medieval and the modern positions. Given this, the reader will want to puzzle out the apparent need of Jews to look elsewhere for their own (ultimately incompatible) models of worship and of the human good. Correlatively, one will ask afresh about the essence of Judaism (itself an un-Jewish query?), an essence that seems at first glance derived, parasitic upon other cultures for its being.

In asking about the essence or nature of Judaism, we have come full circle. We began with the doctrine of divine election in Judaism, a doctrine that has stamped Judaism as the most idiosyncratic of religions and Jews as the most parochial of peoples. And now at the end we are seemingly more distant than ever from having any clear idea, assuming there is one, of the essence of Judaism, what makes Judaism what it is. Jews are at once unique and protean, never changing and yet always changing. Perhaps, at least, this much is clear: the Jews are a people apart, a single people destined to find and make explicit ever new ways to express mankind's eternal struggle to worship its creator.

The eleventh and the twelfth annual conferences of the Academy for Jewish Philosophy provided the occasions for the initial presentation of the essays in this volume. The eleventh conference of the Academy, held June 3–4, 1990, in Philadelphia at the Reconstructionist Rabbinical College and at Temple University, focused on chosenness in Judaism. The twelfth conference, held June 9–10, 1991, in Cincinnati at Hebrew Union College-Jewish Institute of Religion, was given over to aspects of ritual in Jewish philosophical thought. In light of the discussions at the meetings, all the essays included herein have been revised. None has been published previously.

The editor is grateful to Kenneth Seeskin for his generous support of this project. In addition, all the participants in the conferences owe a debt of gratitude to the Reconstructionist Rabbinical College, Temple University, and Hebrew Union College-Jewish Institute of Religion (Cincinnati) for the excellent facilities which they provided; in this latter regard, Jacob Staub, Norbert Samuelson, and Barry Kogan are owed much of the debt.

PART 1

Chosenness

CHAPTER 1

The Election of Israel: Outline of a Philosophical Analysis

David Novak

INTRODUCTION

Before beginning the daily study of the Torah, and before one is called to the public reading of the Torah in the synagogue service, Halakhah mandates the recitation of a specific blessing. Like all blessings, it is both a direct second-person statement to God and an indirect third-person statement for whomever happens to hear it. The blessing states: "Blessed are You, Lord our God, king of the universe, who has chosen us from all the peoples (*asher bachar banu mikol ha'amim*) and who has given us his Torah (*ve-natan lanu et torato*)." This statement is an elementary Jewish proposition in the legal sense, inasmuch as its recitation has never been disputed in the history of the Halakhah.[1] Its recitation has liturgical permanence. Theologically, it is an elementary proposition because, as I shall later argue, it is irreducible to any other theological proposition. Such an elementary proposition, especially in the theological sense, calls for philosophical analysis.[2]

The fundamental logical relations exposed by philosophical analysis in this theological proposition are as follows: (1) Israel is related to God by virtue of God's election of her; (2) Israel is related to God by virtue of God's revelation of the Torah to her; (3) Israel is separate from the nations of the world by virtue of God's election of her.

From this analysis two key questions emerge: (1) What is the relation of the election of Israel to the giving of the Torah? (2) Is

11

Israel's separateness from the nations of the world determined by her election alone or by her election *and* her being given the Torah? Later in this paper, I shall try to show how these two questions themselves are interrelated and that the answer to one necessarily entails the answer to the other. Before that can be done, however, a number of other theological implications, both positive and negative, must be noted.

First, the doctrine of the election of Israel implies that the relationship between God and Israel is essentially historical. It is an ongoing temporal process initiated by a free act of the creator God. The theological alternatives to such a uniquely elective relationship are:

1. God is related to Israel because of natural necessity, in the way children are related to their biological parents because of natural necessity. But, although this type of relationship begins at a point in time and is, therefore, temporal, it does not imply that it is the result of specific choice. Only the latter can be properly termed "historical"; hence, everything historical is temporal, but not everything temporal is historical.[3] Furthermore, even if the relationship is chosen by the parents (who either "wanted" the child by virtue of their own autonomy or chose to observe the biblical commandment "Be fruitful and multiply"[4]), it does not imply that the choosing members of this relationship also have a prior and continuing relationship with a larger number of possible objects of their choice.

2. God chooses Israel, but God is and remains the creator and the sustainer of the nations of the world, indeed of the entire universe. For this reason, then, the election of Israel is not totally analogous to the relationship between adopting parents and their adopted children. For, although the relationship between these persons cannot be considered one of natural necessity (as is very often the case, albeit not always, with biological parents and their offspring), nevertheless, the adopting parents are not choosing from among their own creation.

Moreover, unlike either biological or adoptive parenting, the election of Israel involves not only the free act of God, but also the free act of Israel. The fact of election designated by the word *covenant* (*berit*) is not a bilateral pact mutually initiated by God and

Israel.[5] It is, rather, a historical reality created by God. Nevertheless, this historical reality would have no human meaning without Israel's subsequent free acceptance of it and participation in it. For this reason, then, the fact of covenantal election is more often compared to a marriage than it is to parenting. Yet, even here, there is an important difference. Marriage is initiated and sustained by the natural necessity of eros in both partners. In the covenant, conversely, there is more freedom, inasmuch as the divine partner is not bound by any necessity at all, which is a point emphasized by the doctrine of *creatio ex nihilo*.[6] The relationship between God and Israel is much more political than familial, and that is why the image of God as king is used most often in rabbinic tradition, much more than the image of God as either parent or spouse.

ESSENTIAL PRECLUSIONS OF THE ELECTION OF ISRAEL

The essentially free historical character of the covenantal relationship between God and Israel is basically precluded by two very different views of Judaism. What both of these views do have in common, albeit their vast differences otherwise, is their essentially ahistorical view of the relationship between God and man and/or God and Israel. As we shall presently see, these ahistorical views essentially preclude a constitution of the doctrine of the election of Israel.

The most radical preclusion of the election of Israel comes from the philosophy of the original modern Jewish renegade, Spinoza, who so radically separated philosophy from any connection with historical revelation. For Spinoza, truth is that which is necessary and universal. It is not something revealed by a free act from above at a specific time; rather it is eternal and discoverable at anytime, that is, of course, by anyone intelligent enough to do so. All truth is *sub specie aeternitatis*.[7] Eternity and history are mutually exclusive. But, if this were all that Spinoza asserted, he could still be seen as continuing the tradition of the rationalist theology of the middle ages. Thus, Maimonides, to cite a major example, takes revelation to be the highest level of intellection of eternal truth that is possible for a finite intelligence.[8] For him and the others in this tradition, Jewish vision of the eternal truth about God still holds a privileged historical position, however.[9] The

Torah contains within itself the eternal truth in esoteric form (*sitrei torah*). This truth can be decoded, at least by those properly prepared to do so with a philosophically grounded hermeneutic. Although this type of rationalist theology constitutes neither the event of revelation (apart from the event of human discovery of eternal truth) nor the event of election (apart from this same discovery), it still allots a privileged position to both the people and the Torah of Israel in the universal apprehension of that truth. And, as we shall see later in this chapter, two centuries after Spinoza, Hermann Cohen did much the same thing.

Spinoza broke that fundamental connection between Israel and truth by denying the possibility of a philosophically grounded hermeneutic of the Hebrew Bible. He thus laid the philosophical foundation for the historical critical method of Bible interpretation, which, in its classical form, confines the meaning of all biblical texts to the past time and distant place of their original composition.[10] It is not to the texts of antiquity, with the forced hermeneutic devised to make them philosophically useful, that one is to now turn for truth. Rather, one is to search for the necessary and universal metaphysical presuppositions of the newly discovered natural sciences. It is here where truth is to be found. And the best social and political climate for this pursuit is not, for Spinoza, communities founded on historically contingent revelations. The best climate for scientific philosophy is the ahistorical liberal democratic state, where individual intellects are unencumbered by history. Here historical religion (as opposed to the new religion of reason) is at most a private matter, having no public authority whatsoever.[11] This potent combination of philosophy concerned with necessary and universal truths, and liberal, historically anonymous, democracy, precludes any truth for something so historically contingent as the election of Israel by the creator God. Indeed, Spinoza's God, a God whose very essence is interchangeable with that of nature (*natura naturans*), could not be a creator at all in the traditional sense. The formula *deus sive natura* entails the denial of a transcendent God, one who alone could be absolutely free to choose his people. When one affirms *deus sive natura*, God is viewed as immanent within nature itself (*natura naturata*), as nature is totally immanent within God as the fully self-ordering organism (*causa sui*).[12]

Spinoza's radical project (at least, from the perspective of Jewish tradition) is the basis of Jewish secularism and the atheism it fundamentally assumes. For Spinoza, a relationship with an intelligible and scientifically legitimate God and a relationship with the Jewish people as historically constituted are mutually exclusive. It should not be forgotten that his excommunication by the Portuguese Jewish community of Amsterdam in 1656 was anticlimatic. He had already left that Jewish community and Judaism itself for the sake of the integrity of his philosophical convictions. He opted, then, for God over Israel. In that sense, he was anything but an atheist, at least as we use that term today. Jewish secularism, on the other hand, by opting for the Jewish people, while at the same time assuming that if there is a God it could only be like the God of Spinoza, thereby opted for Israel over God. (More radical than either Spinoza or the Jewish secularists are those Jews who have consistently embraced Marxism. Marxist premises leave no room for either God or Israel.[13]) The point in common between Spinoza, who left the Jewish people, and the secularists, who remained with her, is that the transcendent God of the Bible, the rabbis, the rationalist theologians, and the kabbalists is consistently denied. As such, the election of Israel is necessarily denied as well. Only the transcendent God could have possibly chosen her. Spinoza, and those who are his heirs, if not his actual disciples, already precluded the existence of this God from their worldview.

Spinoza's radical project, along with the secularist Jewish alternative that presupposed it, was clearly rejected by that segment of the Jewish people who insisted that the onslaught of modernity had not broken the connection with Jewish tradition or its authority. For them, Judaism remained the everlasting covenant between God and his people Israel. For traditionalist Jews, the relationship was with the creator God of the Bible and the rabbinic writings. For liberal Jews, the relationship often became one with the God who functions as the ontological anchor of the rational universal moral order—a God of reason out of the sources of Judaism, to paraphrase the title of Hermann Cohen's magnum opus of liberal Jewish theology, *Religion der Vernunft aus den Quellen des Judentums* (unquestionably the most philosophically impressive systematic Jewish theology written from any standpoint in modern times).[14] Contrary to Spinoza (whom Cohen never tired of attacking), for a theology that assumes that more truth about God can be discovered through ethics than through metaphysics, history plays a more central role in that discovery; hence, Jewish historical uniqueness can be constituted even here.

Although seeing the relationship of chosenness between God and Israel quite differently, to be sure, both traditionalist and liberal liturgies, to focus on the most authentic locus of theological doctrine in any religious community, could praise God as the One "who chooses his people Israel in love" (*ha-bocher b'amo yisrael b'ahavah*) with complete integrity. Therefore, despite the large number of departures from various halakhic prescriptions pertaining to specific formulations in the traditional liturgy, Reform liturgies, at least until very recently, continued to affirm the traditional doctrines of the revelation of the Torah and, even more so, the election of Israel.[15]

For Spinoza and the Jewish secularists, the doctrine of the election of Israel affirmed too much and, therefore, had to be dropped. On the other hand, it did not affirm enough for that view of Judaism that became the predominant Jewish theology for at least five centuries: the Kabbalah. Although the researches of Gershom Scholem and his disciples and successors have shown how the Kabbalah is, to a certain extent, conditioned by history, in its own terms, the Kabbalah itself is radically ahistorical. Whereas, for Spinoza, *deus sive natura* means that God is wholly immanent within nature and nature wholly immanent within God, for the Kabbalah, the essential connection of God, Torah, and Israel means that nature qua cosmic order is wholly immanent within God, who both includes it and transcends it (hence, it is panentheism).[16] In the Kabbalah there are no external relationships between God and his separate creation; all relationships are in truth internal relations within the Godhead itself. Anything outside the Godhead can only be considered demonic (*sitra achra*).[17] Everything real is in truth a manifestation of the Godhead. In fact, Israel is the only human manifestation of the Godhead; she is the microcosm, and the full ten *sefirot* are the macrocosm of panentheistic being.[18] As such, Israel and humanity are in essence synonymous. There is no humanity outside Israel. In this divine scheme, the nations of the world have no human reality for all intents and purposes.[19]

In this metaphysical scheme, it is clear why the doctrine of the election of Israel cannot be constituted. Election implies that God chose Israel from among all the nations that he created and that

God did so as a transitive act in history. However, if all relations are in truth internal relations of emanation (*atzilut*) within the Godhead itself, it seems that there can be neither *creatio ex nihilo* nor history.[20] And without *creatio ex nihilo* and without history, Israel's relationship with God could not be the result of an act of free choice anymore than one could choose the body parts to which he or she is necessarily connected. Israel is the Godhead in miniature. She is actually more than human, just as the nations of the world are actually less than human. She cannot be chosen from among the nations of the world because, in essence, she has always been part of God and never part of them.

This does not mean, however, that one can exclude Kabbalah from a philosophical constitution of Jewish theology, as one can exclude the thought of Spinoza. Spinoza himself not only left Judaism (which creates a severe problem for any religious Jewish appropriation of his thought); he also left the Jewish people (which creates a severe problem for a secular Jewish appropriation of his thought, even though he has always been a cultural hero for many Jewish secularists). Kabbalah and the kabbalists, conversely, have played just too important a role in the history of Judaism and the Jewish people for that kind of exclusion. Indeed, I would say that any theological reflection (philosophical or not) on Judaism that does not incorporate at least some kabbalistic elements is deficient.[21] Nevertheless, I do not believe that Kabbalah need be taken as presenting elementary theological propositions. Kabbalah, like medieval rationalist theology, is itself a second-order philosophical constitution of elementary theological propositions from Scripture and the rabbinic writings. But unlike Scripture and the rabbinic writings, one can be much more selective in using kabbalistic concepts, as is also the case when using the concepts of medieval rationalist theology. One ought not eliminate either discipline *ab initio*, however. Thus, even though I cannot incorporate Kabbalah at this point in my theological reflection on the election of Israel, I shall incorporate another aspect of Kabbalah at a later point in this chapter. I cannot incorporate Kabbalah at this point in my reflections because in our time, with the ubiquitous presence of historical thinking, it seems to me that the doctrine of the election of Israel must be constituted primarily upon those classical sources where history is taken to be a reality.

THREE BASIC PHILOSOPHICAL THEORIES OF ELECTION

It would seem that a philosophically constituted theory of the doctrine of the election of Israel must be one in which history can be taken as a realm separate from nature and as a realm where a relationship between God and man is possible. We have seen that, for Spinoza and the Jewish secularists, history is not where God and man are related; for the Kabbalah, there is no history at all. We must, therefore, look to those philosophical theories that are not based on either Spinozistic or kabbalistic premises in order to better conceive the doctrine of the election of Israel. What all these theories must have in common is that God and man can engage in external relationships that are temporal and free, that is, historical. In the case of the doctrine of the election of Israel, it will be helpful to see the scheme of such relationships as being that of the interaction between one singularity and another singularity, and the interaction between a singularity and a more general horizon. This can be illustrated by looking at the following well-known source from the Talmud:

> Rav Nachman bar Isaac said to Rav Chiyya bar Avin, "These *tefillin* of the Master-of-the-universe, what are written in them?" He said to him, "Who is like your people Israel, a singular nation [*goy echad*] on earth!" [1 Chron. 17.21] . . . God said to Israel, "You have made me uniquely beloved in the world [*chativah achat ba'olam*], and I have made you uniquely beloved in the world. You have made me uniquely beloved in the world as Scripture states, 'Hear O Israel: the Lord is our God, the Lord alone [*echad*]' [Deut. 6.4] and I have made you uniquely beloved in the world as Scripture states, 'Who is like your people Israel, etc.' "[22]

The three components of this text are God, Israel, and the world. To continue this theological reflection in a more philosophical way, God has singled out Israel from the greater generality of the world, and Israel has singled out God over and above the greater generality of the world. It seems clear that this mutual singling out cannot be recognized by the world for what it truly is. The world can only recognize Israel's relationship with her "god" as being merely peculiar, having no relevance for the world. All it can recognize is difference. Hence, Balaam states of Israel that she is "a people who dwells alone [*levadad*] and is not considered by the nations" (Num. 23.9). Hence, Haman states to the ruler of most of the earth about the Jews that they are "one people [*am echad*] dispersed and separated among all the peoples in all the provinces of your kingdom and that their laws are different from those of every other people" (Est. 3.5). Hence, Pharaoh states that Israel's "god" can make no valid claims on him: "Who is the Lord [YHWH] that I should listen to his voice to release Israel; I do not recognize [*lo yad'ati*] the Lord" (Exod. 5.2).

From this we see that Israel's general relationship with the world is distinct from her singular relationship with God and that God's general relationship with the world is distinct from his singular relationship with Israel. Nevertheless, one's views of both of these relationships are connected. That is, how one views God's singular relationship with Israel is going to determine how one views God's general relationship with the world, and vice versa. And, how one views Israel's singular relationship with God is going to determine how one views Israel's general relationship with the world, and vice versa.

The correlation of the singular relationship between God and Israel, and the general relationship between God and the world and Israel and the world, is indicated by the presence of the Torah in all of them. Although God has chosen Israel and not the world for a singular relationship and Israel has responded accordingly, God has not deprived the world of Torah. According to Scripture and rabbinic tradition, God gave the complete Torah to Israel and a partial Torah to the world.[23] Furthermore, everything in this partial Torah is included in the complete Torah, even though there is much more in the complete Torah than in the partial one.[24] And although Israel's singular relationship with God is different from her general relationship with the world, both relationships are governed by the same Torah: the former one, by the Torah's more specific precepts; the latter, by its more general precepts. Therefore, it is now appropriate to address the questions raised at the beginning of this paper, namely, (1) What is the relation between the election of Israel and the giving of the Torah to her? and (2) Is Israel's disjunction from the nations of the world determined by her election alone, or by her election *and* her being given the Torah?

In modern Jewish thought, I have been able to discern three basic philosophical theories that approach these questions system-

atically. I shall now briefly outline them and then argue for the
third alternative.

THE PRIMACY OF ELECTION

Jewish secularism, in its emergence as a uniquely modern phenomenon, has amply shown that one can maintain Jewish particularism (at least in theory) without basing it on the theological doctrine of the election of Israel by God.

In its more benign manifestations, which usually emphasize
Jewish "peoplehood," this secularism has simply assumed that
national distinctions are part of the natural order, just like distinct
species of plants and animals.[25] Thus, the Jews are distinct from
other peoples, just like the French or the Chinese or the Zulus are
distinct from other peoples. Nevertheless, the utter naïveté of this
biological (and implicitly racist) analogy should be quickly apparent. Jewish secularism seems to be committed to the survival of the
Jewish people, but Jewish survival could be necessarily maintained
by means of this analogy only if one were operating on the premises of an Aristotelian biology, one that posits the permanence of
species. Since Darwin, however, no reputable biologist holds this
view. Species wax and wane in response to the process of natural
selection.[26] Hence, to assume that the Jews are like a natural species presents no grounds for assuming Jewish survival, or even for
arguing against assimilation, when either individual or collective
survival seems to warrant it. At this time, the inability of secular
Zionism to answer the question of why Jews should emigrate to or
even remain in the state of Israel, when they can perhaps survive
better elsewhere, aptly demonstrates the practical significance of
this point.

In its more virulent manifestations, especially those overtly
nationalistic, Jewish secularism has affirmed the distinctiveness of
the Jewish people to be the result of election in history. But, in this
view of Jewish distinctiveness, that election is not the act of God.
Rather, it is the act of the enemies of the Jewish people. In this view,
Amalek, not the Lord, ultimately determines who is a Jew and why
the Jews cannot lose their distinctiveness, even if they want to lose
it. This is what inevitably comes out from those current views of
Jewish history that make the Holocaust the central orienting event

for Jews.[27] And the irony of this view, whether secularist Jewish nationalists acknowledge it or not, is that its most original enunciation came not from a Jew at all but rather from the atheistic French philosopher, Jean-Paul Sartre, in his seminal book, *Anti-Semite and Jew*.[28]

I mention all this because a philosophical constitution of the theological doctrine of the election of Israel cannot assume that a theory of Jewish distinctiveness is necessarily theological. Such a philosophical constitution must be ever cognizant of how election by God essentially differs from the virulent selection made by Hitler (or anyone else devoted to the extermination of the Jewish people) or from our own more benign attempts to justify our desire to live as Jews by means of a survivalism based on some sort of naturalism.

In contemporary Jewish thought, the person who has argued for the theological primacy of the doctrine of the election of Israel most cogently is Michael Wyschogrod. Let us look at his basic point on this matter as expressed in his recent book, *The Body of Faith: Judaism as Corporeal Election:*

> Why does God proceed by means of election, the choosing of one people among the nations as his people? Why is he not the father of all nations, calling them to his obedience and offering his love to man, whom he created in his image? . . .
>
> We must avoid an answer that does too much. Any answer that would demonstrate that what God did was the only thing he could have done or that it was the right thing to do would be too much of an answer. God must not be subject to necessity or to a good not of his own making. He is sovereign and his own master, and must not be judged by standards external to him.[29]

As Wyschogrod develops his point, he invokes the Buberian model of an I-thou relationship, where the relationship itself is its own justification. Like Buber, Wyschogrod maintains that such a relationship has no antecedents.[30] Unlike Buber and more like Rosenzweig, however, Wyschogrod does see this relationship as having consequents, primarily the Torah.[31] God's election of Israel is a presence, one that itself can lead to other factors, but one that cannot be included in any greater whole.

The questions we must now address to Wyschogrod, which are questions to be addressed to any theorist of the doctrine of the election of Israel, are (1) How is this relationship between Israel and God different from any other relationship between a nation and its "god"? (2) How is this relationship correlated with God's creative relationship with the rest of the universe, especially "all the other peoples"? and (3) How does the Torah function in this relationship between God and Israel?

Beginning with the last question first, Wyschogrod clearly sees the Torah as having been given for the sake of the election of Israel, that is, it is the Torah that structures this relationship and gives it its true content.

> But the law is addressed only to Israel. It is not a universal law, obedience to which is expected of all peoples. Apart from the Noachide commandments, the Torah is addressed only to Israel . . . Israel is not the accidental bearer of the Torah. The Torah grows out of Israel's election . . . the Torah is not a demand that exists apart from the being of Israel.[32]

Along these lines, it is evident why Wyschogrod forcefully argues against any suggestion that Jewish identity is contingent on acceptance of the teachings of the Torah and the practice of its precepts. Obviously, he believes that such acceptance and practice enhance a Jew's sense of his or her election and give it meaning. Nevertheless, he seems to argue that the election of Israel is something *sola gratia* and is true even when Jews ignore the obligations of the covenant, even when they reject them.[33] That is why he insists on the total historicity of the Torah; for the historicity of the Torah presupposes the historicity of the Jewish people. Israel is *there*, and *then* the Torah is given to them in relation to their historical situation. Israel's election by God is the primary event and the giving/receiving of the Torah is the secondary event, which is *for the sake of* the continued meaning of this primary event. It is what makes this event found an unending process. Thus, in support of this view, let us note that the correct meaning of "I am the Lord your God who brought you out of the land of Egypt" (Exod. 20.2) is seen by some exegetes as involving this change of syntax: "Because I brought you out of the land of Egypt, I am now the Lord your God".[34] In this view, there seems to be nothing primordial about the Torah. It is thoroughly within history.[35]

We have already seen that the difference between Israel's relationship with God and the relationship of any other nation with its "god" is that Israel's God is also the creator of the universe. As such, there is a correlation between the way one views God's relationship with Israel as its elector and the way one views God's relationship with the rest of the world as its creator. In fact, only this latter relationship enables Israel's relationship with God to be essentially and recognizably different from the relationship of any other nation with its "god."

In Wyschogrod's particular approach, indeed in the last quote from his book, he refers to "the Noachide commandments." Inasmuch as he has in no way indicated that he advocates anything like natural law theory, one can only assume that he regards these Noahide commandments to be just as historically contingent as is the Torah given to Israel. Both are the product of God's revelation in history. The doctrine of the Noahide commandments indicates the belief that God has not left the rest of the world bereft of his guidance, even after his election of Israel. God did not simply turn the rest of the world loose on its own, as Deism would have it. The question is, How is the revelation to the nations of the world related to the revelation to Israel?

Wyschogrod himself does not raise this question. Nevertheless, it is very much implied by his theological typology and, therefore, it can be raised and an answer attempted by someone interested in the implications of his position on the election of Israel, a position having rich precedent in Jewish tradition.

In a somewhat enigmatic passage, Wyschogrod does state,

> And it is also true that a father loves all his children, so that they all know of and feel the love they receive, recognizing that to substitute an impartial judge for a loving father would eliminate the preference of the specially favored but would also deprive all of them of a father. The mystery of Israel's election thus turns out to be the guarantee of the fatherhood of God towards all peoples, elect and nonelect, Jew and gentile.[36]

Looking at this passage in the context of his views of the historicity of revelation, one might say that God is related to the Gentiles *through* his relationship with Israel. What that means is that the Gentiles learn they too are the children of the living God by accepting the fact that God's fullest relationship is the one with Israel, which is described and given normative content in the Torah; for that Torah also expresses God's ongoing concern with them, however secondary it might be. By acknowledging the truth of that relationship and appreciating at least some of its content in their own collective and individual lives, these Gentiles can be subsequent participants in the covenant.[37]

Such acknowledgment and appropriation, since it is totally within history, can be consistently made only by a prior acknowledgment that Israel is God's elect people and that she has received God's most direct and fullest revelation, a revelation that also includes laws by which these Gentiles are to live in a less direct and more fragmentary relationship with God. And, it would seem that the only Gentiles who have ever made any such acknowledgment, however often they have attempted to change it or deny it, are Christians. Only Christianity has accepted the historical truth of God's election of Israel and the revelation of the Torah to them, however much they have departed from Jewish interpretations and application of it. Nevertheless, those Christians who are today attempting to come closer to the Jewish roots of their Christian faith, Christians with whom Wyschogrod has been a major personality in intimate dialogue, seem to be prepared to acknowledge not only the necessity of Judaism for that faith, but also, equally so, the continued primary presence of the Jewish people for it. Indeed, one can see the current theological project of the Protestant theologian Paul van Buren, which van Buren presents as being about "the Jewish-Christian reality," as the Christian counterpart of Wyschogrod's Jewish theology of the election of Israel.[38] Thus, this new Christian interest in the Judaism of the living Jewish people is the historical demonstration of a Gentile response to God's concern for all of his creation, a concern that can be understood and lived only *through* an ongoing contact with Israel as the elect of God.

Although his emphasis on the irreducibility of the election of Israel corresponds to much classical Jewish teaching, I cannot accept Wyschogrod's theory for two reasons: one theoretical, the other practical.

In classical Jewish teaching, there is a dialectic between a theology of grace and a theology of merit. On the one hand, God has chosen the people of Israel, and that choice is clearly not due to any merit on Israel's part. It is *sola gratia*. Thus, in connection with the gift of the land of Israel as an integral part of the act of election of the people of Israel, the Torah emphasizes, "You shall know that it is not because of your righteousness (*lo be-tzidgatekha*) that the

Lord your God is giving you this good land for a possession, for you are a stubborn people" (Deut. 9.6). And in the preceding verse, the reason for God's election is "in order to uphold the word which the Lord your God promised to Abraham, to Isaac, and to Jacob." That, of course, actually begs the question, since no reason is given for the election of the patriarchs, at least not in Scripture itself.[39] But, on the other hand, the covenant requires that the people of Israel merit it by keeping God's commandments in the Torah. Thus, "even though Israel has sinned, it is still Israel" was a doctrine first taught about the Jewish people collectively and then about each and every Jew individually, it was nevertheless recognized by Jewish tradition that there are cases when Jews can stray so far from the Torah that they do indeed forfeit the privileges of their election, both in this world and in the world-to-come.[40] In other words, Wyschogrod's effective subordination of the Torah to the Jewish people is not adequate to the dialectic between grace and merit, between election and obligation, within classical Jewish teaching. The Jewish people is at least as much for the sake of the Torah as the Torah is for the sake of the Jewish people.

If the Torah is only for the sake of Israel's election, then it appears to be in the interest of her nationalistic self-interest. For if the people Israel is the sole raison d'être of the Torah, there is no room left for any higher standard in it by which nationalistic self-interest can be judged. But, clearly, the prophets of Israel taught otherwise. In their teaching, the Lord of nature and history judges Israel as he judges the whole world. Thus the standard of divine judgment—*mishpat*—must be seen as transcending what is being judged by it. "Do you say that the way of the Lord is not right [*lo yitakhen*]? Each man according to his ways shall I judge [*eshpot*] you, O house of Israel!" (Ezek. 33.20). Israel is required to obey the Torah even when it is not in her nationalistic self-interest. Thus, the compromise of Yavneh, which so influenced all subsequent Judaism, surely indicates that national sovereignty was very much qualified in order that the Torah might be supreme.[41]

The practical implication of assuming that the Torah is solely for the sake of affirming the election of Israel is to see no transcendent standard governing Israel's relationships with the nations of the world. The only relationship possible, then, is one where Gentiles accept Jewish sovereignty and dominance, be it political or only "religious"—in the usual Western sense of that distinction.[42]

This does not mean, of course, that this theological stance necessarily entails political programs in which Jews are to dominate non-Jews. Fortunately, in Jewish tradition, practice is not to be simply deduced from theory, especially from theology.[43] In cases where coercion is the issue, a variety of norms need be considered before any final decision is made. Nevertheless, such a theology can all too easily lend itself to such a practical program of dominance. Indeed, a consistent proponent of it would have no theological arguments with which to argue against such programs, however much he or she might be morally offended by them.

This is the point at which an understanding of the present historical situation of the Jewish people is of great import theologically. In introducing this philosophical option in dealing with the theological doctrine of the election of Israel, I noted that mere Jewish distinctiveness can be maintained, without this theological doctrine, on radically secularist grounds. Therefore, a proponent of this doctrine has to argue for election by God over and above mere distinctiveness in the world. However, if the most cogent (even if not necessary) practical implication of this version of the doctrine is Jewish dominance *anywhere*, then what does the theological component add that we would not already have without it, especially when political coercion is so readily available in the world in which we now live? (To offer a current specification of this general question: How does the "religious" Rabbi Goren differ from the "secularist" General Sharon on any issue of political import for Jews today?) Is not the supposed theological grounding actually dismissable by means of the logic of Occam's razor? Is it not vulnerable to the essential atheistic critique of Feuerbach, Marx, and Freud, namely, that theology is nothing but the self-alienated projection of human self-interest onto the level of the superhuman?

The only way out of this theological-political conundrum, it seems to me, is to philosophically understand the doctrine of the election of Israel so that the doctrine of the giving of the Torah is not reducible to it. It would seem that one has to search the tradition for a view of Torah that applies, equally, even if only on certain points, to both Israel and the nations of the world. Only such a discovery can save us from confusing the doctrine of the chosen people from the odious idea of a *Herrenvolk*, an idea directly responsible for our greatest agony in history. Surely, recent

Jewish experience, an experience that most of us are determined to proclaim to the world, must also be a factor in formulating our theology.

THE PRIMACY OF THE TORAH

The well-precedented theological view that sees the Torah as subordinate to the election of Israel, and its correlate, that the nations of the world are to be subordinate to Israel, is paralleled by another equally well precedented theological view. In this view, the election of Israel is subordinate to the Torah, the Torah being understood as the primordial law of the cosmos itself. And although it does not hold that Israel is to be subordinate to the nations of the world here and now—for that would surely undergird an explicit program of assimilation—it does hold that Israel and the nations of the world are subordinate to an ideal of one humanity, an ideal as yet unrealized. In other words, one might say that the former view favors the particular over the universal; the latter view favors the universal over the particular. Since this latter view has been the more defensible in the philosophical tradition from Plato to Hegel, it should come as no surprise that it was most cogently proposed and developed by that modern Jewish thinker who was also most productive and influential as a secular philosopher, Hermann Cohen.

Like all rationalist theologians who have internalized the classical agenda of Western philosophy, Cohen saw the Torah as containing primary and secondary content.[44] In this whole intellectual tradition, the primary content is what is most rational (*muskal*) and the secondary content is rational by virtue of its teleological function on behalf of the primary content (*mefursam*).[45] Of course, what is primarily rational will vary quite considerably, depending on the metaphysical assumptions of the respective theologian. For Cohen, being so influenced by Kant, the primary content of the Torah is the universalizable moral law it contains. The secondary content, which must be justified as a means to the end of the realization of the primary content, consists of all those laws that seem to presuppose the election of Israel in one way or another.[46]

On purely Kantian grounds, the particularism of the doctrine of the election of Israel seems to be an embarassment. Cohen writes:

> Thus the question remains how could this thought of a unique God [*ein einzigen Gottes*] become manifest uniquely and alone [*einzig und allein*] to the spirit of this people? . . . Does not this universalism call into question not only Israel but every people in its particularity [*seiner Sonderheit*]? . . . How incomprehensible the origin of Messianism in the midst of a national consciousness must appear to us, inasmuch as it had to think and feel the "election" [*Erwählung*] of Israel as a singling out [*Auserwählung*] for the worship of God.[47]

To properly understand this passage, one has to understand the significance of the categories of *singularity* [*Einzigkeit*] and *unity* [*Einheit*] in Cohen's philosophy.

For Cohen, the designation of God as *one* (*echad*) does not mean that God is "one" among many, like the number one; nor does it mean that God is one entity composed of various parts.[48] If God were simply one among many, God would be less than the absolute, and monotheism would ultimately be a trivial henotheism. And if God were a unity of many parts, the distinction between God and nature would be destroyed in pantheism (a point Cohen loved to make against Spinoza, whom Cohen, as both a philosopher and a Jew, vigorously opposed).[49] God is, therefore, *einzig*, namely, the only totally transcendent singularity. God alone is Being per se. Human becoming, which is posited as the infinite task of moral perfection by Cohen, is to lead to the unification (*Einheit*) of humankind in relation to God's Being as this singular ideal.[50] As such, it would seem that any individual people claiming for itself true *Einzigkeit* (singularity) would, in effect, be radically confusing human becoming with divine Being. *Einheit* (universal unity) is the true human goal from which no people should detour. Nevertheless, Cohen has an answer to this charge, and in it he shows himself to be a systematic theologian of remarkable philosophical power.

Although Cohen argues that we cannot dispute that authentic monotheism (which is for him the only sufficient ontological ground for universalizable morality) first arose in Israel, such an argument alone would only indicate that the newly emerging universal order should not forget its historical origin. But historical origin is not enough of a reason to argue for the moral necessity of the continued separate existence of the Jewish people in the present, let alone the necessity of the Jewish people to live until the idealized future. And, for Cohen, moral arguments are the only arguments for rational human action.[51] Rather, he argues that the continued separate existence of the Jewish people is necessary until true *Einheit* (human unity) is achieved. Hence, in the absence of such *Einheit* to date, the Jewish people has to remain closer to divine *Einzigkeit* (singularity) than to the state of the world. In the world at present, there is still only national multiplicity (*Mehrheit*), not true totality (*Allheit*).[52] Any premature surrender to the world-as-it-is would be countermessianic, a charge forcefully leveled by Cohen more than once against Christianity.[53] This is how Cohen justifies all those Jewish practices, such as the Sabbath and the dietary laws, which keep Jews apart from the general culture about them. Israel must be montheistic messianism's vanguard for the time being.[54]

The task of the nations of the world is to see in Israel, and the task of Israel is to see in herself, a symbolic vision of the messianic era. Thus, Israel's election/being-singled-out (*Erwählung/Auserwählung*) is to be maintained until there is a true correlation (Cohen's favorite logical term) between the *Einzigkeit* of God and the *Einheit* of humanity: "But this people is less for the sake of its own nation than as a symbol of mankind. A unique (*einziges*) symbol for the unique idea (*einzigen Gedanken*); the individual peoples have to strive to the unique unity (*einzigen Einheit*) of mankind."[55] And, speaking of Israel being the anchor in present reality (*Wirklichkeit*) of this ideal future, Cohen emphasizes the historical necessity of its continued existence into this future: "From the very outset this symbolism presaged [*Vorbedeutung*] Israel's messianic call, its elevation [*Aufhebung*] into one mankind [*Menschheit*]."[56] Israel's uncompleted, hence still warranted, task is "the messianic realization (*Durchführung*) of monotheism."[57]

What is important to see here with Cohen is that the term he uses for the ultimate fulfillment of Israel's historical mission is *Aufhebung*. This term, of course, is the most significant one in Hegel's theory of the progressive manifestation of Spirit.[58] Now Cohen was usually opposed to Hegel. Indeed, his main accomplishment in German academic philosophy in the latter half of the nineteenth century was to turn attention away from Hegel back to

Kant. Yet, Kant's eschatology is quite insufficient for Cohen's messianism, and so he borrows from Hegel, the philosopher who most strenuously attempted to fuse the philosophical quest for the final Absolute (*telos*) with the historical quest for the endtime (*eschaton*).[59] Hegel's key term for this whole process is *Aufhebung*, which designates the temporal means whereby the now separated particular and universal ultimately emerge together as some new future totality, a totality unlike anything theretofore experienced.

Although Cohen's German patriotism does get the better of him occasionally, and he thus seems to see universalism within the expanding German state, with Israel as a part of it, his more rigorous philosophical principles lead him more often than not to reject any such subordination.[60] (Indeed, despite his acerbic anti-Zionism, one could just as easily develop a theory of Zionist messianism from the very principles Cohen proposes.[61]) Both Israel and the nations of the world—in that order—will be truly and satisfactorily united only when both are elevated-and-transformed (*aufgehoben*) into that new humanity. Nevertheless, the universalizable moral law of the Torah, which Cohen posits as its primary content, must here and now engender a correlation of Jews and non-Jews in a secular state.[62] In the state, equality among all citizens is the basic political norm, and religio-cultural particularities are not prematurely suppressed. All this must be emphasized in order to remove the canard that reduces Cohen to a caricature of a politically blind pre-Hitler German Jew, who ultimately offers nothing more than an intricate rationalization for assimilation. Once Cohen is taken with the seriousness his stature as a Jewish thinker deserves, one can begin a proper critique of his philosophical position concerning the theological doctrine of the election of Israel.

The main point of this critique is that Cohen actually turns the classical doctrine of God's election of Israel into a new idea of Israel's election of God. Now, to be sure, the covenant could not function in the human world if Israel had not, does not, and will not *respond* to God's election of her. However, the response is an acceptance of the prior event of God's choice. When Israel does not respond, which happens all too frequently, God reiterates the choice again and again and again. The covenant is always initiated by God, not by Israel, even when Israel's reiteration of it comes centuries after the initial covenantal event.[63]

At this point, it is Cohen's Kantianism that forces him to make what must be considered a basic distortion of classical Jewish doctrine. For Cohen never rejects, or even criticizes, the fundamental Kantian principle that moral law is grounded in the autonomy of the rational will.[64] Unlike both the doctrine of revealed law and the idea of natural law, for Kant, and for Cohen along with him, morality is not one's becoming part of a higher order already real; rather it is one's rational will intending an ideal order of its own making, one that is yet to be. As such, although God's role in Cohen's philosophical-theological system is far more important than it is in Kant's system, even for Cohen, God is introduced into the system *after* the full constitution of rational autonomy.[65] It is, thus, moral autonomy's full realization that requires God, but it is never God who is the first to require moral freedom and the last to judge it. "I am the first and I am the last and there is no authority [*ein elohim*] besides me" (Isa. 44.6). Relative moral freedom to respond to what it cannot ever make or postulate (*bechirah chofshit*/*liberum arbitrium*) is essentially different from the absolute freedom of the creator of any world, real or ideal (*Willensfreiheit*).[66] For Cohen, then, the human person as rational moral agent can only will and choose; he or she can never be chosen by anyone who addresses him or her from above.

For this reason, the whole subordination of the so-called ritual commandments (*bein adam le-maqom*) to the moral commandments (*bein adam le-chavero*) is an inversion of the teaching of classical biblical and rabbinic Judaism. In terms of the commandments, both types of commandments are equally from God.[67] In terms of the object of the commandments, however, those between man and God directly intend the relationship between man and God. Those between man and man directly intend the relationship between man and man and ultimately intend the relationship between man and God. That is why the latter commandments are included in the realm of the former commandments, but not vice versa. Thus, one guilty of a sin against another human is also guilty of a sin against God, but one guilty of a sin against God is not also guilty of a sin against other humans.[68] This does not mean, of course, that one cannot see evident interhuman goods as being intended by many of the commandments that pertain to interhuman relationships. However, as Maimonides pointed out in his critique of Saadiah and Jewish *kalam* in general, the ultimate intelligibility of all the commandments must be seen in the primacy of the human relationship with God, which, transcending the bounds of the specifically moral realm, is thereby irreducible to it.[69] Cohen's moral universalism, on the other hand, is, therefore, not sufficient to properly constitute the primacy of God, which is the indispensible ground for both the revelation of the Torah and the election of Israel.

Whereas Wyschogrod unbalances the traditional dialectic of grace and merit/election and revelation in favor of a view of election *sola gratia,* Cohen unbalances it in the other direction. It would seem that, for him, only those who merit being Israel—the symbol of ideal humanity—are in fact the elect of God. Yet Jewish tradition has continually affirmed that even those Jews whose apostacy might remove them from communication with normative Jews in this world and in the world-to-come are still part of Israel, God's elect people, and cannot be considered dead and beyond God's call to return (*teshuvah*).[70] Individual Jews, even groups of Jews, can deny their election in the most audacious ways, but from God's point of view, as presented in biblical revelation and rabbinic tradition, they cannot annul a covenant they themselves neither initiated nor are capable of terminating.[71] The covenant is more real than ideal.

Even those who desire to convert to Judaism must cast their lot with the Jewish people in the present, real historical situation, at least as much as they must ideally accept the obligation of all the commandments of the written and oral Torahs.[72] And like the people of Israel herself, converts do not become part of Israel because of their own choice. That is only a precondition. Rather, like Israel herself, they must become elect because they have *been elected.* The members of the Jewish tribunal who accept them, functioning as agents of the divine court, always have the option not to accept them.[73] Their choice is free; they are not functioning out of any necessity.

THE CORRELATION OF ELECTION AND REVELATION

The inadequacy of the respective views of Wyschogrod and Cohen concerning the doctrine of the election of Israel can be seen in the inadequacy of their respective correlations of this doctrine with the doctrine of the revelation of the Torah. And the specific locus of this inadequate correlation can be seen in their invocation of the doctrine of the Noahide laws. For Wyschogrod, on the one hand, the Noahide laws are the exception to his general principle that the Torah pertains exclusively to Israel. Yet he does not explain how that exception can be admitted by his theory of election/revelation. For Cohen, on the other hand, the Noahide laws are the essential content of the Torah precisely because they are exclusively moral, and the essence of the Torah is morality. Yet he cannot explain the whole thrust of Scriptural and rabbinic teaching, which emphasizes that the revelation to Israel is higher and more complete than the revelation to the world at large, that is, that the Torah is concerned with much more than just morality.

The doctrine of the Noahide laws indicates that the normative content of the Torah is twofold: the major part pertaining to the relationship between God and Israel; the minor part pertaining to more general human relationships. The major part of the Torah consists of the 613 commandments; the minor part consists of the 7 Noahide commandments. Elsewhere I have argued that the best way to understand the relation of these two parts is to see the Noahide Torah as the precondition that makes the acceptance of the complete Mosaic Torah possible.[74] The acceptance of the highest law presupposes that those accepting it are *already* living according to law and that their law is open to a higher and more complete realization of its full intent. Furthermore, this preconditional law is incorporated intact into that higher law. It is not sublated (*aufgehoben*) beyond recognition of its original structure and content. Rather, it functions as the moral condition of that higher law.[75] It is a norm for creation, one whereby human persons accept the individual limitations required by the recognition of their mutual transcendence of each other *in* society and the collective limitations required by the recognition of the unilateral transcendence by God *of* their society and humankind per se.[76] Finally, this law, which connects Israel with her pre-Sinaitic past, is also that which connects her with her non-Jewish neighbors. Only when Israel perceives that her non-Jewish neighbors are consistently bound by this law, however they recognize it, can any morally significant relationship with them be maintained.

Wyschogrod, it seems to me, does not account for this relation between his theory of election and his recognition of the Noahide laws, because he does not constitute any antecedents to the event of election. Following Rosenzweig more closely than Buber, however, he does see consequents of the event of election, namely, the normative content of the Torah. His theology involves a consistent commitment to the authority of the commandments and the halakhic system that structures them, interprets them, and applies them. Nevertheless, for him, as we have seen, to constitute antecedents, is to reduce God's free choice to some reality prior to God, a point philosophers have long termed the "Euthyphro problem."[77]

At this point, a Kantian distinction can be helpful. There is a distinction between a cause (*Ursache*) and a condition (*Bedingung*). A cause grounds its necessary effect/consequent. A condition only prepares a possible consequent. Thus, if a causal link is established between A and B, then it is necessary that B follows A. That is the law of sufficient reason.[78] A sufficiently grounds the occurence of B. But, if A only presents a condition making it possible for B to occur, then it is not necessary that B follows A. B cannot occur without A. The mere presence of A in no way guarantees the subsequent occurence of B.[79] Other more direct factors must intervene. To confuse a condition with a cause is to confuse a *conditio sine qua non* with a *conditio per quam*.

If we transpose this etiological scheme to the question of the Torah, we might say that the acceptance of the Noahide laws is a necessary but not sufficient condition for God's election of Israel—the context of the major part of the Torah.[80] God would not have chosen Israel if it had been lawless or living by a law opaque to God's unilateral transcendence; yet this does not explain the cause for God's choice. Thus recognition of *an* antecedent condition does not preclude God's freedom of choice in a way that recognition of *the* antecedent ground or cause would preclude it.

Let it not be inferred from this invocation of Kant that the rejection of the position of Wyschogrod leads me to the position of Cohen. Cohen's theory of election is based on his theory of morality, a theory that proceeds from Kant's second critique, the *Critique of Practical Reason*. My invocation of Kant, conversely, is Kant's theory of the possibility of experience. Of course, this means taking "experience" more broadly than Kant did. He confined it to mute sense experience, whereas I mean it to apply to the experience of verbal revelation. That use of Kant comes from the first part of the first critique, the *Critique of Pure Reason*. For me, the constitution of autonomy as the ground of morality and religion, which Kant presents at the end of the first critique and in the entire second critique, can never escape an essentially atheistic presupposition: man, not God, is the measure of all things.[81] This presupposition remains ubiquitous in all Kantianism, even despite the Herculean efforts to move beyond it made by Cohen.[82]

Cohen sees the election of Israel as having both an antecedent and a consequent. This antecedent and this consequent are essentially identical, and they are both necessary. The antecedent is the idea of universal humanity, which is intended by the moral law. The consequent is the realization of this ideal in the messianic era. Israel is "elected" in the sense that she preserves in her religious/cultural life this ideal, which she has discovered, *until* the rest of humankind is ready to accept it. She is the first to discover it and will not resign her historical particularity until that ideal is realized in world history, that is, until it is recognized and practically accepted by a united humanity. In his use of traditional Jewish terms, Cohen posits the antecedent of Jewish singularity to be the Noahide laws, and this latter is its consequent as well. Israel's ultimate *telos/eschaton* is to return to the (universal) Noahide laws, which she need no longer protect with the "fences" of her historically contingent particularity.[83] Her unique existence, then, is provisional. However, in utter contradistinction to all of this, traditional Jewish messianic doctrine suggests that the nations of the world will ultimately be included in a redeemed Israel. Their universality, not Israel's singularity, will be overcome (*aufgehoben*).[84] Certainly, following the Christian schism, Judaism emphasizes that the commandments of the full Mosaic Torah will not be overcome even in the days of the Messiah.[85]

Although the election of Israel has an antecedent, that election is not reducible to that antecedent, because it functions as a condition, not a ground. As such, the major part of the Torah is not universal law, nor is it particular law functioning for the sake of universal law as it is for Cohen. That is why when the Torah does give reasons, they are historical reasons for its commandments much more often than they are universal ones.[86] This can be seen in the presentation of the three basic types of commandments: (1) *mishpatim;* (2) *edot;* and (3) *chuqqim.*

The *mishpatim* are civil and criminal laws, which, according to the rabbis, reason would have dictated even if they had not been revealed.[87] They are, nevertheless, seen as part of revelation because they participate in a larger covenantal context, one that reason could not dictate since it is rooted in unique historical events, not uniform universal processes. The *edot,* on the other hand, are those laws that testify to covenantal events by symbolic reenactment. They compose that part of revelation that gives tradition its historical intention and continuity. They are most directly concerned with the election of Israel.[88] Finally, the *chuqqim* are those laws having neither universal nor historical reasons, laws accepted because of God's authority alone, laws that have no analogues in the positive law of any other people.[89] In this scheme, the election of Israel—what is most directly experienced in the practice of the *edot*—has two antecedents and one consequent. The antecedents themselves are not identical, nor is either of them identical with the consequent.

The *mishpatim* are the antecedents of the *edot,* inasmuch as Israel is part of the universal human order before she is part of the special covenantal order.[90] The covenant presupposes humanity. Since a presupposition is a condition, and not a ground, the *edot,* therefore, transcend the *mishpatim* in intensity and detail. They are not reducible to them as parts to a larger whole, nor are the *mishpatim* simply the means to the *edot* as ends. The *edot* are the modes of Israel's active, responsive experience of God's elective and ongoing love for her in the covenant. Thus, the *edot* are intercovenantal, involving the collective relationship of Israel with the Lord and simultaneously with each other.[91] The *mishpatim,* though, are included in the covenant, but they are not subsumed by it. As such, the *mishpatim* also govern Israel's extracovenantal relationship with the other nations of the world, her human neighbors in the order of creation.

The *chuqqim* are the antecedents of Israel's election actively experienced through the *edot.* They are antecedents in the sense that they prevent the covenant from becoming a symbiosis between God and Israel, a symmetry between God and Israel as functional equals.[92] Precisely because they have neither universal nor historical reasons, because their sole authority is God's mysterious will, are they able to function as active reminders that Israel is totally immanent *in* the covenant, but that God is both immanent *in* it and *beyond* it. In kabbalistic terms, which most insightfully illustrate this point, God is both *in* the *sefirot* (manifestations) and beyond them as the *Ein Sof* (infinity). The *chuqqim,* then, are as mysterious as creation itself, a point God reiterates to Job when the human temptation to judge God by a common standard arises: "Where were you when I established the earth . . . when I prescribed its limit [*chuqqi*]" (Job 38.4, 10). The ubiquity of the *Akedah* in Jewish consciousness, especially her liturgical consciousness, reiterates this point. The *Akedah* commandment is the archetypal *choq*.[93]

Whereas the *mishpatim*, qua universal order, function as the intelligible precondition or general antecedent of the covenantal *edot*, the *chuqqim*, qua divine fiat, function as their unintelligible precondition or singular divine antecedent. The *chuqqim* declare God's primal authority, which transcends both humanity in general and the specific history of the covenant with Israel. They declare that in the normative order of the cosmos, existence is prior to essence and that God is to be obeyed because "I am who I am" (*ehyeh asher ehyeh*) (Exod. 3.14).[94]

ELECTION, REVELATION, AND THE REDEEMED FUTURE

If one posits the antecedents of the election of Israel or of the giving of the Torah to be causes, then the relation of these antecedents to the ultimate consequents of election or revelation will also be part of this causal continuum, functioning as its telos. One sees this clearly in Cohen. He posits the revelation of the Torah (understood as the *discovery* of universal moral law) as the cause of the election of Israel (understood to be the first *discoverers* of that law). This is then to lead to the messianic era, the historical endtime when that law will have full hegemony over all humanity. Therefore, revelation is the original cause, and redemption is the final result. The election of Israel functions in his theory as the mediating reality between the transcendental origin and the ideal conclusion of history.

If one, however, sees the antecedents of the election of Israel and the revelation of the Torah to her to be only conditions rather than causes, then the final consequents of that election and revelation cannot be seen as simply projections from either state of affairs. They cannot be seen as the fulfillment of the hegemony of the covenant and its content (*torat yisrael*), inasmuch as the Torah in toto is concerned with more than the election of Israel. It is also concerned with the elementary moral norms that the Creator has made discoverable by his unique human creatures in their own nature.[95] And it is also concerned with God's absolute commandments, which seem to have no historical meaning at all and, hence, no covenantal intent. Furthermore, it cannot be seen as the fulfillment of the hegemony of the Torah, qua universal moral law, inasmuch as the Torah is mostly concerned with the nonprovisional singularity of Israel's historical existence. As such, the final redemption cannot be a projection from either of these states of affairs. This is clarified in the fact that a major trend in rabbinic theology emphasizes that at the time of the final redemption neither the original election of Israel nor the authority of the commandments of the Torah will become superfluous. Of course, they both would become superfluous if they were simply *means* to this final end, for once a final end has been achieved, the means leading up to it become superfluous.[96] All that can be known about the final redemption, then, is that the estrangement between God and Israel will be ultimately overcome, and that God's redemption of Israel will be central in his redemption of all his creation—that the Lord will be king of Israel together with his being king over all the earth.[97]

Only when the election of Israel or the revelation of the Torah is seen as a means to another end, namely, the hegemony of the covenantal Torah or the hegemony of the Torah qua universal morality, only then is the redeemed future seen as a simple projection from the present, rather than as a new divine trajectory into nature and history. In the modern age such projections have often presented themselves as some commonly achievable *atechalta de-ge'ulah* (the beginning of redemption).[98] However, as a new divine trajectory into nature and history, the final redemption can only be hoped for; it cannot be predicted. We can only have faith *that* it will come to be (*zehuto*); we cannot have any knowledge of *what* it will come to be (*mahuto*). "No eye has seen but yours O God what you will do for those who wait for you" (Isa. 64.3).[99]

This philosophical approach to the theological doctrine of the election of Israel has profound implications for the two most important political questions facing the Jewish people today: (1) Who is a Jew? and (2) What is the relationship of Jews with non-Jews?

As to the question of who is a Jew, the doctrine of the election of Israel presented here says more than the halakhic answer con-

cerning maltrilineal descent or legally valid conversion. It says that
a Jew is one who, with his or her people, has been chosen by God
in love. That love justifies the commanded response to love God in
return (*ahavat Hashem*) and to love every other member of this
people (*ahavat yisrael*).[100] As such, the doctrine of the election of
Israel teaches that, within the parameters of Halakhah, every effort
must be made to practice that love towards every Jew. Appreciation
of the chosenness of the Jewish people, in correlation with the
authority of the Torah, teaches that no halakhic option be taken
that further exacerbates separation among Jews, when another
more unifying halakhic option can be employed.[101] To add strictures, whose effect is to exclude more and more Jews from one's
conception of Jewish religious community (*keneset yisrael*), is to
reduce the election of Israel to the Torah, that is, one's own view of
the Torah's intent (*da'at Torah*). That, as we have seen, is theologically arguable. But the doctrine of the election of Israel also
teaches that valid halakhic distinctions between Jews and non-Jews
be continually respected, so that a Jew can have an objective criterion for determining who the recipient of his or her Jewish love
truly is. To alter the laws of the Torah for the sake of "Jewish
unity" is to sever the election of Israel from its relation to the
Torah. But it is only the Torah that instructs us *that* Israel is chosen
and *how* her chosenness is to be lived.[102]

As to the question of what is the relationship of Jews with non-
Jews, the doctrine of the election of Israel, as presented here, removes the temptation of chauvinism. It does not say that Israel is
somehow more human than anyone else. It does not place Israel
above the nations of the world in any area of purely human interaction. It says that Israel's election is an intimate matter between her
and God.[103] By not reducing the entire Torah to this relationship,
but rather by emphasizing its universal aspect as well, the doctrine
of the election of Israel enables Jews to function as equals with
non-Jews in those areas where common human issues are at stake.
It does not say that election creates any special privileges in the
world, even those of *noblesse oblige*. And by not seeing the redeemed future as any kind of projection from a present human
state of affairs, Israel cannot claim to be any more redeemed than
anyone else. This lack of redemption, either Jewish or universal, is
a point Jews have always emphasized when the adherents of other
religions and other ideologies have made triumphalist claims

against them, claiming that the world is already redeemed.[104] What God will finally do with the world is as mysterious as what God has been doing with Israel in the past and in the present.

NOTES

Two philosophically formulated terms appear regularly throughout this paper and call for an explanation *ab initio*.

1. *Constitution:* "I use it in the fundamental sense that Husserl did—a reconstruction of a datum within consciousness, as opposed to representation in the empirical sense in which a datum is posited as being viewed as it immediately appears. See Husserl, *Ideas*, sec. 86 . . . I differ from Husserl in that the basis of this constitution is not the ego qua cogito, but a standpoint within Judaism as a living religious tradition to which I am primarily bound" (Novak 1989, p. 159 n. 24).

2. *Relation:* By this term I mean "relation" in the sense of the German *Verhältnis*, viz., the connection of constituted essences as parts of a larger prior whole. Hence, essences or ideas are "related"; and if the relation is symmetrical, they are "correlated." I contrast this with the term *relationship*, which is used in the sense of the German *Beziehung*, viz., the interaction *between* persons (who, not being essences, can never be philosophically constituted). The structure of this interaction flows *from what is between* the persons and does not function as a prior enclosing structure of any kind. See Novak 1985, pp. 131–34.

1. See *Berakhot* 11b and Rashi, s.v. "ve-hi me'ulah"; *Berakhot* 21a re Deut. 32.3; *Y. Berakhot* 7.1/11a; Nachmanides, *Addenda to Maimonides' Sefer ha-Mitzvot* pos. no. 15.

2. See Wittgenstein 1961, 4.2–4.23.

3. The distinction between historical time (*rega/sha'ah*) and physical time (*zeman*) is made by R. Judah Loewe of Prague (Maharal). See *Gevurot ha-Shem* intro. 2.

4. Note that the commandment to procreate (Gen. 9.1; see *M. Yevamot* 6.6; *Yevamot* 65b and *Tos.*, s.v. "ve-lo"; Rabbenu Nissim on *Alfasi: Kiddushin*, chap. 2, beg.) is spoken *to* the first human pair (*lahem*) as opposed to the creation of the animal instinct to procreate, which is only spoken *about* them (Gen. 1.22–see Nachmanides' comment thereon).

5. See Novak 1988b, pp. 54ff.

6. See Kaufmann 1960, pp. 127–28, 298–301. Of course, one can easily show that the strict doctrine of *creatio ex nihilo* might well not be literally biblical. Along these lines, see Levenson 1988, pp. 3ff. Nevertheless, it is an understandable development out of those biblical texts

that emphasize the transcendence of God. See Maimonides, *Guide* 2.13. If God is not the free creator of *everything,* then something else, at least in one sense or other, is coeval with God. See Steinheim 1990, p. 301. Cf. Gersonides, *Milchamot* 4.2.1. For the selection through philosophical hermeneutics of absolute transcendence as God's unique property, see Maimonides, *Mishneh Torah: Hilkhot Yesodei ha-Torah* 1.7–9.

7. See *Ethics 5*, prop. 29.

8. See *Mishneh Torah: Hilkhot Shemitah ve-Yovel* end; *Guide* 2.35, 3.29; Letter to R. Chasdai ha-Levi of Alexandria in *Iggerot ha-Rambam* vol. 2, p. 689.

9. See *Commentary on the Mishnah: Shemonah Peraqim* intro.; *Mishneh Torah: Hilkhot Avodah Zarah* 11.16; *Mishneh Torah: Hilkhot Kidush ha-Chodesh* 17.24.

10. See *Tractatus Theologico-Politicus* chaps. 4–5, 7; also, Strauss 1965, pp. 251ff.

11. See *Tractatus Politicus* 3.10.

12. See Yovel 1989, vol. 1, pp. 148, 161–62; vol. 2, pp. 33, 122.

13. Thus in his early essay, "Zur Judenfrage," Marx's atheism and his anti-Semitism are presented in tandem. See Marx 1975, vol. 3, pp. 151, 174.

14. See Cohen 1972, chaps. 1, 3.

15. See, e.g., *The Union Prayerbook* 1975, pp. 47, 198.

16. See, esp., *Zohar: Acharei-Mot* 3.73a.

17. See Scholem 1980, pp. 187ff.

18. See *Zohar: Bereshit* 1.20b; also, Tishby 1957–61, vol. 2, pp. 3ff.

19. See *Yevamot* 60b–61a re Ezek. 34.31 (cf. *Tos.,* s.v. "ve'ein"; *Zohar: Emor* 3.104b.)

20. See Scholem 1956, pp. 108ff.

21. See Pallière 1985, pp. 169–70, where Pallière reports the critique of the theology of R. Samuel David Luzzatto (d.1865) made by Pallière's teacher and Luzzatto's younger colleague, R. Elijah Benamozegh (d. 1900) for its neglect. See also Novak, introduction to Pallière 1985, pp. x–xiv.

22. *Berakhot* 6a. See Kohut, *Arukh Completum,* vol. 3, p. 372, s.v. "chatav"; also, *Chagigah* 3a, Rashi, s.v. "chativah achat."

23. See the extensive treatment of this whole topic in Novak 1983.

24. See Maimonides, *Mishneh Torah: Hilkhot Melakhim* 9.1.

25. See Kaplan 1957, pp. 180–81.

26. See Darwin 1958, intro.

27. This comes out even in the works of theologians who make the Holocaust the central event of their theology. See, e.g., Fackenheim 1970, p. 81; Fackenheim 1982, pp. 201ff.; Cohen 1981, pp. 10–11.

28.   Originally published as *Réflexions sur la Question Juive*. However, the English translator has captured Sartre's argument quite well in the very syntax of his English title, *Anti-Semite—and Jew*. Hence, Sartre speaks of the "the authentic Jew who thinks himself as a Jew because the Anti-Semite has put him in the situation of Jew" (Sartre 1965, p. 150).

29.   Wyschogrod 1983, p. 58.

30.   See Buber 1970, pp. 62–63.

31.   See "The Builders: Concerning the Law" in Rosenzweig 1955, pp. 77ff.

32.   Wyschogrod 1983, p. 211.

33.   Wyschogrod 1983, pp. 174ff.

34.   See *Mekhilta: Yitro*, pp. 222–23; M. *Berakhot* 2.2; Nachmanides' comment on Exod. 20.2.

35.   For the notion of a primordial, transcovenantal Torah in rabbinic theology, see *Pesachim* 68b re Jer. 33.25; *Bereshit Rabbah* beg.; Rashi's comment on Exod. 33.9.

36.   Wyschogrod 1983, p. 65.

37.   See Novak 1989, pp. 117–18.

38.   See van Buren 1980, pp. 132, 156.

39.   However, for the whole theme in rabbinic theology of Abraham's discovery of God that merited his initial election, see Ginzberg 1909–38, vol. 5, p. 210 n. 16.

40.   *Sanhedrin* 44a re Josh. 7.11. Cf. M. *Sanhedrin* 10.1ff.; Lewin, *Otzar ha-Geonim: Yevamot*, 1936, nos. 76–88, 474–475; *Mordecai: Yevamot*, nos. 12, 28–29; *Rosh: Baba Metzia*, 5.52; Schreiber 1855, no. 89.

41.   *Gittin* 56b.

42.   See Maimonides, *Mishneh Torah: Hilkhot Melakhim*, 8.10, 9.14. Cf. Nachmanides' comment on Gen. 34.13.

43.   *Y. Peah* 2.4/10a; Lewin, *Otzar ha-Geonim: Chagigah*, nos. 67–69.

44.   See Cohen 1972, pp. 351ff., citing a number of medieval Jewish rationalist theologians as precedents for this point.

45.   See, e.g., Maimonides, *Guide* 1.2, 2.33; also, Novak 1983, pp. 280ff.

46.   Note: "God and morality. Only these ends are absolute ends. Only they have value in themselves . . . There cannot be, therefore, any other ends but these two, which are united in one end: God" (Cohen 1972, p. 353). See Cohen 1972, pp. 258, 341, 363.

47.   Cohen 1972, p. 243 = *Religion der Vernunft aus den Quellen des Judentums*, p. 284. For the type of critique that Cohen was attempting to answer (here by anticipation), see Voegelin 1956, vol. 1, p. 327. For an insightful treatment of how the embarassment with the singularity of

historical events in the God-man relationship came to full force in eighteenth century Deism, see Taylor 1989, pp. 273–74.

48. See Cohen, *Jüdische Schriften*, vol. 1, pp. 87–99. Note: "Die Einheit ist nicht die Eins; nicht ein Ding, sondern eine Tätigkeit" (Cohen 1922, p. 66). See Cohen 1922, pp. 169–70, 474.

49. See, e.g., Cohen 1972, p. 45.

50. "Das aber ist der Sinn der Religion der Propheten . . . dass er den Staatenbund der Menschheit vorbereitet in der messianischen Idee der vereingten Menschheit" (Cohen 1923, p. 500).

51. See Cohen 1972, pp. 4ff.

52. "Die Einheit nicht minder Mehrheit gedacht werde . . . Die Sonderung muss ebenso sehr und ebenso bestimmt als Vereinigung werden" (Cohen 1922, p. 60). "Die Mehrheit nicht lediglich als Gegenwart gedacht, sondern in die Zukunft gehoben wird" (Cohen 1922, p. 63).

53. See Cohen 1972, pp. 240, 249, 264.

54. See Cohen 1972, p. 359.

55. Cohen 1972, p. 253 = *Religion der Vernunft*, p. 295.

56. Cohen 1972, p. 260 = German, p. 303.

57. Cohen 1972, p. 267 = German, p. 312.

58. See Kaufmann 1966, p. 144.

59. This meaning of *telos* and *eschaton* is clearly expressed by Hegel at the conclusion of *Phänomenologie des Geistes* (Hegel 1952, p. 564): "*Das Ziel*, das absolute Wissen . . . in der Form der Zufälligkeit erscheinenden Daseins, ist die Geschichte, nach der Seite des begriffnen Organisation aber die *Wissenschaft* des *erscheinden Wissens*, beide zusammen, die begriffne Geschichte, bilden . . . die Wirklichkeit, Wahrheit und Gewissheit." Cf. Heidegger 1961, pp. 49–50.

60. Unfortunately, Cohen's two essays "Deutschtum und Judentum" (note the very ordering in the title) in Cohen 1924 (vol. 3, pp. 237ff., 302ff.) are taken as necessary conclusions of his philosophical position, which they are not.

61. See "Kohen ve-Navi," in Achad Ha'Am 1949, pp. 90–92.

62. See Cohen 1972, p. 123; also, Cohen 1924, vol. 1, pp. 159–60.

63. See *Shabbat* 88a.

64. "Die Selbständigkeit der Ethik beruht auf der Selbständigkeit ihres Gesetzes" (Cohen 1922, pp. 301–2). "Die Autonomie bedeutet das Prinzip der Deduktion in der Ethik . . . Die deduktive Autonomie schliesst ebenso aber auch die absolute Spontanität aus" (Cohen 1922, pp. 581–82).

65. See Cohen 1923, p. 470.

66. See Cohen 1923, pp. 321–25; also, Arendt 1978, vol. 2, pp. 28–29, 89.

67. See *Chagigah* 3b re Exod. 20.1 and Eccles. 12.11.

68. See, e.g., *Sifra: Vayiqra* 27d re Lev. 5.21; *T. Sanhedrin* 9.7 re Deut. 21.23; *M. Yoma* 8.9 and *Yoma* 87a re I Sam. 2.25; *Yevamot* 6b re Lev. 19.3 and *Tos.*, s.v. "kulkhem".

69. See *Commentary on the Mishnah: Shemonah Peraqim*, chap. 6; *Mishneh Torah: Hilkhot Melakhim* 8.11.

70. See *Sanhedrin* 44a re Josh. 7.11; *Yevamot* 47b. The erroneous custom of literally mourning an apostate Jew as dead is based on a famous corrupt reading of an halakhic text. See *Mordecai: Moed Qatan*, no. 896; Schreiber 1855, *Yoreh Deah*, no. 326. Cf. *Rosh: Moed Qatan*, chap. 3, no. 59 re R. Isaac of Vienna; *Or Zarua: Hilkhot Avelut*, no. 428. Designating an apostate Jew as dead was, however, a Karaite practice. See Abrabanel, *Commentary on the Torah: Ki Tetze* (Deut., chap. 21), no. 14.

71. See *Shevuot* 39a.

72. See *Yevamot* 47a.

73. See *Yevamot* 24b.

74. See Novak 1983, pp. 407ff.

75. Thus the famous *midrash* (*Sifrei: Devarim*, no. 343; *Avodah Zarah* 2b), which has God offering the Torah to the Gentiles, when carefully read, actually teaches that their rejection of the Torah is entailed by their prior rejection of the Noahide prohibitions of murder, incest, and theft.

76. See Novak 1974–76, vol. 2, pp. 15ff.

77. See Novak 1975, pp. 29ff.; also, Novak 1989, pp. 152ff.

78. See Kant 1929, B234ff.

79. See Kant 1929, B33, B72, B100, B266.

80. See Novak 1989, pp. 129ff.

81. Only once have I been able to find in Cohen's work a recognition, one he could not justify on his own terms, however, that God's essence transcends its correlation with human moral reason. See Cohen 1972, p. 95. Cf. Cohen 1972, pp. 65, 109.

82. See Novak 1989, pp. 148ff.

83. Cohen 1972, p. 365. Along these lines, Cohen was followed by his student Franz Rosenzweig. See Rosenzweig 1921, p. 382; Rosenzweig 1961, p. 342.

84. Thus the famous view of R. Joshua (*T. Sanhedrin* 13.2) that "there are some (*yesh*) righteous ones among the nations of the world and they have a portion in the world-to-come" means that in the world-to-come they will be included *along with* Israel, all of whom are considered righteous prima facie (*M. Sanhedrin* 10.1 re Isa. 60.21). See *Sanhedrin* 105a re Ps. 9.18.

85. See *Berakhot* 34b re Deut. 15.11; Maimonides, *Mishneh*

Torah: Hilkhot Teshuvah 9.2; *Hilkhot Melakhim* 12.2. Also, see *Niddah* 61b re Ps. 88.6 and note of R. Zvi Hirsch Chajes thereon; *Y. Megillah* 1.5/70d re Deut. 5.19. Cf. *Vayiqra Rabbah* 13.3.

86. See Nachmanides' comment on Exod. 13.16.

87. *Sifra: Acharei-Mot* 86a; *Yoma* 67b re Lev. 18.4.

88. See Nachmanides' comments on Exod. 13.11 and Deut. 6.16 and 6.20.

89. See above, n. 87; also, *Sanhedrin* 21b re Deut. 17.16–17; *Shabbat* 108a re Exodus 13.9 and Deut. 14.21; *Y. Shabbat* 3.3/6a; *Bereshit Rabbah* 44.1; *Bemidbar Rabbah* 19.4; *Midrash Leqah Tov:* Chuqat 119b. In this common rabbinic view of the *chuqqim,* their very unintelligibility is not just apparent, but real. The very phenomenology of their observance requires the suspension of both natural and historical reason. However, for most of the medieval theologians, both rationalist and nonrationalist, the unintelligibility of the *chuqqim* is only apparent. Inherently they are *ratio per se,* even though they are not *ratio quoad nos,* i.e., immediately intelligible to us. See, e.g., Maimonides, *Guide* 3.26 and Nachmanides' comments on Lev. 19.19 and 26.15; *Torah Commentary* of R. Menachem Recanati: Chuqat (Num., chap. 19), beg. a là *Bemidbar Rabbah* 19.3 re Eccles. 7.23. My view of the *chuqqim* is clearly closer to the common rabbinic view than it is to the medieval one common to both rationalists and kabbalists. I think that the dialectical role of *choq* as a surd is important for the philosophical theology presented here.

90. See Nachmanides' comments on Exod. 15.25 and Lev. 18.4.

91. See, e.g., Deut. 5.13–15.

92. Thus the Buberian I-Thou model can be seen as a correlation of man and God, viz., no I (human) without Thou (divine) and no Thou without I. Such a relational God is just as immanent as Cohen's God. This problem affects a number of contemporary covenantal Jewish theologians. See, e.g., Hartman 1985, p. 302. For an insightful, though oblique, critique of Buber on this very point, see Heschel 1951, pp. 45–49, 128–29; also, Tillich 1959, p. 62.

93. See Maimonides, *Guide* 3.24. This may also be the reason why this narrative was once considered by some to be the Torah reading for Rosh Hashanah when it was observed for only one day even in the Land of Israel. For the festival of creation, it expresses the doctrine that creation is rooted in the inscrutable will of God, for which no reason could ever be found. See *Pesiqta de-Rav Kahana,* intro., vol. 1, p. xiv (re Ms. Carmoli). Cf. Mann 1940, p. 178.

94. That is why this phrase is considered to be a proper name of God, not just an attribute of action. See *Shevuot* 35a (cf. Maimonides, *Mishneh Torah: Hilkhot Yesodei ha-Torah,* 6.2; *Guide* 1.61). An attri-

bute of action has a discernible essence and it can be imitated (see *Shab-bat* 133b; Maimonides, *Guide* 3.54); a unique property of God cannot be imitated.

95. See *Avodah Zarah* 3a re Lev. 18.5 and *Tos.*, s.v. "she'afilu" re *Sanhedrin* 59a.

96. For the notion that the original election of Israel in Egypt will not be totally overcome by the final redemption, see *T. Berakhot* 1.10; *Y. Berakhot* 1.9/4a; *Berakhot* 12b. For the notion that the authority of the commandments of the Mosaic Torah will remain even after the final redemption, see above, n. 85.

97. See Zech. 14.8–12.

98. This does not mean, however, that the political necessity of the state of Israel for the Jewish people is being denied or that the sanctity of the Land of Israel (*qedushat ha'aretz*) is being denied. Clearly, as regards the Torah's laws, the Land of Israel is singular (see, e.g., *M. Kiddushin* 1.9). And as regards the election of Israel, the gift of the Land of Israel is an essential part of that gift (see Exod. 6.7–8). See Leibowitz 1976, pp. 181ff. Emphasizing the apocalyptic character of redemption does not entail political and military impotence, as certain chasidic, anti-Zionist quietists would have it.

99. See *Berakhot* 34b.

100. Therefore, the commandment "You shall love your neighbor as yourself" (Lev. 19.18) refers to fellow Jews. See Maimonides, *Mishneh Torah: Hilkhot Deot* 6.3–4; *Hilkhot Avel*, 14.1. Justice, however, is commanded towards all human beings. See *Baba Kamma* 113a–b re Lev. 25.50.

101. See *Sifrei: Devarim*, no. 96 and *Yevamot* 13b re Deut. 14.1.

102. See Saadiah Gaon 1962, 3.7.

103. See *Tanchuma: Ki Tissa*, no. 34.

104. See Nachmanides' disputation (Barcelona, 1263) with the apostate, Pablo Christiani, in Nachmanides 1963, vol. 1, pp. 315–16.

REFERENCES

Abrabanel, Isaac. 1862. *Commentary on the Torah*. Warsaw: Lebensohn.

Achad Ha'Am. 1949. *Kol Kitvei Achad Ha'Am*. Jerusalem: Hozaah Ivrith.

Arendt, Hannah. 1978. *The Life of the Mind*. 2 vols. New York: Harcourt Brace Jovanovich.

Asheri (Rosh). 1898. *Commentary on Babylonian Talmud*. Vilna: Romm.

Bemidbar Rabbah. 1957. New York: Anafim.

Bereshit Rabbah. 1965. Edited by J. Theodor and C. Albeck. 3 vols. Jerusalem: Wahrmann.

Buber, Martin. 1970. *I and Thou*. Translated by W. Kaufmann. New York: Scribner's.

Chajes, Zvi Hirsch. 1898. *Notes on the Babylonian Talmud*. Vilna: Romm.

Cohen, Arthur A. 1981. *The Tremendum: A Theological Interpretation of the Holocaust*. New York: Crossroad.

Cohen, Hermann. 1922. *Die Logik der reinen Erkenntnis*. 3d ed. Berlin: B. Cassirer.

———. 1923. *Die Ethik des reinen Willens*. 4th ed. Berlin: B. Cassirer.

———. 1924. *Jüdische Schriften*. Edited by B. Strauss. 3 vols. Berlin.

———. 1966. *Religion der Vernunft aus den Quellen des Judentums*. Darmstadt: Joseph Melzer.

———. 1972. *Religion of Reason out of the Sources of Judaism*. Translated by S. Kaplan. New York: Frederick Ungar.

Darwin, Charles. 1958. *The Origin of Species*. New York: Mentor Books.

Fackenheim, Emil. 1970. *God's Presence in History: Jewish Affirmations and Philosophical Reflections*. New York: Harper and Row.

———. 1982. *To Mend the World: Foundations of Future Jewish Thought*. New York: Schocken.

Gersonides. 1866. *Milchamot ha-Shem*. Leipzig: n.p.

Ginzberg, Louis. 1909–38. *The Legends of the Jews*. 7 vols. Philadelphia: Jewish Publication Society of America.

Hartman, David. 1985. *A Living Covenant: The Innovative Spirit in Traditional Judaism*. New York: Free Press.

Hegel, Georg Wilhelm Friedrich. 1952. *Phänomenologie des Geistes*. Edited by J. Hoffmeister. Hamburg: Felix Meiner.

Heidegger, Martin. 1961. *An Introduction to Metaphysics*. Translated by R. Manheim. Garden City, N.Y.: Anchor Books.

Heschel, Abraham Joshua. 1951. *Man Is Not Alone: A Philosophy of Religion*. Philadelphia: Jewish Publication Society of America.

Husserl, Edmund. 1962. *Ideas: A General Introduction to Pure Phenomenology*. Translated by W. R. B. Gibson. New York: Collier Books.

Isaac of Vienna. 1862. *Or Zarua*. 2 vols. Zhitomir: n.p.

Kant, Immanuel. 1929. *Critique of Pure Reason*. Translated by Norman Kemp Smith. New York: Macmillan.

Kaplan, Mordecai M. 1957. *Judaism as a Civilization*. 2d ed. New York: Reconstructionist Press.

Kaufmann, Walter. 1966. *Hegel: A Reinterpretation*. Garden City: Doubleday.

Kaufmann, Yechezkel. 1960. *The Religion of Israel*. Translated by M. Greenberg. Chicago: University of Chicago Press.

Kohut, Alexander. 1970. *Arukh Completum*. 9 vols. Tel Aviv: Shilo.

Leibowitz, Yeshayahu. 1976. *Yahadut, Am Yehudi u-Medinat Yisrael*. Jerusalem: Schocken.

Levenson, Jon D. 1988. *Creation and the Persistance of Evil: The Jewish Drama of Divine Omnipotence*. San Francisco: Harper and Row.

Lewin, B. M. 1928–43. *Otzar ha-Geonim*. 13 vols. Haifa and Jerusalem: n.p.

Loewe, Judah. 1582. *Gevurot ha-Shem*. Krakow: n.p.

Maimonides. 1960. *Mishneh Torah*. 5 vols. New York: Otzar ha-Rambam.

———. 1963. *Guide of the Perplexed*. Translated by S. Pines. 2 vols. Chicago: University of Chicago Press.

———. 1965. *Commentary on the Mishnah*. Edited by J. Kafih. 3 vols. Jerusalem: Mossad ha-Rav Kook.

———. 1988. *Iggerot ha-Rambam*. Edited by Y. Shilat. 2 vols. Jerusalem: Ma'aliyot.

Mann, Jacob. 1940. *The Bible as Read and Preached in the Old Synagogue*. Cincinnati: Hebrew Union College Press.

Marx, Karl. 1975. *Karl Marx, Frederick Engels: Collected Works*. Vol. 3. Edited by C. Dutt. New York: International Publishers.

Mekhilta. 1960. Edited by H. S. Horovitz and I. A. Rabin. Jerusalem: Bamberger and Wahrmann.

Midrash Leqah Tov. 1884. Edited by S. Buber. Vilna: Romm.

Mordecai ben Hillel Ashkenazi. 1898. *Commentary on the Babylonian Talmud*. Vilna: Romm.

Nachmanides. 1959–62. *Commentary on the Torah*. Edited by C. B. Chavel. 2 vols. Jerusalem: Mossad ha-Rav Kook.

———. 1963. *Kitvei Ramban*. Edited by C. B. Chavel. 2 vols. Jerusalem: Mossad ha-Rav Kook.

Novak, David. 1974–76. *Law and Theology in Judaism*. 2 vols. New York: Ktav.

———. 1975. *Suicide and Morality: The Theories of Plato, Aquinas, and Kant and Their Relevance for Suicidology*. New York: Scholars Studies Press.

———. 1983. *The Image of the Non-Jew in Judaism: An Historical and Constructive Study of the Noahide Laws*. New York and Toronto: Edwin Mellen Press.

———. 1985. "Buber's Critique of Heidegger." *Modern Judaism* 5:125–40.

———. 1988a. "Natural Law, Halakhah and the Covenant." *Jewish Law Annual* 7:43–67.

————. 1988b. "The Role of Dogma in Judaism." *Theology Today* 45:49–61.

————. 1989. *Jewish-Christian Dialogue: A Jewish Justification.* New York: Oxford University Press.

Pallière, Aimé. 1985. *The Unknown Sanctuary.* Translated by L. W. Wise. New introduction by D. Novak. New York: Bloch.

Pesiqta de-Rav Kahana. 1962. Edited by B. Mandelbaum. 2 vols. New York: Jewish Theological Seminary of America.

Recanati, Menachem. 1595. *Torah Commentary.* Lublin: n.p.

Rosenzweig, Franz. 1921. *Der Stern der Erlösung.* Frankfurt am Main: Kaufmann.

————. 1955. *On Jewish Learning.* Translated by W. Wolf and N. N. Glatzer. New York: Schocken.

————. 1961. *Franz Rosenzweig: His Life and Thought.* Translated by Nahum N. Glatzer. 2d ed. New York: Schocken.

Saadiah Gaon. 1962. *Emunot ve-Deot.* Jerusalem: Meqor.

Sartre, Jean-Paul. 1946. *Réflexions sur la Question Juive.* Paris: Paul Monihien.

————. 1965. *Anti-Semite and Jew.* Translated by George J. Becker. New York: Schocken.

Scholem, Gershom. 1956. "Schöpfung aus Nichts und Selbstverschränkung Gottes." *Eranos Jahrbuch* 25:87–119.

————. 1980. *Pirqei-Yesod Behavanat Hakabbalah.* Translated by Y. Ben-Shlomoh. Jerusalem: Mossad Bialik.

Schreiber, Moses. 1855. *Responsa Chatam Sofer.* 3 vols. Vienna: n.p.

Sifra. 1862. Edited by I. H. Weiss. Vienna: Schlessinger.

Sifrei: Devarim. 1969. Edited by Louis Finkelstein. New York: Jewish Theological Seminary of America.

Spinoza, Benedict de. 1951. *Tractatus Politicus* and *Tractatus Theologico-Politicus.* In *The Chief Works of Benedict de Spinoza.* Translated by R. H. M. Elwes. Vol. 1. New York: Dover.

————. 1955. *Ethics.* Translated by W. H. White. New York: Hafner.

Steinheim, Salamon Ludwig. 1990. *Philosopher of Revelation: The Life and Thought of S. L. Steinheim.* Translated by Joshua O. Haberman. Philadelphia: Jewish Publication Society of America.

Strauss, Leo. 1965. *Spinoza's Critique of Religion.* Translated by E. M. Sinclair. New York: Schocken.

Taylor, Charles. 1989. *Sources of the Self: The Making of the Modern Identity.* Cambridge: Harvard University Press.

Thomas Aquinas. 1949. *On Being and Essence.* Translated by A. Maurer. Toronto: Pontifical Institute of Mediaeval Studies.

Tillich, Paul. 1959. *Theology of Culture.* New York: Oxford University Press.

Tishby, Isaiah. 1957–61. *Mishnat ha-Zohar.* 2 vols. Jerusalem: Mossad Bialik.

The Union Prayerbook. 1957. Newly revised. New York: Central Conference of American Rabbis.

van Buren, Paul. 1980. *A Theology of the Jewish-Christian Reality.* Pt. 1. New York: Seabury Press.

Vayiqra Rabbah. 1953. Edited by M. Margulies. 3 vols. Jerusalem: Ministry of Education and Culture.

Voegelin, Eric. 1956. *Order and History.* Vol. 1, *Israel and Revelation.* Baton Rouge: Louisiana State University Press.

Wittgenstein, Ludwig. 1961. *Tractatus Logico-Philosophicus.* Translated by D. F. Pears and B. F. McGuiness. London: Routledge and Kegan Paul.

Wyschogrod, Michael. 1983. *The Body of Faith: Judaism as Corporeal Election.* New York: Seabury Press.

Yovel, Yirmiyahu. 1989. *Spinoza and Other Heretics.* 2 vols. Princeton: Princeton University Press.

Zohar. 1970. Edited by R. Margaliot. 3 vols. Jerusalem: Mossad ha-Rav Kook.

CHAPTER 2

Chosenness, Not Chauvinism: Maimonides on the Chosen People

Menachem Kellner

In this essay I should like to discuss an issue of ethical concern for Jews everywhere and one that for me, as an Israeli, has important political implications as well. Is it possible to articulate a Jewishly legitimate version of the doctrine of the chosen people that does not lead to chauvinism? Three questions must immediately be posed: (1) What makes a doctrine Jewishly legitimate? (2) If affirming the doctrine of the chosen people raises problems, why not reject it? (It is, after all, an issue that appears so far from the central axis of the Jewish tradition that not one of the medievals who listed principles of faith included it in their lists.);[1] and (3) If, alternatively, it is important to affirm the doctrine, what is wrong with chauvinism?

I am going to sidestep the first issue; instead, I will simply affirm here that if a doctrine was held by Maimonides then it is Jewishly legitimate. That is not to say that Maimonides' holding a doctrine is the one criterion for Jewish legitimacy, nor is it to say that every doctrine that Maimonides held is correct[2] or even well within the mainstream of the Jewish tradition as it had developed to his day. Rather, it is to say that if the "Great Eagle" gave his imprimatur to a position, we cannot reject that position as inconsistent with Judaism.

The issue of chosenness cannot be simply rejected, I think, because without it there is no way to justify adherence to Judaism in the face of adversity. As Emil Fackenehim has taught us, choosing to remain Jewish is not an ethically neutral act. It was the choice of many nineteenth-century Jews not to assimilate that led their descendents into Hitler's gas chambers. If, despite this, we choose to affirm our Judaism, we must have a good reason for it. The fact that God chose the Jews for some special purpose is the best possible reason of all, and the one historically most often affirmed for remaining Jewish. Even Mordecai Kaplan, who explicitly denied the existence of a choosing God, was forced, in his very last book, *The Religion of Ethical Nationhood,* to affirm the notion of chosenness in a sort of backhanded way: the Jews must remain distinct in order to save the world from a nuclear holocaust.

Well, then, why not simply affirm chosenness and, if necessary, chauvinism? This is the route chosen by many figures in Jewish intellectual history (Halevi preeminent among them), and it seems especially widespread today. In his new study, *The Jews in America,*[3] Arthur Hertzberg observes:

> When Jews were asked about their identity, it was possible for many of them to assert that their loyalty was to the Jewish people, and never mind faith in God. The sense of being one people, one family, as the seed of Abraham, had always been central in Jewish consciousness. This self-definition had become more pervasive in the 1950s, as American Jews increasingly identified with the new State of Israel. In Israel, all Jews belonged to the nation, even though many were indifferent to the Jewish religion.

Hertzberg shows how this approach gained steam and cites a 1983 study of the "Jewishness" of American Jewish leaders. The study found that despite a low level of synagogue affiliation and religious observance, 65 percent of the American Jewish community's leadership maintained that the Jews were God's chosen people. Hertzberg then observes:

> Such an assertion did not belong together with their usual rhetoric about ethnic pluralism. An ethnic group cannot assert "chosenness" without falling into chauvinism or worse. In a democratic society, only a religion dare use this term and only to describe believers who are committed to live spiritual lives. (p. 387)

Ethnic Jewish chauvinism may be inappropriate in the democratic societies of North America; when allied with strong religious belief in the state of Israel, it becomes downright dangerous. Chauvinists affirm the superiority of their group and the concomitant inferiority of other groups. It is views like this that underlie the common assumption in Israel that Arabs are in some way intrinsically different from Jews and inherently untrustworthy. Where Jews think of themselves as motivated by rational considerations of self-interest, Arabs are thought to be motivated by an irrational desire to drive every last Jew into the sea. Given the way in which the Germans in many cases sabatoged their war efforts towards the end of World War II in order to continue the destruction of the Jews, one cannot reject this fear of the Arabs as simple paranoia; but it certainly gets in the way of attempts to find out whether or not it is possible to arrive at some sort of *modus vivendi* with them. Theological positions that give "aid and comfort" to such approaches must be examined carefully, and, if possible, rejected or modified.

Thus, as a committed Jew, I must affirm chosenness; as an Israeli seeking peace with my neighbors I must reject chauvinism (there are, of course, other good reasons for rejecting chauvinism!). What can I do? Well, it turns out that Maimonides can be of assistance here. An examination of Maimonides' writings on the nature of the Jewish people in general and on the notion of chosenness in particular presents a Jewishly legitimate way of affirming chosenness without ethnic chauvinism.

That the Jews are distinct from the Gentiles is an axiom of Jewish faith and a lesson of Jewish history. But what is the basis of that distinction? Jacob Katz has pointed out that the distinction has been explained in two very different ways. One approach grounds it in theological terms and sees it as "a mere divergence in articles of creed."[4] Katz contrasts this to what we may call an "essentialist" view, one that traces "religious and historical differences to the dissimilar character of Jew and non-Jew respectively." On this view, "a qualitative difference was involved for which the individual was not responsible and which he [or she] could not change." There was, in other words, an *essential* difference between Jew and Gentile. Katz finds the origin of this view in Midrash, sees its development in Halevi, and explains its widespread acceptance among late medieval Jews to the impact of the *Zohar*.

I have written a monograph, *Maimonides on Judaism and the Jewish People*,[5] in which I argue, *inter alia*, that Maimonides could not adopt an essentialist view of the nature of the Jewish people on the grounds that he was committed to an Aristotelian philosophical psychology. The monograph is, I hope, a disinterested historical and philosophical study. That it has implications for current questions of Jewish ethics and policy is an expression of the fact that Jewish life, especially in Israel, cannot be divorced from questions of Jewish thought.

For Aristotle, the soul is the form of the body, that is, the animative principle whereby a human being is a human being. It is the soul that actualizes the potential given us by nature to be human beings.[6] But for Aristotle, form does not exist independently of the matter it actualizes. Contra Plato, there is no hint of preexistent souls "zapped" into the body at the moment of conception or birth. But if the soul does not preexist the body, can it, or some part of it, survive the death of the body? In Hellenistic and medieval times a theory was developed, elaborating on some ambiguous comments of Aristotle's, that accounted for the possibility that some humans, at least, would achieve immortality. For our purposes, the most important aspect of the Aristotelian theory, especially as it was developed by Aristotle's later interpreters, is that our rational capacities are not given to us fully formed. That part, element, or aspect of our souls that most truly distinguishes us from other living beings, that element through which human beings are truly human,[7] exists in us only as a capacity when we are born.

On this view, human beings are born, contra Plato, without innate knowledge, but with a capacity or potential to learn. This capacity is called, depending on the specific version of the theory that one encounters, "hylic intellect," "material intellect," or "potential intellect." If one takes advantage of one's capacity to learn (a process in which God or the Active Intellect plays a crucial role) and actualizes one's potential for study, then one will have acquired what Maimonides calls "an intellect *in actu*,"[8] often called the "acquired intellect." The question of how one must perfect one's intellect in order to acquire an intellect *in actu*, that is, the question of what one must master, was a matter of debate. In the version of the theory often ascribed to Maimonides, one perfects one's intellect only through the apprehension of metaphysical truths. In the version of the theory adopted by Gersonides, the achievement of true knowledge in any discipline is sufficient to give one at least a measure of intellectual perfection.[9] To the extent that immortality is affirmed, it is the acquired intellect that is seen as immortal.

Since one can actualize one's potential intellect to different degrees, it follows that one's perfection, and thus one's share of immortality, depends on the degree to which one perfects himself or herself intellectually.[10]

For our purposes, the crucial elements in this theory are the claims that (1) no human being is born with a fully developed soul—we are, rather, born with the *potential* to *acquire* what can be called a soul—and (2) the only way one can possibly actualize his or her potential to acquire a "soul" is through intellectual activity. On the one hand, this theory commits one to an extremely parochial position: only the intellectually gifted and energetic can ever fulfill themselves as human beings. This form of intellectual elitism leaves most of the human race out in the cold.[11] On the other hand, the theory also forces one to adopt a very nonparochial stance: anyone born with a measure of intelligence and a willingness to apply it to the exacting demands of intellectual labor can achieve some measure of perfection. Race, creed, sex, or national origin are simply not issues.

Consistent with his philosophical psychology, Maimonides develops a theory of ethics according to which human beings at birth are *tabulae rasae*, upon which education, training, and acculturation write out our moral characters. All humans are born with basically the same moral potential and the same absence of fully formed character traits. This being the case, moral qualities that we have acquired can be changed if we are willing to work at it, especially if we avail ourselves of the guidance of the wise, the "physicians of the souls." Obedience to the Torah leads to high moral virtue; in this sense Jews, Maimonides held, are morally superior to Gentiles. But that is a matter of education, not inborn character.

This philosophical psychology forces Maimonides to adopt a number of unusual positions on questions of a more narrowly religious or parochial nature. Among these are providence, prophecy, and immortality. In each case it is shown in my aforementioned monograph that, for Maimonides, the simple fact that one is a Jew plays no role in determining whether one will enjoy God's providence or prophecy or inhabit the world-to-come. In each case it is intellectual perfection that is crucial.

Another such issue is the question of the status of Gentiles in the messianic era. Many Jewish authorities assume that until the end of days the distinction between Jew and Gentile will remain; after the Messiah's coming, the Jews will rule the Gentiles, who at present rule them. Maimonides rejected this view, anticipating a time when all Gentiles would become Jews, either through formal conversion, as I believe, or because the distinction would cease to be relevant, as Ya'akov Blidstein maintains.[12] This position was made both possible and necessary by Maimonides' philosophical psychology. Since all human beings will devote themselves to the pursuit of the knowledge of God in the messianic era, that which truly distinguishes Gentiles from Jews will disappear.

Similarly with the question of conversion. While there are conflicting views within the tradition about proselytes, some very positive, some very negative, the rabbinic tradition has never encouraged proselytization. For Halevi, converts could become the equals of native Jews only after many generations of intermarriage between them. For certain strands of the Midrash and for the *Zohar*, conversion as such was not possible. Converts were actually persons of Gentile parentage into whom intrinsically Jewish souls happened to find their way. Conversion, then, was not so much the issue as was returning an errant soul to its proper place. Gentiles not having such souls could never truly convert to Judaism. Maimonides rejected these views altogether, welcomed sincere proselytes wholeheartedly, allowed for proselytization, and adopted a warmly positive attitude towards the whole issue of conversion. Given that we are at root the same, and given that one day all humans would convert to Judaism, Maimonides had no reason to have reservations about sincere proselytes and may even have seen in the welcoming of proselytes an anticipation of the messianic era. Whether this latter is true or not, Maimonides' views on this issue are a consequence of his philosophical psychology.

Maimonides' views on dogma were absolutely unprecedented in the Judaism which developed to his day. The essence of being and becoming a Jew, and of earning a place in the world-to-come, Maimonides teaches, involves the acceptance or rejection of certain views. Defining a Jew in terms of the views that he or she accepts goes hand in hand with a view of human nature that insists that all humans are at root alike, distinguished, to the extent that they are distinguished, only by the views they adopt. Thus, Maimonides' philosophical psychology plays a role in one of his religiously most unusual claims, that concerning the place and nature of dogma in Judaism.

What sort of views are those the adoption of which is crucial for being Jewish? These turn out to be the science of the Torah in its true sense, which, in turn, is *ma'aseh bereshit* and *ma'aseh merkavah,* physics and metaphysics. The body of knowledge to be mastered, then, if one wishes to become a Jew, or, if already a Jew, to become a perfect Jew, is difficult but not occult or esoteric. Any intelligent person can master it to one degree or another. One sees yet again the footprints of Maimonides' nonessentialist definition of what a Jew is, which, in turn, is a consequence of his philosophical psychology.

In my monograph, then, I prove that Maimonides adopts a variant of the theory of the acquired intellect and examine the consequences of that adoption for his positions on ethics, providence, prophecy, immortality, the place of Gentiles in the messianic era, the nature of proselytes, the definition of a Jew, and the nature of Torah. In this paper I would like to examine Maimonides' conception of the nature of the Jewish people.

Maimonides' attitude towards the Jewish People ("Israel" in his terminology) was one of great national pride. He was convinced that the Jews, as a national group, were in every way superior to other national groups.[13] Unlike Halevi, however, he did not make an entire metaphysic out of this pride.[14] The superiority of the Jews derived from two sources: God's promise to Abraham that his progeny would enjoy special benefits and, most importantly, the Torah.[15]

Maimonides' comments on the nature of the Jewish people mirror these two sources of Jewish superiority. The Jews are, on the one hand, a people defined by their descent from Abraham and, on the other hand, a community defined by the Torah. While both these understandings of the Jewish people find expression in Maimonides' writings, the latter is much more important than the former. It is my intent in this study to prove this last claim and explain its significance.

In order to make my discussion clearer, I will introduce a distinction that is not textually grounded in Maimonides' writings but that will help us keep in mind the twofold nature of his writings about the Jews. Those individuals constituted as a national group by their shared descent from Abraham I will call "Jews," while that religious group constituted by its adherence to the Torah I will call "Israel." Maimonides was not always careful to keep these two meanings distinct and may even have occasionally inadvertently fudged them. The distinction is in any event hard to keep sharp since in historical and halakhic terms "Jews" and "Israel" denote the same entity. Despite all this, ignoring the distinction makes understanding Maimonides very difficult.

Indirect but compelling evidence to the effect that Maimonides adopted the distinction here outlined can be found in *Laws of Kings* 10.8:

> The Rabbis said that the sons of Keturah, who are of the seed of Abraham, who came after Ishmael and Isaac, are obligated to be circumcised. But since today the descendants of Ishmael have become intermingled with the descendants of Keturah, all of them are obligated to be circumcised on the eighth day, but are not executed because of it.[16]

Here we have a *commandment,* not one of the seven Noahide laws, devolving upon a group of non-Jews because of their Abrahamic descent. The commandment of circumcision was given to Abraham and to his descendants (Gen. 17.9–14). Maimonides takes that literally and imposes upon the Ishmaelites (Muslims), who had married into the descendants of Abraham, the obligation to circumcise their children on the eighth day after birth (as mandated by Gen. 17.12). Can there be clearer proof to the effect that Maimonides distinguishes between Abrahamic descent on the one hand and membership in the people of Israel on the other hand?[17]

Just as Maimonides refuses to accept an essentialist definition of who an individual Israelite is, he also rejects essentialist definitions of Israel the people. Maimonides never denies, indeed he is eager to affirm, that the Jews should be proud of their Abrahamic descent and that this descent confers great benefits upon them. But, withal, Maimonides repeatedly affirms that what makes Israel, Israel is the Torah and not any inborn characteristic, inherent quality, or shared biological origin.

We can see this in many ways. First, in his letters to Obadiah the Proselyte, Maimonides emphasizes the importance of commitment to Torah over and above actual physical descent from Abraham: "Let not your lineage be base in your eyes, for if we link our lineage to Abraham, Isaac, and Jacob, you link your lineage to He Who spoke and the world came into being."[18]

Examining Maimonides' comments on the nature of the activities of Abraham himself is also illuminating. In *Laws of Idolatry* 1.1–2 Maimonides explains how humankind, originally monotheist, fell into error (literally) and began to worship idols. "The world moved on in this fashion," Maimonides says in 1.2,

> till that pillar of the world, the patriarch Abraham, was born. After he was weaned . . . his mind began to reflect . . . : "How is it possible that this sphere should continuously be guiding the world, and have no one to guide it and cause it to turn round; for it cannot be that it turns round of itself?" He had no teacher . . . but his mind was busily working and reflecting till he had attained the way of truth and apprehended the correct line on the basis of his own correct intellect and knew that there is one God, that He guides the sphere, that He created everything, and that among all that exists there is no god beside Him.[19]

Abraham, then, is presented as a natural philosopher who came to recognize that God exists, is one, and created the world, on the basis of his unaided reason.[20] What then did Abraham do? He tried to convince his neighbors, rationally, of their error:

> He realized that the whole world was in error. . . Having attained this *knowledge* he began to *refute* the inhabitants of Ur of the Chaldees, *arguing* with them . . . and commenced to instruct the people. . . When he prevailed over them with his *arguments*, the king sought to slay him . . . When the people flocked to him and questioned him regarding his assertions, he would instruct each one according to his *intellect,* until he had returned them to the way of truth.[21]

Abraham, having achieved philosophic certainty, sought to share his knowledge and certainty with others, by way of rational argumentation.

Maimonides presents a similar picture in the *Guide of the Perplexed,* although there the emphasis is on distinguishing the Patriarchs, who sought rationally to convince their fellows of the truths of God's existence, unity, and creation, from Moses, who brought the Torah, which includes these truths but also includes commandments and was sent by God. Moses was distinguished from the Patriarchs because he was able to "make a claim to prophecy on the ground that God had spoken to him and sent him on a mission." The Patriarchs, however, "were addressed in regard to their private affairs only; I mean only in regard to their perfection, their right guidance concerning their actions, and the good tidings for them concerning the position their descendants would attain."[22] Unlike Moses, who came with commandments from God, the Patriarchs "addressed a call to the people by means of speculation and instruction." Once again we see that Abraham, Isaac, and Jacob[23] came to know God on the basis of rational, philosophical grounds and sought to share the truth thus discovered with their contemporaries. Thanks to this, God promised their descendants many benefits.

The same point is reiterated in *Guide* 2.39. Protecting the uniqueness of the Torah, Maimonides asserts the uniqueness of Mosaic prophecy. No other prophet has ever said to a group of people, "God has sent me to you and commanded me to say to you such and such things; he has forbidden you to do such and such things and commanded you to do such and such things." Prophets other than Moses,

> who received a great overflow, as for instance Abraham, assembled the people and called them by way of teaching and instruction to adhere to the truth that he had grasped. Thus Abraham taught the people and *explained to them by means of speculative proofs* that the world has but one deity, that He has created all the things that are other than Himself, and that none of the forms and no created thing in general ought to be worshipped.[24]

The founder of the Jewish nation, then, is presented in both the *Mishneh Torah* and the *Guide of the Perplexed* as a philosopher who achieved knowledge of God through rational examination of the world around him and sought rationally to convince others of the truths he had discovered. This is made clear here in this passage from the *Guide*. Abraham received an "overflow" (i.e., emanation) from God, such an emanation, as Maimonides explains in his chapters on prophecy (2.32–48), being a consequence of intellectual perfection. As a reward, Abraham was promised that special benefits would be conferred upon his progeny. The foundation of the Jewish people as an entity defined in terms of its Abrahamic descent is itself a consequence of a philosophic appreciation of God.

Maimonides' explanation of how the descendants of Abraham were constituted into the entity called "Israel" is particularly illuminating. Maimonides compares the creation of Israel with the process of conversion: "With three things did Israel enter the covenant: circumcision, immersion, and sacrifice . . . And so it is for all generations, when a Gentile wishes to enter the covenant and shelter [literally, "stand at the threshold of"] under the wings of the *Shekhinah*, and accept upon himself the yoke of Torah, he needs circumcision, immersion, and the bringing of a sacrifice."[25] Maimonides makes the essential element of conversion to be the acceptance of (philosophic) teachings concerning God.[26] I do not think that it is pressing the issue too much to impute to Maimonides the view that the philosophic acceptance of the existence and unity of God was no less essential to the mass "conversion" of the Jews from the tribe of Abraham to the people of Israel at Sinai than it is for the conversion of individuals through the ages.

This interpretation of Maimonides is strengthened by his account of the theophany at Sinai. Maimonides denies that all the Jews prophesied at Sinai,[27] but he does insist that the assembled people rationally understood the philosophic import of the first two statements in the Decalogue. "It is clear to me," Maimonides says, opening *Guide* 2.33, "that at the gathering at Mt. Sinai, not everything that reached Moses also reached all Israel. Speech was addressed to Moses alone . . . and he, peace upon him, went to the foot of the mountain and communicated to the people what he had heard" (pp. 363–64). The people of Israel did not then share Moses' prophetic apprehension. But in explaining the rabbinic dictum to the effect that Israel heard the first two statements of the Decalogue directly from the "mouth" of God,[28] Maimonides says,

> They mean that these words reached them just as they reached Moses our Master and that it was not Moses our Master who communicated them to them. For these two principles, I mean the existence of the deity and his being one,[29] are knowable by human speculation alone. Now with regard to everything that can be known by demonstration, the status of the prophet and that of everyone else who knows it are equal; there is no superiority of one over the other. These two principles are not known through prophecy alone. The text of the Torah says: "Unto thee it was shown"[30] [Deut. 4.35]. As for the other commandments, they

belong to the class of generally accepted opinions and those adopted in virtue of tradition, not to the class of the intellecta. (p. 364)

Here we are told by Maimonides that Israel at Sinai apprehended by philosophical demonstration the truth of precisely those two principles (God's existence and unity), which are taught to the convert and by virtue of the acceptance of which he or she becomes a proselyte to Judaism. Israel became Israel by virtue of its acceptance of these two principles. This is convincing proof of the congruence between the process of conversion and the creation of Israel. At the moment of its inception, therefore, Israel was constituted as such by the rational acceptance of true philosophic teachings concerning God. This is as far from an essentialist definition of Israel that one can get!

The same point becomes clear when we examine how individuals are excluded from *Klal Yisrael*, the community of Israel. Maimonides asserts that "anyone who destroys one of these foundations which I have explained to you [Maimonides' "Thirteen Principles"] has left the community of Torah adherents."[31] Maimonides imposes harsh penalties on the heretic, sectarian, and *epikoros*. In *Laws of Repentance* 3.7 Maimonides defines a sectarian as one who denies any of the first five of his thirteen principles of faith. In *Laws of Idolatry* 2.5 he affirms that "Israelite sectarians are not like Israelites at all" and that it is forbidden to converse with them or return their greeting. He compares them to idolators and says that even if they repent they are never accepted back into the community. The *epikoros* is defined in *Repentance* 3.8 as one who denies prophecy, Mosaic prophecy, and God's knowledge. In *Laws of the Murderer* 9.10 and in *Laws of Mourning* 1.10 Maimonides informs us that the *epikoros* is not considered part of the community of Israel; in the latter place we are bidden not to mourn them on their deaths. We are bidden to destroy them in *Laws of Idolatry* 10.1 and are told that they are no better than informers, the lowest of the low in Jewish estimation. That the *epikoros* has no place in the world to come is the burden of *Laws of Testimony* 11.10; we are also informed there that it goes without saying that their testimony is not acceptable in a court, since they are not Israelites at all. In this paragraph we are bidden to kill the *epikoros*.[32] The parallelism here is compelling: one exits the community of Israel by *denying* certain teachings parallel to the way in which that community was constituted, namely, through the rational *acceptance* of certain (philosophic) teachings.[33]

Further evidence of Maimonides' nonessentialist understanding of the nature of the community of Israel can be found, of all places, in his "Epistle to Yemen." I say "of all places" because this text was written in order to bolster the confidence of a Jewish community suffering from Muslim persecution. Part of Maimonides' strategy here is to denigrate the Muslims and praise the Jews. That, at least, appears to be what he is doing at first glance. In actuality, he denigrates *Islam* and praises *Judaism*. Even in this context, then, his nonessentialist approach to the definition of Israel is apparent.

Maimonides begins that part of his discussion relevant to our concern by citing Deut. 10.15: "Yet it was to your fathers that the Lord was drawn in His love for them, so that He chose you, their lineal descendants, from among all the peoples." That verse could be used to underline an essentialist definition of the nature of the Jewish people, distinguishing them from all other peoples by virtue of their lineal descent from Abraham. But Maimonides uses it for other purposes, explaining "that ours is the true and divine religion, revealed to us through Moses, chief of the former as well as the later prophets. By means of it, God has distinguished us from the rest of mankind."[34] This choice, Maimonides goes on to say after citing Deut. 10.15, "was not made thanks to our merits, but was rather an act of grace, on account of our ancestors who were *cognizant* of God and obedient to Him" (pp. 96–97).

Maimonides further emphasizes the point under discussion here: ". . . God has singled us out by His law and precepts, and our preeminence over the others was manifested in His rules and statutes" (p. 97). We are singled out by the Torah, not by anything inherent in our collective or individual character. We are indeed superior to other nations, not because of some inborn quality, but because of the rules and statutes of the Torah.

Maimonides' approach to the issue comes out even in his discussion of how other nations sought to attack the Jews. It was, according to him, not a matter of what we today would call anti-Semitism or Jew-hatred, but rather of anti-Torahism and anti-Judaism. Jealous of Jewish preeminence (a consequence of the Torah), all the nations, instigated by envy and impiety, rose up against us in anger, and all the kings of the earth, motivated by injustice and enmity, applied themselves to persecute us. They wanted to thwart God, but He will not be thwarted. Ever since the time of revelation every despot or rebel ruler, be he violent or ignoble, *has made it his first aim and final purpose to destroy our Law and to vitiate our religion* by means of the sword, by violence, or by brute force. Such were Amalek, Sisera, Sennacherib, Nebuchadnezzar, Titus, Hadrian, and others like them.[35]

Attacks on the Jews, that is, are really attacks on Judaism.

There is one place in the "Epistle to Yemen" where strong emphasis is placed on Abrahamic descent. It is also one of the few (perhaps only) places in his writings where Maimonides makes explicit reference to the notion of the chosen people: "When God spoke to Abraham He made it amply clear that all the blessings that He promised and all his children to whom He will reveal the Law and whom He will make the Chosen People—all this is meant only for the seed of Isaac. Ishmael is regarded as an adjunct and appendage in the blessings of Isaac."[36] Three points must be made. First, the immediate context of this passage, and the passage itself, make clear that Maimonides is primarily interested in refuting the Muslim claim that the favored son of Abraham was Ishmael, not Isaac. Second, it is reasonable to read this passage as saying that Israel will become the chosen people because of the fact that the Torah will be revealed to them, not because of some inherent essence or nature of the Jews. Third, it is true that the Jews did receive the Torah, and thus became constituted as the faith community of Israel, as a reward to Abraham; but this in no way implies that the Jews as such are qualitatively different from other peoples.

There is one last place in the "Epistle to Yemen" that supports the reading of Maimonides offered here. Toward the end of the work Maimonides expresses a messianic wish. Referring to the Jews of Yemen, he says, "May God increase your numbers and hasten the day of gathering you with the entire *religious community*."[37] Even in the context of a prayer for the messianic ingathering, Maimonides makes reference to a *religious community* (defined, we have seen over and over, in terms of its having accepted the Torah) and not to a *people* defined in some essentialist fashion.

I noted above that Maimonides rarely makes reference to the

notion of the chosen people. This alone is suggestive. While the Torah plays a central role in his thought and finds central expression in his "Thirteen Principles,"[38] the notion of the chosen people is almost entirely absent from his writings and plays no role whatsoever in the "Thirteen Principles" or in the *Laws of the Foundations of the Torah*. Indeed, in that latter work, the term *Israel* shows up for the first time only at the end of chapter 4.[39]

Further illustration of this point can be had by examining Maimonides' use of biblical verses that form the basis for the notion of the chosen people. I examined a variety of these verses (Gen. 18.1, 18.18–19; Exod. 19.5–6; Deut. 7.6–8, 14.2, 18.5). Some of them Maimonides never discussed, and others are used in ways that throw no light on Maimonides' ideas concerning the nature of the Jewish people. Usages that are relevant, however, invariably support the interpretation of Maimonides here put forward (as is exemplified by his use of Deut. 10.15 in "Epistle to Yemen," discussed above). A number of examples will make this clear. One of the earliest expressions of the idea of the chosen people is Gen. 18.18–19:

> And Abraham shall surely become a great and mighty nation, and all the nations of the earth shall be blessed in him. For I have known him, to the end that he may command his children and his household after him, that they may keep the way of the Lord, to do righteousness and justice; to the end that the Lord may bring upon Abraham that which He hath spoken of Him.

According to Rav Kafih's index of bibical citations in his works, Maimonides makes no reference at all to Gen. 18.18, while verse 19 is cited seven times.[40] While some of these citations have nothing to do with the issue under discussion, others are most suggestive.

Thus, Maimonides opens the last chapter of *Laws of Gifts to the Poor* (10.1) by telling the reader that one must observe the commandment of charity more scrupulously than any other positive commandment, "for charity is the sign of the righteous seed of Abraham, our Father, as it says: "For I have known him, to the end that he may command his children . . . to give charity"[41] and neither can the seat of Israel be firm nor the true religion stand without charity." Here we have the "righteous seed of Abraham" referred to and even distinguished by a special characteristic: charity.

But Maimonides immediately explains that the seed of Abraham are not intrinsically charitable; rather, they are *commanded* to give charity; it was because they were going to receive that commandment that they became constituted as the "righteous seed of Abraham," and it is by fulfillment of that commandment that they are recognized as such. The persuasive nature of Maimonides' argument here is clear as well. He is trying to encourage the Jews to give charity; if they do so naturally, due to some intrinsic character, the argument would be otiose.[42]

Our verse shows up four times in the *Guide*. In 2.39 (p. 379) it is used to show that Abraham did not convey God's commandments to his household. In 3.24 (p. 502) Maimonides cites the verse to support his claim that "Abraham our Father was the first to make known the belief in Unity, to establish prophecy, and to perpetuate this opinion and draw people to it." In 3.43 (p. 572) it is explained that the descendants of the Patriarchs enjoy benefits thanks to the promises God made to their forbears. These promises, in turn, were made because Abraham, Isaac, and Jacob "were perfect people in their opinions and their moral character." In the last citation of the verse in the *Guide* (3.51:624) we are reminded that the Patriarchs sought "to bring into being a religious community[43] that would know and worship God"—a religious *community*, not a *people* defined by some essential characteristic, and a community defined by its mission: to know and to worship God.

Maimonides also cites the verse in his first letter to Obadiah the Proselyte.[44] That letter opposes any possibility of reading Maimonides as one who holds that the Jewish people have some inherent, essential characteristic that distinguishes them from other nations. In the particular context under discussion, Maimonides uses the verse to support his contention that all those who adopt Judaism are of the household of Abraham.

Our review of Maimonides' use of Gen. 18.19, then, confirms the thesis proposed above: Maimonides plays down the notion of the chosen people, denies that the Jews have any inherent, essential characteristic that distinguishes them *prima facie* from other nations, and emphasizes instead the importance of the community of Israel as constituted by the Torah, which in turn means the rational acceptance of the philosophical truths of God's existence and unity.

A further example is Exod. 19.5–6:

Now therefore if ye will hearken unto My voice indeed, and keep
My covenant then ye shall be Mine own treasure from among all
the peoples; for all the earth is Mine. And ye shall be unto me a
kingdom of priests, and a holy nation.

Here is Maimonides comment:

For a sudden transition from one opposite to another is impossible. And therefore man, according to his nature, is not capable of
abandoning suddenly all to which he was accustomed. As therefore God sent Moses our Master *to make out of us* "a kingdom
of priests and a holy nation"—*through the knowledge of Him.*
(*Guide* 3.32:526, emphasis added)

Israel, then, is *made* into a holy nation (i.e., it is not intrincially or
inherently holy) through its being taught by Moses correct knowledge concerning God. Here we see again that there is nothing
inherently or essentially special or unique about Israel; it is the
rational appropriation of metaphysical truths about God that constitutes Israel as a "kingdom of priests and a holy nation."

Other evidence for Maimonides' nonessentialist interpretation
of the Jewish people is found in a text that seems, at first reading,
to teach the opposite. At the end of a discussion of certain astro-
nomical phenomena, and, more importantly and immediately, a
discussion of the nature and activities of the separate intellects
(*Guide* 2.11:276), Maimonides points out he has already explained that "all these views do not contradict anything said by
our prophets and the sustainers of our Law. For our community[45]
is a community that is full of knowledge and perfect, as He, may
He be exalted, has made clear through the intermediary of the
Master who made us perfect, saying: "Surely, this great nation[46] is
a wise and understanding people [Deut. 4.6]." " Here we have a
text in which Maimonides says that the Jewish nation or people is
"full of knowledge and perfect." Does this not run counter to the
reading of Maimonides urged here, according to which the Jewish
people, in and of itself, as an ethnic entity, has no special, inherent,
essential characteristics?

Not only does this text not run counter to my thesis, it
strengthens it. When Maimonides says that the Jews are "full of
knowledge and perfect," he means that they are full of knowledge
and *therefore* perfect. This is proved by the sequel:

However, when the wicked from among the ignorant nations ruined our good qualities, destroyed our words of wisdom and our compilations, and caused our men of knowledge to perish, so that we again became ignorant, as we had been threatened because of our sins—for it says: "And the wisdom of their wise men shall perish, and the understanding of their prudent men shall be hid [Isaiah 29.14]"; when, furthermore, we mingled with these nations and their opinions were taken over by us, as were their morals and actions . . . when, in consequence of all this, we grew up accustomed to the opinions of the ignorant, these philosophic views appeared to be, as it were, foreign to our Law, just as they are foreign to the opinions of the ignorant. However, matters are not like this.

We see here that the perfection of the Jews[47] is not an inborn characteristic but a consequence of their knowledge. When that knowledge is corrupted through assimilation to ignorant and immoral nations, the Jews behave as foolishly and wickedly as those who have influenced them. We further see here that it is the philosophic views embodied in the Torah that make us a "wise and understanding people." This is seen by the context of our discussion here in 2.11 and by the conclusion of the passage just quoted: It is because of our having grown accustomed to the opinions of the ignorant that the philosophic views discussed in 2.11 appeared foreign to the Torah. Had the Jews understood that these views were not foreign to the Torah, they would still be a "wise and understanding people."

I have shown here that Maimonides, in effect, distinguishes the ethnic group, defined in the first instance through Abrahamic descent, from the faith community Israel, defined in the first instance by its acceptance of certain true philosophic views. Texts discussed included Maimonides' letters to Obadiah the Proselyte, his discussions of Abraham the philosopher in both the *Mishneh Torah* and the *Guide of the Perplexed,* and Maimonides' argument to the effect that the Jews (the seed of Abraham) became Israel through a process of conversion that involved the acceptance of certain philosophic teachings. We further saw that exclusion from Israel, like joining it, depends upon the holding of certain views (in this case, heretical ones). Maimonides' nonessentialist reading of the nature of the Jewish people was supported through an analysis of texts from his "Epistle to Yemen," his near total avoidance of the notion

of the 'chosen people,' and his use of Gen. 18.19 and Exod. 19.5–
6, verses ordinarily interpreted as supporting an essentialist reading of the nature of Israel.

Maimonides' understanding of the nature of the people of Israel, like his understanding of ethics, prophecy, providence, and immortality, his conception of the place of Gentiles in the messianic
era, his approach to proselytes and proselytization, his understanding of dogma, and his understanding of the nature of the
Torah, is a further consequence of his having adopted the psychological theory according to which human beings are born equally
ignorant and equally capable of overcoming that ignorance.[48]

Leaving the historical discussion and returning to the issues
raised at the beginning of this chapter, we see that Maimonides has
shown us a way to affirm chosenness and reject chauvinism: The
Jews are God's chosen people because they have accepted the
Torah. A Jew as such, that is, a descendant of Abraham, is in no
way inherently superior to a non-Jew. The superiority of the Jew
resides in the fact that he or she is also an Israelite, that is, a person
who has accepted the Torah. Any human being can become such
through the process of conversion, and, Maimonides and I both
agree, all human beings will become such in the messianic era.
Gentiles, then, must be treated, not as second-class human beings,
but as Jews[49] *in potentia,* future partners in the messianic reformation of the world.

NOTES

I wish to dedicate this essay to the sacred memory of Steven
Schwarzschild. I am grateful to Rabbi Yisroel Miller, Col. Yizhak Gross,
and Professors Daniel J. Lasker and Michael Schwartz for their helpful
and insightful comments and criticisms.

1. See Kellner 1986, pp. 200–207.

2. A view that seems to be affirmed by Chabad and that brings
some of their spokespersons to interesting intellectual gymnastics.

3. Hertzberg 1989, p. 329.

4. See Katz 1971, p. 26. Subsequent citations from Katz are drawn
from this page and the following one.

5. Kellner 1991.

6. *De Anima* 2.1 (412aff.). For some of the necessary qualifica-
tions, see Hyman 1981.

7.   As Maimonides says, "through it [the conception of intelligibles which teaches true views concerning metaphysics] man is man." See Maimonides, *Guide* 3.54:635 (Pines).

8.   See, for example, *Guide* 3.27:511.

9.   See Harvey 1977.

10.   See Fakhry 1976, p. 139: "The whole process of human cognition thus becomes a gradual progression or ascent from the lowest condition of potentiality to the highest condition of actuality, or the apprehension of those intelligibles stored away in the active intellect. The name that ibn Sina and his successors gave to this progression is not union with, or even vision of, but rather conjunction or contact (*ittisal*) with the active intellect." For the theory of the acquired intellect in ibn Sina and al-Farabi, see Davidson 1972, pp. 137–44 (al-Farabi) and 160–68 (ibn Sina). The question of the nature of the contact with the active intellect became crucial in medieval Muslim and Jewish philosophy but need not detain us here. The bibliography on medieval Muslim and Jewish philosophical psychology is enormous. Studies that may be consulted with profit include Rahman 1952; Harvey 1973, p. 28 n. 1; Feldman 1984, pp. 71–84; and Feldman 1978. All of these studies contain references to the relevant scholarly literature.

11.   Maimonides' notorious intellectual elitism is an expression of this. See, for example, *Laws of the Foundations of the Torah* 4.11; *Guide* 1, Introduction:16 (Pines); and especially 3.18:475 (Pines).

12.   See Blidstein 1983, pp. 227ff.

13.   This comes out very clearly in many places. In his "Epistle to Yemen" (Maimonides 1985), for example, he speaks of the preeminence of the Jew (pp. 96–97) and of the "pure and undefiled lineage of Jacob" (p. 103); see also *Laws of Repentance* 2.10.

14.   Fairness to Halevi demands that we take note of the special circumstances surrounding the adoption of his position and that we not accuse him of or blame him for twentieth-century racism. Halevi flourished in a place and time in which conflicting national and religious groupings each advanced their own claims to nobility and belittled the character of their opponents. Spanish Christians affirmed their superiority over Jews and Muslims; Muslims affirmed their superiority over Jews and Christians; Muslim Arabs affirmed their superiority over non-Arab Muslims; Halevi affirmed the superiority of the Jews over the Christians, Arabs, and North Africans. My thanks to Bernard R. Goldstein for drawing my attention to this point.

15.   Studies of Maimonides' attitude towards the Jewish people include Levinger 1971, 1984; Ben-Sasson 1969–74, pp. 165–96; Raffel 1978, pp. 119–22; and Kaplan 1985.

16.   I.e., if they neglect it.

17. Compare Isadore Twersky's more muted formulation of this point: "Maimonides' spiritual conception of Judaism, in which biological factors are rather insignificant." In Twersky 1980, p. 486.

18. See Maimonides 1988, p. 235.

19. I cite from Hyamson's translation (Maimonides 1974), p. 66b, with emendations. It appears that Maimonides here combines aggadot with the sort of philosophical tale his slightly older contemporary, ibn Tufayl developed in his *Hayy ibn Yaqzan*. See Ginzberg 1968, pp. 195–98, and ibn Tufayl 1983.

20. Abraham, that is, came to knowledge of God through philosophic conviction, not religious faith. On this distinction, see Kellner 1992.

21. Maimonides 1974, pp. 66b–77a, with emendations and emphasis added.

22. *Guide* 1.63:153–54 (Pines).

23. In the continuation of the text quoted above from *Idolatry* 1.2, Maimonides makes clear that Isaac and Jacob were as motivated by philosophic considerations as was Abraham.

24. *Guide* 2.39:379 (Pines); emphasis added.

25. *Laws of Forbidden Intercourse* 13.1.

26. See Kellner 1991, chap. 6; Kellner 1986, pp. 19, 226–27.

27. Compare Halevi, *Kuzari* 1.87: "The people prepared and became fitted to receive the divine afflatus, and even to hear publicly the words of God . . . They distinctly heard the Ten Commandments . . . from God . . . The people saw the divine writing, as they had heard the divine words" (pp. 60–61).

28. *Makkot* 24a.

29. Precisely the principles of faith that Maimonides says must be taught to the prospective convert: "He should then be made acquainted with the principles of the faith, which are the oneness of God and the prohibition of idolatry. These matters should be discussed in great detail" (*Forbidden Intercourse* 14.2).

30. I.e., proved.

31. *Commentary to Mishnah Sanhedrin* 10.3.

32. For more details, see Kellner 1989, pp. 251–53. Further on the need and obligation to kill heretics, see Maimonides 1985, p. 114.

33. In Kellner 1986, pp. 42ff., I show how the first five of Maimonides' thirteen principles, which are rationally demonstrable (actually, the first four are, while the fifth, not to worship any entity but God, is a consequence of them), are for him the most important and crucial of the thirteen. Our discussion on this point allows us to solve a puzzle. There are two areas in which Maimonides does not apply his strictures against the heretic, etc.: with respect to marriage and to the taking of interest.

Why does he not inform us that a marriage entered into by a heretic is not invalid (compare *Laws of Forbidden Intercourse* 13.17 and *Laws of Marital Relations* 4.15), and why does he not inform us that we may take interest from a heretic? The reason, I submit, is as follows: The heretic, sectarian, and *epikoros* have excluded themselves from the community of Israel, but that does not change the brute biological fact that they are Jews by birth. Marriage restrictions are first and foremost a matter of lineage; we are forbidden to take interest from our *brother* (Lev. 25.35–37; Deut. 23.20–21); thus Maimonides did not and could not impose his strictures on theological deviants in these two cases.

34.   Maimonides 1985, p. 96. On this point, compare Saadia's well-known dictum, "Our nation of the Children of Israel is only a nation by virtue of its laws." See Saadia, *Beliefs and Opinions*, 3.7:158 (Rosenblatt).

35.   Maimonides 1985, p. 97; emphasis added.

36.   Maimonides 1985, p. 108. On Maimonides' general lack of attention to the notion of the chosen people, see Silberman 1971, vol. 5, col. 501.

37.   Maimonides 1985, p. 114; emphasis added. The Arabic for "religious community" is *milla*, which means exactly that, as opposed to *umma*, or "nation." To the best of my knowledge there is no study of Maimonides' use of the term. For its use in al-Farabi, see Kraemer 1979, p. 151; Vajda 1970, p. 256; Berman 1969, p. 108; Berman 1974, p. 165; and Berman and Alon 1980, p. 264.

38.   See Abravanel 1982, pp. 98–105.

39.   For details, see Kaplan 1985.

40.   Kafih 1972.

41.   "To give charity" is an alternative translation for the words translated as "to do righteousness" in 18.19.

42.   Another text from the *Mishneh Torah, Laws of Forbidden Intercourse* 19.17, might be cited as a counterexample to my reading of Maimonides, since he there asserts that Jews are by nature merciful. In *Laws of Slavery* 9.8, however, he explains that Jews are merciful because the Torah has educated them to be merciful. My attention was drawn to these passages by Levinger 1989, p. 89.

43.   Arabic: *milla*.

44.   Maimonides 1988, p. 234.

45.   Arabic: *milla*. Pines translates this as "community," offering "nation" as an alternative. Since Maimonides immediately cites Deut. 4.6, where the term *am* (nation, people) appears, we have further evidence for our thesis: Maimonides in effect here translates the Hebrew *am* (nation, people) into the Arabic *milla* (religious community).

46.   Hebrew: *am*. Pines renders this as "community," an odd trans-

lation of the Hebrew and one obviously influenced by Maimonides' use of the Arabic *milla*.

47. As Norbert Samuelson correctly notes in his rejoinder to this essay, this should read "Israel."

48. That is to not say that Maimonides had no biblical or rabbinic warrant for what he was trying to do with the notion of the chosen people. An example of a text that he could have cited in support of his position is the following: "For had it not been for My Torah which you have accepted, I would not recognize you or look upon you more than any other idol-worshippers" (*Exodus Rabbah* 47.3). For a full discussion of my understanding of Maimonides' attitude towards his Jewish sources, see Kellner 1991, chap. 10.

49. Samuelson is once again correct, and I should have written "Israel" here.

REFERENCES

Abravanel, I. 1982. *Principles of Faith (Rosh Amanah)*. Translated by M. Kellner. London: Associated University Presses.

Ben-Sasson, H. 1969–74. "The Uniqueness of Israel according to Twelfth-Century Thinkers" (in Hebrew). *P'raqim* (Schocken Institute Yearbook) 2:145–218.

Berman, L. 1969. "A Re-Examination of Maimonides' Statement on Political Science." *Journal of the American Oriental Society* 89:106–11.

———. 1974. "Maimonides, the Disciple of Al-Farabi." *Israel Oriental Studies* 4:154–78.

Berman, L.; and Alon, I. 1980. "Socrates on Law and Philosophy." *Jerusalem Studies in Arabic and Islam* 2:263–79.

Blidstein, Y. 1983. *Ekronot Medini'im bi-Mishnat ha-Rambam*. Ramat Gan: Bar Ilan University Press.

Davidson, H. 1972. "Alfrabi and Avicenna on the Active Intellect." *Viator* 3:109–78.

Fakhry, M. 1976. "The Contemplative Ideal in Islamic Philosophy: Aristotle and Avicenna." *Journal of the History of Philosophy* 14:137–45.

Feldman, S. 1978. "Gersonides on the Possibility of Conjunction with the Agent Intellect." *AJS Review* 3:99–120.

———. 1984. Introduction to Gersonides' *Wars of the Lord*. Translated by S. Feldman. Vol. 1. Philadelphia: Jewish Publication Society.

Ginzberg, L. 1968. *Legends of the Jews*. Vol. 1. Philadelphia: Jewish Publication Society.

Halevi, J. 1964. *Kuzari*. Translated by H. Hirschfeld. New York: Schocken Books.

Harvey, W. 1973. "Hasdai Crescas's Critique of the Theory of the Acquired Intellect." Ph.D. diss., Columbia University.

————. 1977. "Rabbi Hasdai Crescas and his Critique of Philosophic Happiness" (in Hebrew). *Proceedings of the Sixth World Congress of Jewish Studies* 3:143–49.

Hertzberg, A. 1989. *The Jews in America*. New York: Simon and Schuster.

Hyman, A. 1981. "Aristotle's Theory of the Intellect and Its Interpretation by Averroes." In *Studies in Aristotle*, edited by Dominic J. O'Meara, pp. 161–91. Washington: Catholic University of America Press.

Ibn Tufayl. 1983. *Ibn Tufayl's Hayy ibn Yaqzan*. Translated by L. Goodman. Los Angeles: Gee Tee Bee.

Kafih, J. 1972. *Ha-Mikra be-Rambam*. Jerusalem: Mossad ha-Rav Kook.

Kaplan, L. 1985. "Maimonides on the Singularity of the Jewish People." *Da'at* 15:v–xxvii.

Kaplan, M. 1970. *The Religion of Ethical Nationhood: Judaism's Contribution to World Peace*. New York: Macmillan.

Katz, J. 1971. *Tradition and Crisis: Jewish Society at the End of the Middle Ages*. New York: Schocken Books.

Kellner, M. 1986. *Dogma in Medieval Jewish Thought*. Oxford: Oxford University Press.

————. 1989. "A Suggestion Concerning Maimonides' Thirteen Principles and the Status of Non-Jews in the Messianic Era." In *Tura—Oranim Studies in Jewish Thought: Simon Greenberg Jubilee Volume*, edited by Meir Ayali, pp. 249–60 (in Hebrew). Tel Aviv: Ha-Kibbutz ha-Meuhad.

————. 1991. *Maimonides on Judaism and the Jewish People*. Albany, N.Y.: SUNY Press.

————. 1992. "The Virtue of Faith." In *Neoplatonism and Jewish Thought*, edited by L. E. Goodman, pp. 195–205. Albany, N.Y.: SUNY Press.

Kraemer, J. 1979. "Alfarabi's *Opinions of the Virtuous City* and Maimonides' *Foundations of the Law*." In *Studia Orientalia: Memoriae D. H. Baneth Dedicata*, edited by J. Blau, et al., pp. 107–53. Jerusalem: Magnes Press.

Levinger, Y. 1971. "Prophecy Among the Gentiles According to Maimonides" (in Hebrew). *Ha-Ma'ayan* 12:16–22.

————. 1984. "The Uniqueness of Israel, Its Land, and Its Language According to Maimonides" (in Hebrew). *Mil'et* (Open University Studies in Jewish History and Culture) 2:289–97.

————. 1989. *Maimonides as Philosopher and Codifier* (in Hebrew). Jerusalem: Mossad Bialik.

Maimonides. 1963. *The Guide of the Perplexed*. Translated by S. Pines. 2 vols. Chicago: University of Chicago Press.

———. 1974. *Book of Knowledge*. Edited and translated by Moses Hyamson. Jerusalem: Feldheim.

———. 1985. *Crisis and Leadership: Epistles of Maimonides*. Translated by A. S. Halkin; discussions by David Hartman. Philadelphia: Jewish Publication Society.

———. 1988. *Iggerot ha-Rambam*. Edited and translated by Ya'akov Shilat. Jerusalem: Ma'aliyot.

Raffel, D. 1978. "The Status of the Nations and Their Purpose in the Teachings of R. Judah Halevi and Maimonides" (in Hebrew). In *Mishnato he-Hagutit shel R. Yehudah Halevi*. Jerusalem: Ministry of Education and Culture.

Rahman, F. *Avicenna's Psychology*. London: Geoffrey Cumberlege for Oxford University Press.

Saadia Gaon. 1948. *The Book of Beliefs and Opinions*. Translated by Samuel Rosenblatt. New Haven: Yale University Press.

Silberman, L. 1971. "Chosen People." In *Encyclopaedia Judaica*. Jerusalem: Keter.

Twersky, I. 1980. *Introduction to the Code of Maimonides (Mishneh Torah)*. New Haven: Yale University Press.

Vajda, G. 1970. "Langage, philosophie, politique et religion, d'apres un traite récemment publie d'Abu Nasr al-Farabi." *Journal Asiatique* 257:240–60.

Response to Menachem Kellner

Norbert M. Samuelson

KELLNER'S GOAL

Menachem Kellner suggests that Maimonides' conception of the Jewish people/Israel provides us with "a Jewishly legitimate version of the doctrine of the chosen people that does not lead to chauvinism" (51).[1] He eliminates the possibility of excluding this doctrine altogether, even though "not one of the medievals who listed principles of faith included it in their lists" (51). Furthermore, he uses Maimonides as an authority for a legitimate Jewish interpretation, even though Rambam "rarely makes reference to the notion of the chosen people" (64–65), his "views on dogma were absolutely unprecedented in the Judaism which developed to his day" (56), and the dominant later traditional views[2] also differ significantly from Maimonides' position.

Kellner devotes a single paragraph (51–52) to the possibility of simply dismissing chosenness as a central faith doctrine. He asserts that without this belief in chosenness, "there is no way to justify adherence to Judaism in the face of adversity" (51). He supports this claim by invoking Fackenheim's emotive analysis of the theological significance of the Holocaust and Kaplan's affirmation that "the Jews must remain distinct" (52) in the light of the threat that nuclear weapons pose to the world. Kellner's own invocation of Kaplan illustrates the deficiency of this argument. Throughout his life[3] Kaplan both rejected the traditional doctrine of chosenness and affirmed the moral value of Jews remaining a distinct people.[4] The philosophical basis of his affirmation was the doctrine of nationalism, namely, all people who have a distinct history, language, and culture have an inherent right to exist; and the Jewish people have a distinct history, language, and culture. Furthermore, this "right" entails an ought. On purely secular terms, without an appeal to a doctrine of chosenness, Kaplan and his followers, no less than Orthodox Jews, could make their commitment to the survival and perseverance of the Jewish people a primary value before, during, and after the Holocaust.

My point is not that secular nationalism offers a viable alternative to traditional chosenness as a philosophical principle whose "cash value" is that Jews can commit themselves to survival as Jews in the face of radical adversity. Rather, my point is that, contrary to Kellner, chosenness is not the only possible alternative. In other words, the value of the survival of the Jewish people does not constitute a transcendental deduction (à la Kant) for chosenness. People are willing to risk their lives for all sorts of principles that have nothing to do with being chosen.[5]

There are two possible valid lines of reasoning to continue to believe in chosenness that have nothing to do with Kellner's argument. First, there can be a philosophical/scientific argument, based on empirical data or moral imperatives, whose conclusion is that this belief is true or right. Second, there can be a legal/political argument to the effect that to reject altogether any traditional doctrine, because its previous use tends to be false and/or bad, is worse than to interpret it in such a way that it can be affirmed, with honesty, as true and/or good. In other words, a "best reading" of a traditional text is preferable to a possible reading that, in spite of its historical popularity, is a "less-than-best reading." In fact, what I would consider to be a "best reading" of Kellner's enterprise in this essay is the latter line of reasoning. Kellner uses a traditional rabbinic source, namely, Maimonides' doctrine of the Jewish people/Israel, to interpret chosenness in such a way that it can be affirmed, with honesty, to be worthy of belief, even though Rambam's interpretation is atypical of most traditional rabbinic thinkers.

KELLNER'S INTERPRETATION

Kellner's interpretation of Maimonides' doctrine of chosenness rests on drawing a sharp distinction, which Rambam himself does not make, between two different senses of the terms *Jews* and *Israel*. Kellner reserves the term *Jews* for the "national group" that has a "shared descent from Abraham" and *Israel* for a "religious group constituted by its adherence to the Torah" (58). The former is defined by a "shared biological origin" (58),[6] and the latter, by its commitment to Torah. What "commitment to Torah" turns out to mean is belief in God's existence and unity (58ff).

Based on this distinction, Kellner advocates the following interpretation of Maimonides' writings as the best reading of the traditional doctrine of chosenness. The Jewish people are a people, no better and no worse than any other. However, they have benefitted from the historical fact that out of their nation has developed the religion of Israel, whose most central claim is that God exists and is one. This religion is called "Judaism." All who commit themselves to it are part of Israel; all who do not make this commitment are not. Today, many, but not all, Jews make this commitment. In the messianic era, Judaism will be the common religion of all mankind, both Jews and Gentiles.

In fact, my statement of Kellner's position is itself a "best reading." Kellner does not always keep the terms *Jews* and *Israel* as sharply separated as he intends, and it is not clear what he means by "commitment to the Torah." For example, at the end of his paper he says that "Jews are God's chosen people because they have accepted the Torah" and that "Gentiles . . . must be treated . . . as Jews *in potentia*, future partners in the messianic reformation of the world"(69). The use of the term *Jews* in both statements is not correct. Nothing that either he or Rambam said suggests that at the end of days everyone must become part of the national group. Rather, what is claimed is that they will become part of the religious group. Hence, Kellner ought to say that Israel, not the Jews, is God's chosen people and that Gentiles, no less than Jews, have the potential to enter the people Israel. In fact, this is precisely the claim about Israel that is commonly made in traditional expressions of Christian thought. In other words, Maimonides' analysis of chosenness, the one advocated by Kellner, turns out to be conceptually the same as the use of the term *Israel* often found in Christian theology. Kellner has escaped his feared consequence of Jewish "chauvinism," only to fall into the affirmation of an inherently Christian understanding of divine election.[7]

The proper source of the above *reductio* is the equivocality of Kellner's use of the expression, "commitment to the Torah." Although he never says so explicitly, what he means is commitment to the system of beliefs and practices developed in Judaism through the ongoing tradition of interpretation of the Pentateuch by classical and Orthodox rabbis. In short, "commitment to the Torah" is commitment to all 613 *mitzvot*, and not just, contrary to what he explicitly says, commitment to the commandments to believe that God exists and God is one.

If "commitment to the Torah" means acceptance of the obligation to fulfill all 613 *mitzvot*, then it follows that all non-Orthodox Jews, be they secular or liberal-religious,[8] are not part of Israel. On the Rambam/Kellner view, it is alright for Israelites to marry non-Israelite Jews because marriage is a question of biology rather than faith. However, by implication, it ought not to be alright to count non-Israelite Jews in an Israelite minyan. Furthermore, non-Israelite Jews ought not to be counted in an Israelite court as witnesses, because this also is a matter of a shared faith community rather than blood. In other words, it would seem that on Kellner's interpretation, the status of non-Israelite Jewish males within Judaism is reduced to that of Israelite women. Still, this is a fairly benign interpretation of the implications of Kellner's view. Worse interpretations are possible.

Kellner seems to imply that if Jews affirm Maimonides' first two principles, then they will affirm all thirteen, and if they affirm all thirteen, then they will commit themselves to all 613 *mitzvot*. Of course, the antecedents in each case are insufficient to entail the consequents. In Maimonides' world all educated and reasonable people affirmed that God exists and is one, and the greater majority of them were not Jews. More of them were Christians, and most of them were Muslims, none of whom recognized the validity of the system of *mitzvot*. Nor did Maimonides himself believe that his own first two principles entail the others. Maimonides distinguished between the sectarian and the *epikoros*. The sectarian is distinguished by denying the first five principles; the *epikoros*, by denying prophecy, Mosaic prophecy, and God's knowledge. The question is whether Rambam/Kellner intends these groupings to be joined by a disjunction or a conjunction; that is, is an *epikoros* someone who denies prophecy and/or Mosaic prophecy and/or God's knowledge, and is a sectarian someone who denies all or any one of the first five principles? Presumably Rambam/Kellner intends the disjunction rather than the conjunction. Note that Maimonides says that Israelites are forbidden to converse or even greet Jewish sectarians, and one may not even mourn the death of an *epikoros*. Even worse, Maimonides also says that "we are bidden to kill the *epikoros*" (62). Now consider who these heretics are. The greater majority of Jews in the world, including Israelis, are at best agnostic about the existence of God. On Maimonides' terms, that makes them sectarians. Similarly, no Reform, Conservative, or Reconstructionist Jews accept the principle of Mosaic prophecy on Maimonides' terms. That means that they belong to the category of the *epikoros*, which entails that Kellner ought not to have greeted us at the conference of the Academy for Jewish Philosophy, let alone conversed with us on questions of Jewish philosophy.

In sum, the price that Kellner has paid for a nonchauvinist doctrine of chosenness is the principle of *Klal Yisrael*. Now, as far as I am concerned, *Klal Yisrael* is no more an ultimate principle of Judaism than chosenness is. However, between the two, I would think that *Klal Yisrael* takes precedence.

If we take Kellner to mean that Israel consists of people who affirm God's existence and unity, then an entirely different, but no less troubling, set of consequences follow. To be an Israelite is reasonable, but being an Israelite in no way entails being a Jew. In fact, what Maimonides has done is taken over the classical theological interpretation of what it means to be a Muslim, namely, someone who submits to God, and used it to interpret the meaning of the term *Israel*. A Muslim, in the sense of "one who submits," is not a Moslem, in the sense of someone who belongs to a particular religious nation whose origins are in the community of Muhammad's followers. Rather, both the terms *Muslim* and *Israelite* in this sense mean followers of something like what the successors of Spinoza meant by a universal religion or what Hermann Cohen meant by the religion of reason. In the former case, being part of Israel is totally independent of any particular religion, including Judaism. In the latter case, the term *Israel* would express an ideal that is embodied in the particular religion of Judaism but differs radically from the version of Judaism to which most Orthodox Jews are committed.

I mention Cohen last because Kellner dedicates this essay to Cohen's student, Steven Schwarzschild, and Kellner is Schwarzschild's student. The essay that Schwarzschild wrote that relates most closely to Kellner's concerns in this chapter is "Do Noachites

Have to Believe in Revelation?" It is included in Kellner's edition of Schwarzschild's Jewish writings.[9] This is not the setting in which to discuss this essay, other than to say that Schwarzschild's article clearly is the source for and probably is the inspiration behind Kellner's choice of this topic. In that spirit I am in full agreement with what Kellner has tried to do here, namely, to develop a non-chauvinist interpretation of chosenness that deals seriously with what Maimonides has to say on the subject. I do not believe that Kellner has as yet succeeded in his goal. However, I "believe with perfect faith," because I know Kellner, that he will subsequently revise what he has said and produce an interpretation more in keeping with his own instincts and the tradition of his teachers in philosophy—Hermann Cohen and Steven Schwarzschild.

NOTES

1.   This and subsequent numbers enclosed in parentheses are page references to Professor Kellner's essay in this volume.

2.   Most notably, those of Nachmanides and Chasdai Crescas, as Kellner himself demonstrates in Kellner 1986.

3.   And not just in his last book (Kaplan 1970).

4.   In fact, in all probability the primary motive for all of his work was to contribute to preserving the Jewish people as a distinct entity.

5.   For example, communists and homosexuals both were victims of the Holocaust who died in the name of their commitments, neither of whom considered their groups to be a chosen people. Furthermore, Gypsies, like Jews, also were victims, not because they had any particular beliefs, but because they are what they are because of "blood," and Gypsies continue after the Holocaust, no less than Jews, to take pride in their identity and to promote the welfare of their people.

6.   To call the origin "biological" is not precisely right. It is biological to the extent that being a Jew is a question of biological parentage. However, converts do not share in this biological link, but their biological children do. It is possible, for example, for a male convert to marry a female convert whose offspring are no less Jews than anyone else. The category of origin has more in common with politics, sociology, and anthropology (i.e., identity through a national, communal, and/or familial line) than it does with biology (i.e., identity through a "blood" line).

7.   On the problems inherent in this consequence, see Novak 1993 for Novak's critique of Wyschogrod 1983.

8.   E.g., Reform, Conservative, or Reconstructionist.

9.   Schwarzschild 1990, pp. 29–59.

REFERENCES

Kaplan, Mordecai. 1970. *The Religion of Ethical Nationhood: Judaism's Contribution to World Peace.* New York: Macmillan.

Kellner, Menachem. 1986. *Dogma in Medieval Jewish Thought.* Oxford: Oxford University Press.

Novak, David. 1993. "The Election of Israel: Outline of a Philosophical Analysis" (chapter 1 of this volume).

Schwarzschild, Steven. 1990. "Do Noachites Have to Believe in Revelation?" In *The Pursuit of the Ideal: Jewish Writings of Steven Schwarzschild,* edited by Menachem Kellner. Albany, N.Y.: SUNY Press.

Wyschogrod, Michael. 1983. *The Body of Faith: Judaism as Corporeal Election.* New York: Seabury Press.

Reply to Norbert Samuelson

Menachem Kellner

Norbert Samuelson raises several important issues concerning my chapter. I will concentrate here on what I see as the most important and interesting of the issues on which we disagree.

MAIMONIDES

Samuelson, trying to do me justice, presents what he calls a "best reading" of my chapter. According to this "best reading," I am trying to present a "best reading" of Maimonides. That is not really what I am trying to do. My paper has two sharply distinguishable parts: a historical core surrounded at the beginning and end by an attempt to apply that historical core to contemporary concerns. In the historical portion of the paper I do the best job I can to present Maimonides' own views on the nature of the chosen people. I am old-fashioned enough to think that there is some value in trying to determine what Maimonides intended to say, as opposed to reading his texts with no reference to what he wanted them to say.

Having established Maimonides' views on the nature of the chosen people, I then quite self-consciously make use of them in order to suggest that one can affirm chosenness without chauvinism. Maimonides' position is not typical of the tradition, but it is surely part of that tradition. Using Maimonides' views in this fashion, of course, does not commit me to adopting every position ever put forward by Maimonides; thus, many of Samuelson's arguments with Maimonides, correct or not, are irrelevant to my paper.

CHOSENNESS AS A PRIMARY VALUE

There are, of course, plenty of reasons why individuals might want to affirm their identity with a distinct people. When we attempt to convince individuals that they *ought* to identify as Jews and act on that identification, especially in the light of recent Jewish history, we should have stronger arguments than the claim that the Jews have no less a right than other people to maintain their separate national existence. Jews in North America today must *choose* whether to be Jewish or to assimilate and disappear as Jews. The option is theirs. It is for this reason that Samuelson is wrong to dismiss as only "emotive" Fackenheim's argument that choosing to remain Jewish after the Holocaust is not an ethically neutral act. Given that Jews today (especially in North America), if they wish to remain Jews, must actively choose to do so, Fackenheim's argument is absolutely correct: choosing to be a Jew is a morally serious matter.

Of course Kaplan rejected the traditional doctrine of chosenness; but in the end, even he felt forced to adopt a variant of the doctrine of chosenness. In his last book Kaplan seeks to convince Jews to be Jewish because through their unique supernational existence the Jews hold the key to showing the world that a people can lead a national existence without degenerating into chauvinistic patriotism; this sort of paradigmatically Jewish form of existence, Kaplan insists, is the one hope the world has of avoiding nuclear annihilation. Despite the fact that he does not believe in a God capable of choosing the Jews, Kaplan provides what he would call a "functional reinterpretation of the concept of the chosen people." Indeed, Kaplan makes the Jews even more important than most traditional representations of the notion of the chosen people.

MY READING OF MAIMONIDES

Samuelson is right: in a number of places I failed to keep *Jews* and *Israel* as sharply separated as I should have. It is indeed Maimonides' position that Israel, not the Jews as such, is God's chosen people, and that at the end of days all human beings will be part of Israel. Samuelson asserts that this is a Christian interpretation of the nature of Israel and thinks that that is enough to show my interpretation of Maimonides to be absurd. Why is it absurd to think that some elements of Christianity reflect normative Jewish views? The debate between Judaism and Christianity is not between one (Christianity) that affirms a fully universalistic vision of the messianic era and the other (Judaism) that does not; rather, the debate here is over the question of whether or not the messiah has in fact already arrived. Christianity, believing that the messiah has already arrived, insists that all believers are part of "Israel." Maimonidean Judaism denies that the messiah has arrived, but affirms that after the messiah's coming all human beings will be part of Israel, even if most of them are not descended from today's Jews.

COMMITMENT TO TORAH

I do not say or affirm that commitment to Torah must mean nothing other than the punctilious observance of the 613 commandments. That indeed is Maimonides' position; it is not mine. I may personally be convinced that most liberal interpretations of Judaism are incorrect, but I do not for a moment doubt the sincere attachment to Torah as God's revelation of their adherents and leaders.

It is indeed Maimonides' position that non-Orthodox Jews are not part of Israel. Building on Maimonides' writings to develop a nonchauvinist interpretation of chosenness does not mean that we are forced to accept everything Maimonides ever wrote. It is furthermore true that for Maimonides non-Israelite Jews cannot testify in a Jewish court of law; he says this explicitly in the *Mishneh Torah*. It is received and widely accepted halakhah. But so what? It should surprise no one that Maimonides is not a theological pluralist; it should surprise no one familiar with his writings (both halakhic and philosophic) that he is perfectly willing to impose horrifying penalties on theological deviants. Again, so what?

Furthermore, Samuelson's "worst reading" of Maimonides, according to which I am forbidden to converse with my friends in the Academy for Jewish Philosophy, indeed should seek their immediate downfall and destruction, does not reflect halakhic realities. Contemporary Orthodox decisors, including figures as "ultra-Orthodox" as the Chazon Ish, insist on seeing non-Orthodox

Jews, rabbis and laity alike, as "captured children," not responsible for their rejection of Halakhah. Confused by the shifting currents of modernity and discouraged by the fact that God's providence is not clearly manifest in today's world, non-Orthodox Jews, on this reading, cannot be held liable for their failure to observe Judaism. This is, of course, not a view congenial to most liberal Jews, who do not see themselves as unsophisticated innocents led astray, and it may even be advanced more as a legal fiction than anything else, but it certainly shows that one can reject theological pluralism and not be immediately committed to ferocious witch-hunts.

THE CRUX OF THE DEBATE

This last comment highlights the real debate between Samuelson and myself. It has nothing to do, I submit, with the fact that in my private belief and practice I am an Orthodox Jew, while in his private belief and practice Norbert Samuelson is a Liberal Jew. Rather, the debate reflects the fact that we are frightened of different things. I am frightened of super-chauvinism here in Israel and of a North American Jewry that refuses to take its Judaism seriously and immerses itself in a shallow, self-glorifying ethnicity. For me, therefore, it is extremely important to find a way of affirming traditional Jewish beliefs without being forced to affirm the native superiority of Jews over Gentiles; it is equally important for me to seek to convince my fellow Jews that being Jewish is not enough—becoming "Israel" is what is important. Norbert Samuelson finds the specter of witch-hunts in Judaism more frightening and therefore affirms the preeminent value of Jewish ethnic identity. "*Klal Yisrael*," he says, "is no more an ultimate principle of Judaism than chosenness is. However, between the two, I would think that *Klal Yisrael* takes precedence" (81). I agree that neither *Klal Yisrael* nor chosenness are "ultimate principles" in Judaism. But since the notion of 'chosenness' makes little or no sense without the concept of 'revelation' (Kaplan notwithstanding), while one can make excellent sense of *Klal Yisrael* without recourse to revelation, I must differ with Samuelson and insist that, of the two, chosenness must take precedence.

STEVEN SCHWARZSCHILD

Nothing could be more foolish than arguing over who is the truer "Schwarzschildian," and I will not do so, especially since, although Steven Schwarzschild influenced me forcefully, I am not and have never been an orthodox follower of all his views (something he would not have wanted in any event). All this said, it is still the case that Steven Schwarzschild clearly held that there is one correct, normative version of Judaism. He was no more of a theological pluralist than was Maimonides. Indeed, it was his Cohenian insistence on seeing Judaism as ultimately rational, as more of a philosophy than a way of life, that forced him to adopt the position that there is one correct, "orthodox" if you will, version of Judaism. "Israel" and "the Jews" were not coterminous for Schwarzschild, any more than they were for Maimonides.

CHAPTER 3

Judaism and Chosenness: On Some Controversial Aspects from Spinoza to Contemporary Jewish Thought

Ze'ev Levy

The concept of 'chosenness' or 'election' has been a central idea throughout the long history of Jewish thought from the Bible, through the Talmud, rabbinic thought, medieval Jewish philosophy and mysticism, to modern and contemporary Jewish philosophy and theology. It certainly was and still is one of the most perplexing and controversial concepts of the Jewish religious tradition and, at the same time, one of the most important and decisive ones for Jewish life and history.

In the modern era, Jewish philosophy encountered new problems, and many traditional concepts underwent significant mutations and acquired new connotations. This is very much true of the concept of *chosenness* which was replaced, in the liberal trends of modern Judaism, by the idea of the *mission* of Judaism. Therefore, every discussion of chosenness today has to take into consideration two chief distinct aspects:

1. The important role that the concept of chosenness fulfilled in Jewish life and history in the past;
2. The questionability of its essential meaning today from theoretical, ethical, and humanist viewpoints.

As concerns the first aspect, no one will deny that the belief in "Thou hast chosen us from among all the nations," together with

91

the belief in the coming of the Messiah, were among the most important unifying factors of Judaism in its confrontation with a hostile world. These beliefs gave Jews a sense of superiority. Despite all the persecutions, massacres, derision, and discrimination which befell their lot throughout the ages, they felt superior on account of the particular *covenant* between God and Israel which, according to the Bible, was motivated by God's *love* for "his" people (Deut. 7.7–8, 9.5–6). This idea of superiority had its origin in the Bible where God referred to the people of Israel as "*am segulah*": "The Lord thy God has chosen thee to be a special people unto Himself above all people that are upon the face of the earth" (Deut. 7.6). But do these verses really affirm the sentiment of superiority? From the religious point of view, chosenness (election) is an act of divine *grace*. It is not a recompense for any achievement. Stiff-neckedness certainly does not merit any reward. It seems much more credible that because the patriarchs chose God (in contradistinction to the prevailing polytheistic and idolatrous religions of the time), he in return chose them. It was therefore out of love that he chose the Hebrews as "a kingdom of priests and a holy nation." These beliefs were also corroborated by the allegorical interpretation of Song of Songs and by the idea that God—*ha-Shekhinah*—accompanies Israel everywhere in the exile.

For many generations Jews believed that the absence of illiteracy among them, their pronounced moral standard in family life, their greater attention to rules of hygiene, and so forth were a result of this election. This tendency to self-praise was, of course, not unique to the Jewish people; the ancient Greeks displayed it as well. Herodotus, in describing his travels to Asia, was inspired by pride in being a Greek, a member of a nation endowed with higher intellectual skills than any other. Aristotle expressed a similar feeling when he defined all non-Greeks as "barbarians," incapable of caring for themselves, because of their alleged intellectual inferiority, and therefore "by nature" suited to be slaves. There is no lack of similar examples throughout history.

However, this feeling of spiritual superiority, accompanying Judaism throughout the generations, only seldom led to arrogant boasting. It served as a powerful support against Christianity and represented a source of hope in times of persecution and despair. "It was the conviction of 'Chosenness' that enabled the Jews to defy the powers of destruction and to reverse the normal patterns of history."[1]

The idea of chosenness became more pronounced and influential in proportion, or as a reaction, to oppression and suffering. One may say that the concept of the 'chosen people' constituted a sort of ideological self-compensation for the inferior status of the Jewish people in the diaspora. Buber once remarked that the important thing "is not whether we feel or do not feel that we are chosen . . . [but] that our role in history actually has been unique."[2] Yet, belief in chosenness is one thing; its being a fact is another. Moreover, can uniqueness be cherished as a value?

In medieval Jewish philosophy the belief in chosenness reached its height in Judah Halevi's *Kuzari*, a work stressing the special supernatural providence awarded the Jewish people, in contradistinction to the destiny of all other peoples, who were subjected to the crude laws of nature. Moreover, the people Israel was privileged to receive the Torah as a result of its inherent superiority, a superiority inherited from Adam, Noah, and the patriarchs. As Kaplan demonstrated, this became later the characteristic view of neoorthodoxy.[3] Most of the other medieval Jewish philosophers, however, denied this "racial" superiority and derived their concept of chosenness from the giving of the Torah, and not vice versa. On the whole, it was a minor point of interest for them.

This notion of chosenness and superiority invariably led to a certain isolation of the Jewish people from the other nations. Spinoza, whose criticism of the concept of chosenness will be discussed below, called attention to this too: "At the present time there is absolutely nothing which the Jews can arrogate to themselves beyond other people . . . As to their continuance so long after dispersion, there is nothing marvellous in it, for they so separated themselves from every other nation as to draw down upon themselves universal hate."[4] The belief in divine election thus turned the Jews into "outsiders" and became a mark of their anomalous position in (Gentile) society.

This idea of chosenness began to erode in the modern era. The very expression "chosen people" acquired a discordant ring. What had been a useful and important notion in the past failed to meet modern needs or to conform to modern understanding. Other people too used to regard themselves as "chosen"; Dostoevski, for example, believed the Russians to be the chosen people. Ultrareactionary views, as in Germany in the nineteenth and twentieth centuries, caused terms such as *chosen people, chosen race,* or even *chosen class* to sound offensive. Whenever one regards oneself or one's people or some other group as "chosen" by supreme providence or by history, one is inevitably in danger of entertaining an unjustified feeling of arrogant superiority. It is as if one, endowed with unique attributes not available to his fellow human beings, is required to save everyone else, or, what is worse, to rule over everyone else. There are today many Jews in the diaspora, regardless of their religious affiliation, who find it difficult to accept that God "chose" them specially to worship him and to fulfill his mission. For them, the concept of election has become an anachronism, an idea that is obsolete and irrelevant to modern life.

Even in ancient times, several thinkers recognized the tenuousness of the concept of election. In the first century, the pagan philosopher Celsus commented with ironic hostility on Judaism and Christianity:

> Jews and Christians appear to me like a host of bats, or ants who come out of their hiding places, or like frogs who sit in a swamp, or like worms who hold a meeting in the corner of a manure pile and say to one another: "To us God proclaims and reveals everything. He does not trouble himself with the rest of the world; we are the only beings with whom he has dealings . . . To us is subjected everything: the earth, the water, the air, the stars. Because it has happened that some among us have sinned, God himself will come or will send his own son in order to destroy the wicked with fire and to give us a share in eternal life."[5]

Despite the poisonous language, the inaccuracies, and the misconceptions, the words of Celsus indicate the discomfiture, on the philosophical level, occasioned by a phrase like "the chosen people." For similar reasons, modern Jewish philosophers felt uncomfortable with the belief that God has singled out the Hebrews from all other people in order to make them his "chosen people." Therefore, they turned their attention more and more to the second of the two aforementioned aspects. They clearly sensed the problematic nature of the notion of chosenness in its traditional form. Growing rationalism and universalist tendencies as well as the spread of emancipation and of a liberal sensibility all contributed to the weakening of its conventional connotation. Modern Jewish thinkers, therefore, preferred the notion of *mission,* but, as will be shown later, this terminological change did not really entail any substantial difference.

The first philosopher of modernity to come to grips with the concept of chosenness was Spinoza. In his *Thelogico-Political Treatise,* he devoted a whole chapter ("On the Vocation of the Hebrews") to the issue. There he tried to respond to the traditional arguments for the "eternal election" of the Jews.[6] His conclusion is that any claim to election based on allegedly intellectual or moral superiority is philosophically untenable. Since Spinoza's argument served as a paradigm for most further discussions on this issue, it seems useful to dwell on it more extensively. His starting point is unmistakably ethical:

> Every man's true happiness and blessedness consist solely in the enjoyment of what is good, not in the pride that he alone is enjoying it, to the exclusion of others. He who thinks himself the more blessed because he is enjoying benefits which others are not, or because he is more blessed or more fortunate than his fellows, is ignorant of true happiness and blessedness, and the joy which he feels is either childish or envious and malicious. For instance, a man's true happiness consists only in wisdom, and the knowledge of the truth, not at all in the fact that he is wiser than others, or that others lack such knowledge: such considerations do not increase his wisdom or true happiness.[7]

The same idea is formulated in the *Ethics* much more outspokenly:

> If we think that someone enjoys something that only one person can possess, we shall endeavor to bring it about that he shall not possess that thing.[8]

But there is also a philosophical aspect of a more general nature to the problem. Nations can be set apart by their languages and social habits, but never by reason, the distinctive feature of man qua man. Nature creates not nations, but individual human beings. From this angle, Spinoza anticipated Lévi-Strauss, who also advocated the universality of the human mind, rejecting very sharply any ethnocentric conception such as, for example, Lévy-Bruhl's notion of "prelogical mentality." (Will Herberg, too, noted that the moral argument that "the doctrine of 'chosenness' is little better than ethnocentrism, in which a particular group regards itself as the center of the universe and develops doctrines that will flatter its pride and minister to its glory."[9])

In order to ascertain the reason for the belief in the election of the Hebrews, Spinoza first of all gives a secular explanation to some traditional theological concepts: "guidance of God" or "help of God" are, according to his philosophical view, synonyms of "the universal laws of nature."[10]

> We can now easily understand what is meant by the election of God. For since no one can do anything save by the predetermined order of nature, that is, by God's eternal ordinance and decree, it follows that no one can choose a plan of life for himself or accomplish any work save by God's vocation choosing him for the work or the plan of life in question, rather than any other.[11]

Now, there are, according to Spinoza, different forms of preserving a society:

> That society will be most secure, most stable, and least liable to reverses, which is founded and directed by far-seeing and careful men; while, on the other hand, a society constituted by men without trained skill, depends in great measure on fortune, and is less constant.[12]

From this, Spinoza reaches the following conclusion in regard to the chosenness of the Jews:

> Nations, then, are distinguished from one another in respect to the social organization and the laws under which they live and are governed; the Hebrew nation was not chosen by God in respect to its wisdom nor its tranquillity of mind, but in respect to its social organization and the good fortune with which it obtained supremacy and kept it so many years. This is abundantly clear from Scripture. Even a cursory perusal will show us that the only respects in which the Hebrews surpassed other nations are in their successful conduct of matters relating to government, and in their surmounting great perils solely by God's external aid; in other ways they were on a par with their fellows, and God was equally gracious to all. For in respect to intellect . . . they held very ordinary ideas about God and nature, so that they cannot have been God's chosen in this respect; nor were they so chosen in respect of virtue and the true life, for here again they, with the exception of a very few elect, were on an equality with other nations: therefore their choice and vocation

consisted only in the temporal happiness and advantages of independent rule.[13]

I have quoted this passage at length because it is of great significance to the issue at hand. Spinoza's exegetical examples from the Bible, which are not always very convincing, need not concern us here. They were meant to corroborate his claim

> that the Jews of that time were not more beloved to God than other nations . . . [and] the election of the Jews had regard to nothing but temporal physical happiness and freedom, in other words, autonomous government, and to the manner and means by which they obtained it.[14]

Spinoza thus describes the notion of election or chosenness as an historical necessity that *separates* the Jews from all other people, while for traditional Jews the belief in election represented a metaphysical privilege that *distinguished* the people of Israel from other peoples. Likewise, in the famous concluding passage of the chapter where Spinoza ponders the prospective renewal of the Hebrew state and even speaks about the possibility "that God may a second time elect them [the Jews],"[15] he hastens to affirm:

> Lastly, if any one wishes to maintain that the Jews, from this or any other cause, have been chosen by God for ever, I will not gainsay him if he will admit that this choice, whether temporal or eternal, has no regard, in so far as it is peculiar to the Jews, to aught but dominion and physical advantages (for by such alone can one nation be distinguished from another), whereas in regard to intellect and true virtue, every nation is on a par with the rest, and God has not in these respects chosen one people rather than another.[16]

What he is here suggesting is that the laws of nature (and also of history), which apply to every people, hold for the Jewish people as well. The possibility of reestablishing the Jewish state exists not on account of "divine election," but rather on account of general historical laws.

Some scholars assume that these polemical passages of the *Theologico-Political Treatise* were perhaps remnants of the "Apology," which Spinoza had written to justify his rupture with the Jewish community following his excommunication. He clearly attacks here the particularist trends of Judaism for the sake of universalism. The deflation of divine election to favorable political circumstances perhaps expresses some resentment against the Jews who had expelled him from their midst.

Spinoza's discussion of 'election' comprises the principal elements of all subsequent discussions about the concept of the 'chosen people'. Although it would be naive to explain the fact of Jewish separateness or the idea of chosenness in terms of anti-Semitism, or anti-Semitism as a result of Jewish separateness and alleged chosenness, one cannot dismiss the existence of some relationship between the two notions. In a certain way they foster each other. But even Spinoza, notwithstanding his critical or hostile attitude, was somehow attentive to the fact that the "choosing" was also a "calling"; after all, he entitled the relevant chapter "On the *Vocation* of the Hebrews."

I have not dwelled here on Spinoza's general philosophical conception of God. If Spinoza's God (i.e., Nature), *ex definitio*, does not desire anything, he, of course, cannot choose, either. Therefore, when speaking about election, he employed a similar line of argument as when interpreting Hebrew theocracy as an *idea*—"this state of things existed rather in theory than in praxis."[17] This latter was indeed a very effective idea, one that nurtured the self-consciousness of the people of Israel after their liberation from Egyptian slavery. Similarly, election was a useful idea from the political-historical standpoint. However, in this case it is not only philosophically wanting, but also morally indefensible.

Moses Mendelssohn, more than one hundred years after Spinoza, also dissociated himself philosophically from the notion of election. Even though his view that God revealed himself only once in the course of human history, namely, at Sinai, and then only in order to reveal a Law to one single people, lends a certain credibility to the traditional doctrine of election, Mendelssohn refrained from using the term *chosen people*. It simply happened once that God acted as a divine lawgiver to one particular people, but that was a unique occurrence in the distant past. So, although Mendelssohn's concept of the 'ceremonial law' as the distinctive feature of Judaism entails several philosophical difficulties, engendered by Mendelssohn's twofold loyalty to Deism as a philosopher and to the Law (the Torah) as a Jew, he nowhere upholds the idea of Jewish superiority. Yet, nevertheless, if one accepts the view that God singled out the people of Israel for his unique and sole revelation, the concept of chosenness is unavoidable. To wit, why did he give the Torah to this people alone, not to others as well? Further-more, on several occasions, mainly in his letters, Mendelssohn expresses the view that Judaism is commensurate with reason, whereas Christianity is not. In his answer to the Hereditary Prince of Braunschweig-Wolfenbüttel he wrote the following:

> The distinction that I draw between the books of the Old and the New Testament consists in this: The former is in harmony with my philosophical conviction or at least does not contradict it; the latter, on the other hand, requires a belief that I cannot afford.[18]

But he did not connect any of this with the notion of a chosen people. On the contrary, *Jerusalem* was expressly written in order to defend the thesis that Jews as human beings are entitled to the same rights as all other citizens. Equality, not superiority, was Mendelssohn's goal. His plea was that Jews ought to enjoy an equal share in the spiritual, cultural, and social life of their co-citizens. Perhaps one can discern in Mendelssohn's views on Juda-ism a predilection for the concept of 'Jewish mission,' although it comes to the fore mainly in the later interpretations of Men-delssohn's concept of Judaism by Jewish scholars of the nineteenth century. Liberal Jewish thinkers indeed supported this view, which was taken up, at the same time, by S. R. Hirsch, the founder of *neoorthodoxy*. All of them tried to avoid the concept of a chosen people and to place the main emphasis on the concept of *mission*. The mission of Israel, as Moses Hess, the precursor of Zionism, was fond of saying, ought to replace the concept of election, and even though the latter term was laden with emotional content, it was no longer acceptable to modern Jewish thinkers. The mission is fulfilled through the dissemination of the moral message of the Bible, especially as expressed by the Prophets, and the conse-quences in the arena of social action drawn from them. The bibli-cal message is universal and humanitarian, namely, to spread the idea of "ethical monotheism." This became the favorite expression of the liberal Jewish thinkers of the nineteenth century, epitomizing the "mission of Judaism." This was particularly true of German Jewry where the young "Sciences of Judaism" (*"Chokhmat Israel"*) were most influential at the time. The questionable aspects of this expression are still to be discussed. However, the particularist ele-ment that characterized the concept of the election of Israel now gave way to the universal element, expressed by the phrase "the mission of Israel."

This latter interpretation of 'election' drew some of its inspiration from the Bible itself, and, in a certain way, represented it faithfully. In the Bible, election implied not any sort of superiority but *conditional* chosenness. The election of Israel imposes duties and responsibilities. It does not award rights or privileges: "Superiority and sanctity do not belong to historical Israel, to concrete individuals, but to a mythical Israel, held up as a model and ideal, defined by submission to God's commandments and respect for the covenant."[19] This interpretation of election certainly conforms much more easily to modern views; however, it is liable to give rise to the analogous argument of Christian theology, that it is the church that now embodies the "true Israel." Christianity does not deny the notion of election as such, but claims that the Jews, by rejecting Jesus, have forfeited their right to it. The Church has now become the truly elected. But whether advocated by Judaism or Christianity, the concept of chosenness, whatever its formulation, entails a preferential status vis-à-vis the secular state and society. This conflict, which has provoked tense relations between church and state for so many centuries, has not been absent from the Jewish scene either, and it still creates numerous difficult problems on the political scene in Israel today.

It follows from all this that the concept of chosenness has to be taken up with great care and caution. Rosenzweig called attention to this in his famous correspondence with Eugen Rosenstock:

> That is why even today, when the idea of being elected has become a coloring reagent in every nation, the election of the Jews is something unique, because it is the election of the "one people," and even today our peculiar pride or peculiar modesty, the world's hatred or the world's contempt, rejects an actual comparison with other peoples. Though its content has now become something universal, it has lost nothing of its metaphysical weight . . .
>
> For the Jewish idea of election is from the outset anything but naive. If it had been, you would have been right in comparing it with the race born from Zeus and nurtured by Zeus. But it is not in the least naive. It discovers its "origin" only when it has learnt about its "destiny" . . . On Sinai (not, say, by terebinths of

Mamre), so says an old punning legend, Israel has inherited the
"sinna," the hatred of the peoples.[20]

Some of Rosenzweig's formulations might remind us of Spinoza's
argument that the hatred of the Jews by the other nations is the
cause of the perpetual distinctiveness of the Jewish people. There
is, however, a certain disanalogy. As previously noted, Spinoza
treated the Jewish people as subordinate to the same historical
laws as all other peoples; but for Rosenzweig, the Jewish people
differs from all other peoples and religions by not being subject to
history; its chosenness implies eternity. Israel achieves its unique
functions, derived from its chosenness, *outside* of history, while
Christianity accomplishes them on the historical plane. Rosenzweig's metahistorical conception of Judaism is indeed one of the
most controversial aspects of his philosophy.[21]

For Leo Baeck, Israel's chosenness is the focal point of his
Jewish religious thought. Interestingly, he also shares some of
Rosenzweig's ahistorical approach. Baeck conceives of chosenness
as derivative of revelation, which is Israel's unique experience; the
more certain the act of revelation, the more pronounced the sense
of chosenness derived from it. But for Baeck, this is an article of
faith and not a historical judgment. It involves Israel's responsibility towards other people. This implies, evidently, the concept
of the *mission* of Israel again: "The idea of election has as its
unconditional correlation the idea of humanity."[22] The people of
Israel is chosen, for Baeck, because it is part of humanity and
accomplishes the latter's task in the world. From its very beginning
Judaism was a missionary movement, and with the expansion of
the diaspora this mission was addressed to the whole world. Baeck
thus links together the concepts of revelation, chosenness, and
mission; they form the theological expression of that Jewish particularity that was destined to become universal. However, while for
Rosenzweig this universal mission implies the concept of Israel as a
metahistorical people, Baeck conceives of it as the outcome of his
historical theology, although at the same time transgressing historical definitions and limitations.

At first glance one might ask: Do these terminological changes
from chosenness to mission express a substantial change in ideational content? Is not the view that Israel carries a purpose, a

special mission, merely a repetition of the concept of election in a more refined garb? After all, the assertion of a privileged relationship remains intact. In reply, some scholars have maintained that Judaism was not chosen a priori for the fulfillment of this mission. However, the fact that, because of unique historical circumstances, it was the first to accept ethical monotheism makes Judaism uniquely positioned to engage in spreading this concept. Parenthetically, it should be noted that in the Bible itself it was already stated that God did not choose Israel for its superior qualities, but for other reasons:

> The Lord did not set his love upon you, nor choose you, because ye were more in number than any people; for ye were the fewest of all people. But because the Lord loved you, and because he would keep the oath which he had sworn unto your fathers . . . Not for thy righteousness, or for the uprightness of thy heart dost thou go to possess their land; but for the wickedness of these nations the Lord thy God doth drive them out from before thee, and that he may perform the word which the Lord sware unto thy fathers, Abraham, Isaac and Jacob. Understand therefore, that the Lord thy God giveth thee not this good land to possess it for thy righteousness, for thou art a stiffnecked people (Deut. 7.7–8, 9.5–6).

In sum the following ought to be kept in mind: It is true that the concept of election is unacceptable in the light of scientific and philosophical criticism, and it is a contravention of the humanist view that sees every person and every nation as an embodiment of equal value of one humanity and one human spirit. Yet, the foregoing should not get in the way of appreciating the important function that the concept of chosenness has played in the development of unity and self-confidence of the Jewish people in times when they were the object of ubiquitous hatred and persecution. Just as the secular Jew is able to recognize and value the unique place and function of faith in the long history of the diaspora and is capable of respecting religion without himself accepting its beliefs or obeying its commandments, so, too, in the case of the concept of chosenness. Without identifying with its ideational content, which is incompatible with a consistent humanist viewpoint, one may still appreciate the function that it has played in the historical and spiritual circumstances that Jews encountered in the past, and respect the belief in it by previous generations.

To conclude: The concept of chosenness, due to its significant role in Jewish life and history, certainly must not be disparaged as scandalous; but it is now utterly incompatible with a modern worldview, based on the ethical essentials of humanism and universalism. In this regard, Kaplan states very clearly, "As a psychological defense to counteract the humiliation to which the Jewish people was subjected, the doctrine of "election" had its value as an expression of the sense of spiritual achievement in the past, it had some justification in fact."[23] But Kaplan hastens to add that nowadays "from an ethical standpoint, it is deemed inadvisable, to say the least."[24] After Spinoza, it is Kaplan who discarded the notion of chosenness more systematically than any other Jewish thinker. He does not hesitate to name the chapter devoted to it "The Chosen People an Anachronism."[25] Unlike Spinoza, he does not deny its importance in the past (though now it belongs "to a thought-world which we no longer inhabit"[26]). To hold on to the concept of chosenness now is no more than "self-infatuation." This equally applies, according to Kaplan, to the attempts to replace it by the doctrine of "mission," which he characterizes, using again a very strong term, as "religious imperialism."[27] It also clashes with "the ethical basis of democracy."[28] Both are not merely undesirable concepts, but useless claims. Therefore Kaplan looks for a substitute, to be reached by their reinterpretation.[29]

However, when summing up his criticism of the concepts of 'chosen people' and 'Jewish mission,' what he proposes as their substitute is a no less problematic notion, one denounced already by Spinoza, namely, the doctrine of *vocation*. He presents it as "a valid substitute for the doctrine of election."[30] It seems to me, however, that this conclusion undercuts his previously convincing arguments; it is indeed a substitute, but an unsatisfactory one. His conclusion is rather disappointing.

From this it becomes understandable why not only secular Jews, but also many religious Jews, feel awkward with the concept of chosenness. The rationalist notion of a universal God cannot be reconciled with the personalist conception of a "choosing" God. It does not befit him to be a "choosing" God in the first place. On the other hand, for a modern religious Jew, the rationalist concept of an absolutely universal and impersonal God would not be much less devoid of sense than for a Jew holding to traditional belief. Both try to sustain the belief in a "living" God, "who meets man in personal encounter in the context of life and history."[31] But in this case, the argument is reduced again to the ethical question of whether God would choose one particular people over all others. This, as we have seen, was, and still is, the Achilles' heel of the whole problem, against which Spinoza already took a firm stand. Modern Jewish religious thinkers try to overcome such an "ethnocentric fallacy" by emphasizing those verses in the Bible that underscore the universal "missionary" purpose of chosenness. But does this interpretation really undo the implicit arrogance involved? This seems dubious.

So however one turns in elucidating the concept of chosenness, one encounters inevitable obstacles. It can be (partially) justified only from the *historical* angle, that is, by an objective evaluation of its spiritual and moral contribution to Jewish life throughout the immemorial exile, persecution, and suffering. Chosenness has indeed been a powerful agent of consolation and hope, especially during the darkest hours of Jewish history. A fair and equitable judgment of the historical role of the concept of chosenness, therefore, ought not to be belittled by the rightful criticism of its essential meaning today. Contemporary anthropological theories do not merely proclaim the inherent universal equality of all people qua human beings; they also stress the *equivalence* of all human cultures. There are no inferior and superior peoples or cultures but only different, *other,* ones. Alas, the concept of chosenness entails ethnocentrism, for the better (in the past) or for the worse (today). Chosenness does not go hand in hand with otherness, that is, with unconditional respect of otherness.

NOTES

1. Herberg 1970, p. 279.
2. Herberg 1970, p. 273.
3. Kaplan 1934, p. 145.
4. Spinoza 1951, p. 55.
5. Origen: *Against Celsus,* vol. 4, p. 23; quoted in Herberg 1970, p. 262.
6. Chap. 3, "*Of the Vocation of the Hebrews, and whether the gift of prophecy was peculiar to them*"; Spinoza 1951, pp. 43–56.
7. Spinoza 1951, p. 43.
8. *Ethics,* pt. 3, prop. 32; Spinoza 1982, p. 123.
9. Herberg 1970, p. 280.

10. Spinoza 1951, p. 44.
11. Spinoza 1951, p. 45.
12. Spinoza 1951, p. 46.
13. Spinoza 1951, pp. 46–47.
14. Spinoza 1951, p. 48.
15. Spinoza 1951, p. 56.
16. Spinoza 1951, p. 56.
17. Spinoza 1951, p. 220.
18. Mendelssohn 1929, p. 229.
19. Atlan 1987, p. 56.
20. Rosenstock-Huessy 1971, p. 131.
21. Rosenzweig 1937, pp. 12–25.
22. Baeck 1905, p. 46.
23. Kaplan 1934, p. 43.
24. Kaplan 1934, p. 43.
25. Kaplan 1948, pp. 211–30.
26. Kaplan 1948, p. 211.
27. Kaplan 1948, p. 222.
28. Kaplan 1948, p. 224.
29. Kaplan 1948, p. 228.
30. Kaplan 1934, chap. 19, pp. 253ff.
31. Herberg 1970, p. 281.

REFERENCES

Atlan, Henri. 1987. "Chosen People." In *Contemporary Jewish Religious Thought*, edited by A. A. Cohen and P. Mendes-Flohr. New York: Scribner's.

Baeck, Leo. 1905. *Das Wesen des Judentums*. Berlin: Schriften der Gesellschaft zur Förderung der Wissenschaft des Judentums.

Herberg, Will. 1970. "The 'Chosenness' of Israel and the Jew of Today." In *Arguments and Doctrines, A Reader of Jewish Thinking in the Aftermath of the Holocaust*, edited by Arthur A. Cohen. New York: Harper and Row.

Kaplan, Mordecai M. 1934. *Judaism as a Civilization: Toward a Reconstruction of American Jewish Life*. New York: Macmillan.

———. 1948. *The Future of the American Jew*. New York: Macmillan.

Mendelssohn, Moses. 1929. *Der Mensch und das Werk: Zeugnisse, Briefe, Gespräche*. Berlin: Heine Bund (Weltverlag).

Rosenstock-Huessy, Eugen. 1971. *Judaism despite Christianity: The "Letters on Christianity and Judaism" between Eugen Rosenstock-Huessy and Franz Rosenzweig*, edited by Eugen Rosenstock-Huessy. New York: Schocken Books.

Rosenzweig, Franz. [1919] 1937. "Der Geist und die Perioden der jüdischen Geschichte." In *Kleinere Schriften*. Berlin: Schocken Verlag.

Spinoza, Benedict de. 1951. *Theologico-Political Treatise*. In *The Chief Works of Benedict de Spinoza*. Translated by R. H. M. Elwes. Vol. 1. New York: Dover.

————. 1982. *The Ethics and Selected Letters*. Translated by Samuel Shirley. Indianapolis: Hackett Publishing Company.

PART 2

Ritual

CHAPTER 4

Rational Law/Ritual Law

L. E. Goodman

Ritual has a more pervasive influence on human life than many a naturalistic or utilitarian philosophy is inclined to admit—or, indeed, to allow. Yet those who disparage the role of ritual the loudest are often quickest to condemn the women whose nylons have crooked seams, the man who appears in different colored socks or shows up for dinner at a restaurant without a tie—or the student who fails to appear at a formal dinner wearing a brightly colored beanie topped by a red plastic propeller, if that is what is expected just this year, say, of freshmen. Much of what passes as a conflict between ritual and freedom, or even between ritual and reason, is in fact a conflict among rival ritual claims, and one of the questions we must ask, if we are interested in the norms by which people live or would like to live (or would like *others* to live), is why and how rituals dare make any claim at all.

All students of Jewish thought know that Saadiah Gaon, following a rabbinic distinction between commandments that would have been unknown without revelation and those we should have been obliged to invent had they not been revealed, distinguished rational from positive (or revealed) commandments. The rabbinic distinction was built upon a presumed scriptural distinction between ordinances (*mishpatim*) and statutes (*chuqqim*). It became a focal point of discussion because it seemed to suggest that *mishpatim* were apprehensible or even deducible from the precepts of unaided reason while *chuqqim* were impossible to anticipate or even to comprehend on the basis of reason alone. Thus Saadiah is thought to have distinguished a realm of obligations that are strictly a matter of prudence and another realm of obligations that are ritual or ceremonial in nature and therefore not obligations of reason but simply a matter of obedience to the will of God.[1]

Some thinkers have celebrated Saadiah's rationalism on this ground, and others have deplored it. But I shall argue to begin with that Saadiah did not make the distinction commonly attributed to him but held a subtler, simpler, and more sensible view. Where Saadiah's chief and most recent detractors attempt to find conceptual incoherence and ambiguity in his words, I shall show the internal coherence of his thinking on the relations between law, reason, and ritual and argue for its consilience with the best of the teachings of the rabbinic sages and with the philosophy of law and ritual that grows out of Saadiah's approach in the authoritative juridical and philosophic writings of Maimonides. Beyond these issues of historical accuracy, exegesis, and the inner coherence of the tradition that Saadiah and Maimonides faithfully represent, I shall argue that in fact all laws have a ritual aspect (a point Maimonides seems clearly to anticipate) and that all sound laws are rational in the same sense that can be used to ascribe rationality to any laws. That is, I shall argue that all laws are rituals and that all sound laws are rational. If these points about the logic of law can be established, I think it will be clear why Saadiah did not draw the sharp dichotomy so commonly ascribed to him: The simple reason is that it is false.

DOES SAADIAH DISTINGUISH RATIONAL FROM RITUAL COMMANDMENTS?

Let us consider first what Saadiah said in introducing[2] the very topic of the commandments:

> Having established that God is eternal and without counterpart, I must premise at the outset of this Third treatise what we recognized at the end of the First as to God's reason for creating, that He acted purely out of grace and goodness. The same point, that God is good and bountiful, is to be found in scripture too, as the Bible says, "God is good to all, and His mercies are on all His works" (Psalms 145.9).
>
> He commenced His bounty toward creation with the bestowal of being, giving creatures existence, which they did not previously have, as He says regarding the most distinguished of them, "All that are called by my name, whom I created for my

glory" (Isaiah 43.7). But beyond that, He gave them the means of attaining perfect happiness and undisrupted bliss, as it says: "Thou makest known to me the path of life. The full of joy is Thy presence, and at Thy right hand, blessedness eternal." This refers to the commands and prohibitions God gave to that special class of those whom He created.

The first question that enters the mind of one who reflects on such a claim is this: "God had it in His power to give us perfect blessedness and everlasting bliss without issuing any commands or prohibitions. Wouldn't it suit His grace and serve our interests better to give us our happiness in that way and spare us the burden of responsibility?"

To clear up this point, let me say, on the contrary, that it was better and more generous to give us the means of attaining eternal blessedness for ourselves, by fulfilling the commandments God set out for us. For reason discerns that one who attains a good by working to earn it achieves many times over what one does who simply receives it without any effort, as a favor. Reason sees no comparison between the two.

This being so, our Creator preferred us to the richer portion, so that our profit from its requital would be many times greater than the profit of one who expended no effort. As it says, "Lo, the Lord God cometh with power, and His arm will rule for Him. Lo, His reward is with Him, and His recompense before Him" (Isaiah 40.10).

Saadiah thinks that the commandments were given, not as a penance, a fruitless discipline, or a merely arbitrary exercise, but as an enhancement to the human condition, an enhancement even beyond mere (!) eternal bliss. For an earned and deserved benefit is better than an unearned or undeserved one.

This means two things: (1) that God's justice allows him to enhance the reward of those who are more deserving, so that the assigning of responsibility is no mere arbitrary burden but a challenge that deserves to be rewarded and (2) that the world is the better for being a place in which rewards can and must be earned. This is the sense that Saadiah gives his important thesis that the world was created for the sake of justice. It means that the world was created as the arena in which man in general and Israel in particular can earn and become worthy of a transcendental reward, thus *instantiating* the rule of justice, letting God manifest his justice in fact and in act, rather than merely *possessing* it as an attribute.

It is in this context, in the context of this metaphysic of morals, that Saadiah introduces his thoughts about the character and purposes of the commandments:

Reason calls for a response to any good received, either by a return of the favor, if the giver is in need of such reciprocity, or by rendering thanks if the giver has no such need. Since this is a universal requirement of reason, it would be incongruous for the Creator to ignore it in His own case. In fact, it was imperative that He command His creatures to serve Him and thereby express their gratitude for their creation.

Reason likewise demands of the wise that they not permit themselves to be insulted or abused. So it was imperative as well that God restrain His creatures from such behavior.

Reason again requires that creatures be kept from trespassing against each other in all sorts of ways. So it was necessary as well for a wise God to prohibit this too.

And reason judges it appropriate for the wise to find employment for those who can be useful in some way and reward them with what they deserve for their work, in recognition of the special effort they have expended in behalf of some particular good. For this benefits the worker and in no way harms the employer.

But if we sum up all four of these requirements, together they would comprehend all the laws our Lord commanded us:

He required of us that we know and serve Him and devote ourselves to Him with sincere intention, as it says: "And thou, Solomon my son, know the God of thy father and serve Him with a perfect heart and a willing soul, for all hearts doth the Lord search and every inclination of thought doth He comprehend" (1 Chronicles 28.9).[3]

Futher, He forbade us to address Him with any ugly disrespect. Not that it would harm Him, but simply because it is out of keeping with wisdom to tolerate this. Thus, for example, it says: "If any man shall curse his God, he shall bear his sin" (Lev. 24.15).

And He did not permit us to infringe upon or wrong one another, as it says: "Ye shall not steal or defraud or lie to one another" (Lev. 19.11).[4]

At this point, where we would expect some mention of the fourth class, Saadiah instead generalizes his thesis about the first three, arguing that all acts of worship and piety are included under the first rubric, all forms of polytheism and impiety under the second, and all forms of human goodness, justice, truthfulness, fairness, and generosity under the third. It should be clear why no separate discussion of the commandments falling under the fourth requirement of reason are mentioned: There are no further goods. All of the commandments serve the goods already mentioned. They express our gratitude and acknowledgement of God, eschew the disrespect that impiety or obscenity would entail, or seek to avoid wronging our fellow human beings.

In keeping with the Mosaic conception of justice and injustice, our positive obligations toward one another are subsumed under the prohibition of injustice. For to deprive another of his due is injustice, and the deserts of our fellows in the Mosaic conception include aid, support, and love, not merely the avoidance of actual aggression.[5] Beyond the duties of man to man and man to God, there are no other goods to pursue. God has a fourth reason for giving commandments, but there is no further good for those commandments to serve. Either they serve one or a combination of the goods already listed, or they serve no good at all. It is at this point that Saadiah introduces his famous distinction:

> Implanted in our minds is an innate approbation of each of the three foregoing categories of acts commanded (or disapprobation of the corresponding forbidden acts), just as Wisdom, which is reason, says: "Truth doth my palate love, and wickedness is loathsome to my lips" (Proverbs 8.7).
>
> But the second great division is of those things that reason does not regard as good or evil intrinsically, which our Lord added to the tally of our commandments and prohibitions so as to augment our reward and the happiness we attain through them, as it says: "The Lord delighted for His righteousness' sake to make the Torah great and glorious" (Isaiah 42.21). What is commanded in this category becomes good, and what is prohibited becomes evil, as a result of its being commanded, since it serves as a way of worshipping God. It is thereby assimilated in a derivative way to the first category.[6]

Rosenblatt, in translating this passage, seems embarrassed at the thought of what is neutral in itself becoming good when commanded by God. He may equate this claim with the theistic subjectivism that Saadiah emphatically rejects. Perhaps desiring to avoid a contradiction, Rosenblatt renders: "What is commanded of this group of acts is, consequently [to be considered as] good, and what is prohibited as reprehensible; because the fulfillment of the former and the avoidance of the latter implies submissiveness to God. From this standpoint they might be attached secondarily to the first [general] division [of the laws of the Torah]."[7] But Saadiah does not say that intrinsically neutral acts come to be *considered* good or evil when commanded by God but that they *become* good or evil. He also explains why: These neutral acts are given significance as acts of worship. In what follows I think it will become clear that no theistic subjectivism (or any other form of relativism) is implied in the idea that divine commands, or other ways of situating actions in a context, can transform an intrinsically neutral act into a significant and therefore morally freighted act.

If we ask now how Saadiah distinguishes rational commandments in the Torah from those which are not rational, the answer is that he does not distinguish them at all. All the commandments are rational, and none differs from the rest in terms of rightness or prescriptivity. Saadiah distinguishes what he calls "rational commandments," not by their rationality, but by their intrinsic rightness or wrongness, characteristics which we have the innate ability to recognize. Other commandments deal with actions for which we do not immediately recognize an intrinsic good or evil. They may be neutral, considered strictly in themselves. But the Law itself assigns or finds for them a significance in context that makes them anything but neutral. They may seem to be matters of discretion, as though one could freely choose to perform or neglect them. But such a judgment would be mistaken, the product of maintaining an artificially abstract perspective on each act. Purely symbolic observances, for example, can serve a good, the one mentioned under Saadiah's fourth rubric, of giving us useful employment and allowing us legitimately and properly to receive the reward of our labors.

Further, once an act is made a proper act of worship, its intrinsic neutrality is replaced by the value it serves. In the same way, we must add, any act that is morally neutral in isolation will acquire a moral significance in context, by the significance it bears in our relationships with one another, with nature, or with God. We cannot evaluate a piece of behavior as an act without knowing the social and symbolic significance it may have. Some might imagine that this means that no action has moral significance apart from what is arbitrarily or conventionally assigned to it. On the contrary, what it means is that no action is ever without a moral significance, often complex and ramified. The isolation of an act from its moral environment is an abstraction. Beyond this general corollary of ours to Saadiah's point, Saadiah wants to argue that the actions he concedes to be neutral in themselves, at least at first blush before the tribunal of untutored reason, prior to a religious significance being assigned to them, may not be in fact entirely without moral significance. Thus he adds, with regard to actions that he classifies under his second broad category: "Moreover, on closer consideration, one must recognize that these have some slight benefits and partial explanations from the point of view of reason, just as the first category has major benefits and momentous significance from the point of view of reason." This refers to the actions taken narrowly, without regard to their adoption as means of worship. Such means, in the nature of the case, are symbolic; and a symbol, by definition, has a (partly) arbitrary relation to its object: A bow is not submission but an expression of submission. Clasping our hands in prayer (as Jews did in ancient times) is not humility but an expression of humility. No symbol can operate *as* a symbol, that is, expressively, unless it is distinct from what it expresses or represents. Nonetheless, Saadiah reasons, the acts that become morally significant by being taken up as acts of worship need not be wholly neutral in themselves. A red rose symbolizes love not because there is any intrinsic connection between redness and love—and yet there is an intrinsic connection, or, better, a structural relation, between the intensity of red and the intensity of love, between the associations of red with blood and of blood with life and death and of these again with love. The acts and objects that will serve as symbols in the worship of God are never purely neutral. I have shown at length, for example, how purity is made a symbol in that worship;[8] and, of course, spiritual purity is never wholly arbitrary in the physical symbols it chooses to represent it, never wholly unconnected to the bodily and moral and hygienic dimensions of itself, even at its most spiritual.

Reason has ready access to the categories implanted in it. It knows the value and the point of serving God, and it recognizes the immensity of consequence not only in the acts and omissions on which hinges our ultimate reward, but also in the conduct by which we ensure the justice or injustice of our comportment toward one another. When it comes to the special employment God has allotted us, reason finds itself on foreign soil, able, as it were, to catch only a syllable or two of significance in the language that is spoken. But is that language insignificant? Does our inability to understand more than a fraction of it entail that it means nothing? That certainly is not Saadiah's view. To maintain that God will augment our reward for the performance of *useless* or *pointless* actions would be to contradict the very heart of Saadiah's rationalism and to destroy his central thesis that the purpose of creation is the expression of God's justice.

The inability of human reason to comprehend more than a smattering of the wisdom in the special commandments by which Israel is to distinguish herself is no sign that those commandments lack wisdom. Saadiah repeats throughout his writings the claim that such commandments seek a higher good and express a higher reason than human reason knows. He in fact develops a theory of the way in which such commandments help us toward the happiness and perfection that is meant to be their reward. And it is appropriate that he should. For if they did not, and the explanation of their sense depended solely on the notion that they are acknowledgements of our loyalty and wholehearted devotion to God, the question would be very much unanswered: Why did God choose to be worshipped in this fashion rather than some other? That is a question that some theistic positivists would insist *is* unanswerable, even meaningless. But Saadiah cannot share that view as long as he holds that God's actions are meaningful, that creation is not, as he puts it, just a bad joke, that the burdens God imposes are not just burdens, not just busywork, but legitimate responsibilities and meaningful endeavors, *useful* work. For Saadiah maintains, not simply that God does as he pleases, but that God is good and does what is right.[9]

Consider the anatomy of scripture that Saadiah offers. All scriptures, he argues (suggesting his familiarity at least with the Qur'ân, whose language he sometimes echoes[10]), are tripartite in composition, embodying law, sanction, and the historical episodes that link the two:

> All the books of prophets and sages of every nation, regardless how many we study, comprise only three elements: (1) a system of commands and prohibitions, (2) rewards and punishments, which are their fruit, and (3) the accounts of those who lived virtuously in the land and therefore succeeded and of those who

lived corruptly in the land and therefore perished. For human well-being is made perfect only by these three components.[11]

One might suppose that, because Saadiah speaks here of sacred scriptures in general, his argument is not intended to apply to the Torah. But the context is one in which he is seeking to demonstrate how essential tradition is to the project of scripture conceived precisely in biblical terms, *as law*. Without tradition we would lack the clear connection between legislative norms and success or failure that enables us to call the life of sincere devotion to the precepts of the Law virtuous, wholesome, or good. Without these models or paradigms of the worldly working of the Law, we would not have the clear nexus of obedience, assent, and appropriation that enables us to recognize violation of the principles enunciated in the Law as vice and to understand its inherent or consequential destructiveness. Nothing here is arbitrary, such that God (as in the teachings of the Ash'arite school, whose theistic subjectivism Saadiah opposed[12]) might have commanded just the opposite of what he ordained, or condemned what he commanded. On the contrary, we know God's goodness and can vouch for the authenticity of the revealed text precisely because we can recognize the authority and legitimacy, that is, the goodness of its commandments.[13] Saadiah illustrates his point with the example of a patient and a physician, comparing the physician's advice to the method of scripture: not just, "Do this and don't do that," but "Do this and don't do that, because it will cure or prevent your headache, as it did for so-and-so."[14]

Developing this medical homily, which Maimonides will further refine, along with much else in Saadiah's metaphysic of the *mitzvot,* Saadiah addresses the question why God gave commandments to the virtuous, who do not seem to need legislative medicine. He finds four reasons: First, so that the virtuous may know God's will. Good intentions are not enough. If one wants to serve God, one needs to know what God desires of one.[15] Here we see the theme of concretizing general principles that will become so central to Maimonides. As Saadiah puts it:

> Reason ordains thanksgiving to God for His bounties but does not specify what form it should take, what verbal formulations, what times and what manners of expression it should use. So

reason itself depends on messengers to give definition to this expression and to give it the name of prayer, to assign it specific times and special formulae, its own distinctive postures, the direction in which one is to face. Similarly, reason rejects fornication but tells us nothing specific about how a woman is to be espoused exclusively to one man—whether merely orally, or by a simple monetary exchange, or by her consent and that of her parents alone, or whether there must be two witnesses, or ten, or all the people of the town, or by wearing her husband's insignia, or his brand. So the prophets come and give us dowries, wedding contracts, dual witnesses. Again, reason rejects thievery but tells us nothing about how people are to acquire property so as to make it their own.[16] Do goods belong only to the maker, can they be acquired through trade or inheritance, or appropriated from what belongs to no one in particular, as in hunting and fishing? Does a sale occur when a price is paid, or only on possession, or simply on a verbal commitment? . . . Again, with regard to crime and punishment. Reason deems that every crime has its proper sanction but does not specify what it should be— whether a reprimand is enough, or castigation should accompany it, or flogging as well, and if so, how many stripes . . . or whether only capital punishment will suffice. Does every criminal who commits a given crime deserve the same punishment, or should some be treated differently from others?[17]

Saadiah is emphatic that reason alone is incapable of specifying its own general requirements. Prophecy is needed, "not only for the positive religious commandments, to make them known, but also for the rational commandments, since people cannot fulfill them in practice without emissaries to show them how."[18]

Beyond this specifying and instituting of human obligations, Saadiah argues, God gives commandments to the virtuous to ensure them their full reward. Alluding to the talmudic theme (*Kiddushin* 31a) of the superiority of acting from obedience over acting out of inclination,[19] he argues that an act performed without a command, spontaneously, merely, say, because one is good natured, would merit no reward. He heightens this point in his third reason, responding to an argument of the Ashʿarite *mutakallimûn* by arguing (in appropriately *kalâm*—specifically, Muʿtazilite—style) that if it were fitting for God to reward unprescribed acts, it would be fitting for him to punish un*pro*scribed acts, a plan *reductio ad absurdum*, if God's justice is to be preserved, since justice allows no punishment without a prohibition. Finally, citing Ezek. 3.21, Saadiah argues that the virtuous need laws as reminders, to keep them on guard against any weakening of character or moral backsliding.[20]

Throughout Saadiah's discussion, what God commands is identified with virtue; what he prohibits is identified with vice. It is never arbitrary. What might have seemed arbitrary in itself becomes morally right or wrong when commanded by God, not merely (as in Ash'arite theology) *because* it is commanded, but because it is made part of a system of virtues and vices by which we are to be perfected and rewarded or corrupted and destroyed. We can see now why Saadiah says, not that the objects of God's commandments are *deemed* fair or foul as a result of their being commanded, but that they *become fair or foul* as a result of their subsumption in a system of legislation. For that system has our perfection as its goal.

We might suppose that Saadiah's saying that certain actions become right or wrong as a result of such subsumption leaves room for him to regard at least some of those actions as arbitrary, thus vindicating the sharp dichotomy that scholars have habitually ascribed to him, distinguishing between commandments that are rational and those that have "slight" if any rational basis. But such a view would ill consort with Saadiah's emphatic rejection of the theistic subjectivism that was widely discussed in his time. And in fact it is rejected by him, not only implicitly, as when he speaks about the benefits that all the commandments bring, but also explicitly, in his treatment of the direct, causal impact of the commandments.

Saadiah pointedly includes the reward of the commandments among their benefits, so one might have supposed that God, on his account, rewards us consequentially for observances that have no value constitutively. But if so, there would be no internal connection between the character of some of our actions and their reward or punishment by God, a notion that ill consorts with Saadiah's commitment to God's justice. What Saadiah says in fact is that our obedience or disobedience to God's commandments leaves its impact on the soul, purifying or corrupting us and making us not only more or less deserving, but also more or less susceptible to our merited requital. This theory of character and virtue has its roots in the Mu'tazilite objectivist riposte to the theory of the

Ashʿarites and is developed further by Maimonides. Saadiah finds frequent reference to it in the biblical imagery connecting light and darkness with the righteous and the wicked.[21] But his aim is not simply to echo but to gloss that imagery:

> Our Lord has made it known to us that obedience on the part of His servants, when preponderant, is called virtue; and disobedience, when preponderant, is called vice . . . and that these acts leave their imprints upon the soul, rendering it pure or sullied, as it says, in the case of sin, "he shall bear his iniquity," "he shall bear his sin," "and they set on their soul their iniquity," "its iniquity shall rest upon that soul" (Leviticus 5.1, 24.15, Hosea 4.8, Numbers 15.31). Even though these things may be hidden from human beings, or not plain to them, they are patent to Him, as it says: "I the Lord search the heart and try the kidneys" (Jeremiah 17.10).[22]

God's justice is exercised, not in rewarding or punishing us for arbitrarily selected behaviors, but in rewarding us for *and through* our virtues and vices.[23] The Torah does not waste words simply to inform us tautologously that one who disobeys God is guilty of disobedience. Nor does it simply inform us that disobedience is wrong—as though one who contemplated disobeying God would be moved by another commandment to obey the commandments or by the knowledge that such rebelliousness is undesirable. Rather, the Torah tells us that wrongdoers will bear the consequences of their wrongdoing, not upon their heads, but upon their souls. Their guilt (and the corresponding merit of those who obey God's commandments) redound to their injury (or benefit) constitutively, through the dynamic of their actions, making them weaker and less free (or better and stronger) persons, as well as affecting them consequentially, through God's justice, his requital of good and evil acts:

> Having established God's justice as an axiom, I can refer to this principle any questions that people may raise about the fate of the soul, and argue that since the soul does not act in isolation, sheerly by its own constitution, it needs something coupled with it to accompany it, through which it can act in its own interest. For it is only through actions that it will reach lasting blessedness and perfect happiness, in accordance with what I explained in the Fifth Treatise, that obedience augments the luminosity of the

substance of the soul, and disobedience muddies it, as Scripture plainly states: "Light is sown for the righteous," etc. (Proverbs 13.9).[24]

Far from an extrinsic justice, God acts directly on the substance of the soul and through its very nature. The concept of reward here is very compact with that of the *mitzvot* and the life of the *mitzvot*, as is not surprising in view of the biblical rootedness of Saadiah's thinking.[25] The same substance that sustains the soul and renders it capable of action bears the consequences of its actions, their "fruits," as Saadiah calls them, not external responses, but expressions of the inner dynamic of choice itself, by which, as Saadiah sometimes puts it, one and the same divine light sheds joy and blessedness on the righteous but torment and agony on those who flout God's commandments of righteousness.[26]

One final piece of evidence for our claim that Saadiah regards none of the *mitzvot* as arbitrary but takes all of them to exemplify rational principles (even in cases where human reason glimpses only a smattering of the principles at stake) can be drawn from his rejection of the free method of allegorical exegesis, which the Arabs called *"ta'wîl."* Saadiah's arguments against the arbitrary application of *ta'wîl*[27] boil down to a colorful and extended demonstration that if such a method is given its head, anything can be proved: The prohibition of leaven at Passover can be taken to mean that harlotry is forbidden, the prohibition against lighting a fire on the Sabbath might mean that armies are not to be brought into the field. To head off such arbitrariness, Saadiah devised a rigorous set of hermeneutical rules, which he scrupulously obeyed himself and which he founded on the canons of reason, science, language, and tradition.[28] Without some such discipline, as many modern students of hermeneutics are painfully discovering today, exegesis becomes arbitrary and turns to woolgathering and narcissism.

What Saadiah's method (and indeed any workable method of hermeneutics) requires is a *thematic* exploration of the canon to which it is addressed. This Saadiah has done in outline when he groups the *mitzvot* under the goods they serve. Without such a linkage, guided by our moral understanding and by the traditions that aid that understanding to direction, focus, and coherence, there would be no way of knowing where and how to take scripture literally, where and in what direction to extend or confine its apparent dictates, or even how to disentangle its literal from its figurative intensions. To make such an observation is not a blanket endorsement of every exegetical aperçu that Saadiah may have offered; it is to recognize with him and with the rabbinic tradition for which he speaks that if the *mitzvot*, any of the *mitzvot*, are treated as brute positive demands, we are in that measure deprived of access to an understanding of what it is that they demand.

Saadiah's objectivism about values and his resultant recognition of the affinity of Platonism with the biblical fusion in God of the highest phases of being and value allow him not only to respond to the Epicurean dilemma, but also to see through the notion that what God would command, or what we could appropriately construe as the will of God, would be anything other than the good. Glossing Job 34.17–19, which he renders, "How can one who hateth justice prevail in his own affairs? Or wilt thou overrule Him who is great in justice? Is 'scoundrel' to be said unto the king or 'unfair' to the openhanded, who favoreth not princes and sustaineth not lavishness in the presence of the poor, since they are all His work?" Saadiah discovers seven arguments "refuting the notion of divine injustice" and establishing that the very power of God and legitimacy of his sovereignty rest upon his justice. The three arguments that Saadiah takes as basic aim at the Epicurean dilemma, arguing that God is not weak, venal, or unknowing. But crucial for our present purpose are three of the four that he calls subsidiary:

> First, *Doth one who hateth justice prevail?* (v. 17). This means that when a man is unjust and hates just rule, his own affairs are not well ordered or successful, as it says, "A man is not established by iniquity" (Proverbs 12.3). But He, whose concerns run in perpetual order and stability, is on a plane which precludes His being unjust. Second, *Or wilt thou condemn Him who is great in justice?* (v. 17). This means that the doings of the Creator cannot be impugned and His judgment overruled by some denier. For it is absurd to impugn the Truth Itself. Third is his saying, *Is "scoundrel" to be said unto the king?* (v. 18). Here Elihu makes clear that the king deserves to rule only for his justice. So it is absurd that He be a rightful king and yet be vicious.[29]

Someone who holds the incoherent notion that power means arbitrary authority might imagine that God simply commands whatever he pleases and that there is no need for his commandments to be just or appropriate, that he might reward behaviors which he arbitrarily assigned for that very purpose. But Saadiah holds no such notion of power or of God. God's power, like all legitimate authority, is founded on justice, and God's rewards are assigned for the performance of work that is valuable, even if human reason does not immediately or instinctively detect the full measure of the value in it.

IS SAADIAH'S VIEW INCOHERENT?

In a paper first published in the early 1970s, Marvin Fox argues against the very idea of rational commandments:

> Whatever interpretation may be put upon those talmudic passages which seem to support the claim that some commandments are rooted in reason, it is clear that Saadia is the first major Jewish writer to refer to certain commandments specifically as *sikhliyyot* . . . There is no philosophically acceptable sense in which Saadia can be said to have shown that there are rational commandments.[30]

Thus, where I have argued against the conventional view by showing that according to Saadiah all of the commandments are rational, although we may not have the immediate means of detecting the rationality of some, Fox argues that none of the commandments are rational and that it was wrongheaded of Saadiah to attempt to show that any are.

Fox rests his case on an alleged incoherence in Saadiah's conception of rationality: "When we pay close attention to the variety of ways in which Saadia uses the various terms for 'reason' and 'rationality' in his book, we see that no simple explanation of these terms will suffice. In fact, it may not be possible at all to emerge with a completely satisfactory explanation, precisely because Saadia appears to say a variety of things that are not internally consistent."[31]

Fox hedges his position by disowning as part of his topic not only the rabbinic discussions in which Saadiah anchored his thematic conception of rationality, but also the *kalâm* discussions in whose idiom the issue was characteristically discussed in Saadiah's day. He voices this refusal to contextualize as though it were the outcome of an effort to address Saadiah on his own terms: "Whatever the origins of his doctrines and whatever purposes they may have been intended to serve, we must still try to see and understand them in their own context. Saadia's readers are not required by him to know the entire intellectual history of the concepts and arguments that he develops."[32] This disclaimer from a historian of ideas, coupled with the demand for a "completely satisfactory," "simple explanation" seems to load the dice in the direction of failure.

But in fact, in his commentary on Job, Saadiah does offer readers who may not be wholly familiar with the entire history of human speculation on what Saadiah takes to be perennial and universal issues about the metaphysic of morals quite a straightforward and indeed simple standard of what would count as rationality in his terms: He says that individuals who are tested with sufferings but maintain their integrity and allegiance to God, as Job did, will discover, when they receive the recompense to which this extra measure of devotion entitles them, that the enhanced blessings they receive were well worth their suffering. Listing God's bounties toward his creatures, Saadiah makes the point graphically, using imagery clearly intended to make plain what is at stake for the benefit of readers who are not conversant with the pertinent rabbinic and *kalâm* discussions:

> The third is recompense for tribulations with which He has afflicted us and which we have borne with fortitude. This, accordingly, can be called a reward. For the tribulations are not on account of some past sin on the servant's part. They are spontaneously initiated by God. Their purpose, therefore, lies in the future, as the prophet makes clear: "Fortunate is the man Thou chastenest, O Lord, and whom Thou teachest in Thy Law" (Psalms 94.12). The Allwise knows that when we are visited with sufferings they are abhorrent to our natures and harrowing to us in our struggle to surmount them. So He records all to our account in His books. If we were to read these ledgers, we would find all we have suffered made good, and we would be confirmed in our acceptance of His decree.[33]

Here in his discussion of the extreme case, the case of undeserved sufferings, Saadiah makes it perfectly clear what his standard of rationality in human choices is: It is our objective interest. The discussion is relevant to our present concern with rationality because it is the apparent disparity between God's justice and the suffering of innocents that in Saadiah's view makes the strongest case for theistic subjectivism and leads those who ponder the human condition, as Job did prior to his enlightenment and as the Ash'arite theologians did in Saadiah's time, to conclude *not that God is unjust* but that his expectations are arbitrary.[34]

Saadiah makes a point of saying that God does not conform creation to our desires or wants. "Wisdom," he writes, "is not identical with what creatures yearn for, nor is the right course of action that which human beings are pleased with. . . . The proper object of concern is not whether the decrees of the Allwise gladden His creatures or grieve them. For what is agreeable to them is not the standard of His wisdom. Rather His wisdom is the standard for them."[35] But God does maximize our interests, and in a way that we would recognize if we had objective knowledge of the case—a way that we *shall* recognize when that knowledge is made open to us. Even martyrdom, Saadiah argues, if its recompense is borne in mind, "is actually better than continued life in the world. Of this it says, 'For Thy favor is better than life' (Psalms 63.4)." It is for this reason that Saadiah can equate reason or rationality with wisdom.

Fox attempts to drive Saadiah into an equivocation or inconsistency by noting that he sometimes takes rationality in a purely formal sense, as in denying the rationality of the claim that fire is cold, or in neglecting the requirements of syllogistic entailment. But none of the commandments of the Torah "is rational by this standard," that is, none of them states an analytic truth.[36] Readers who have a genuine interest in the *material* sense that Saadiah gives to the idea of reason will find the core of it spelled out brilliantly and faithfully in Spinoza: "Since reason demands nothing contrary to nature, it demands that everyone love himself, seek his own advantage, what is really [sc., objectively] useful to him, want what will really lead man to a greater perfection, and, absolutely, that everyone should strive to preserve his own being as far as he can. This, indeed, is as necessarily true as that the whole is greater than its part."[37] Spinoza goes on to explain the senses in which our personal well-being depends on that of others and cannot be achieved to their detriment or by any sacrifice of virtuous principle. That explanation is important, if we are to avoid confusion, since many modern exponents of rationality in decision making have presumptively equated rationality with the reductively defined interests of the atomic ego. Saadiah would no more make such an equation than he would equate objective interests with their subjective apprehension.

Crucial to us in the passage from Spinoza is the argument on which he rests his claim: The warrant for our knowledge that the requirement to pursue our own interest is a truth of reason as solid as "The whole is greater than its part" is that the essence of each existent is its striving to preserve its own being. For a being to exist is for it actively to affirm its essence, to strive to preserve and promote its own distinctive mode of being, that which affirms its own character. For it to fail to do so would be for it to deny or reject itself. Now some can debate, or pretend to debate, whether a being *ought* to preserve or express its own being. But no one can deny that there can be no obligation more basic. Correspondingly, there is a fundamental incoherence in self-negation, that is, in the pressing or affirmation of one's own existential negation or annihilation. It is in this sense that self-interest can and must be considered an imperative of reason, not in the sense that, say, suicide is impossible or unintelligible, but in the sense that it involves a contradiction of what the very intension of any action affirms. It is not *formally* inconsistent to deny our own being in this sense, but it is ontically so, in that the being that seeks to negate itself simultaneously affirms itself. It seeks protection, surcease, peace, in the very act by which it destroys the basis of the very claims its being makes for affirmation and existence. Less dramatically, we find a parallel negation, ontic self-denial, in morbid shyness, agoraphobia, fear of success, and kindred pathologies, including several forms of addiction and compulsive behavior, where self-protective impulses are perverted, deceived, or self-deceived into self-negation, self-thwarting, emotional self-crippling, perhaps through the introjection or internalization of ambient, even depersonalized hostilities encountered in a competitive or indifferent social environment.

Philosophers who choose to deny the centrality and elementality of self-affirmation as the dynamic core of the essence of any being can still see the sense of Saadiah's argument. For even if our own active existence is claimed not to involve self-affirmation, one can grasp what would be meant by rationality in Saadiah's discussions, if one simply posits one's own interests as a desideratum and takes rationality as Saadiah uses it here to mean "conducive to one's (true or objective) interest." If we want to understand

Saadiah's treatment of 'reason' fully, we have only to generalize Spinoza's thesis, as Spinoza himself does in social terms, when he makes piety the desire for all others of what one desires for oneself. Saadiah identifies reason as the recognition of *any* real value, not solely the value of self-affirmation or self-expression. Given Saadiah's moral objectivism or realism, and abandoning the perspectivism of the Cartesian primacy of the subjective, we can also recognize why Saadiah regards, say, acceptance of the truth as a demand of reason. For reason would call upon us to recognize *any* objective value and thus would encompass the acknowledgment of truth, the appropriateness of gratitude for favors rendered, the legitimacy of just rewards, and the illegitimacy of unjust punishments. But recognition of the possibility of such a conception of reason requires a willingness to budge from the dogmatic equation of reason with tautology. Where such a willingness is withheld, the formal fit of desert to recognition, or of merit to acknowledgment, of legitimacy to acceptance, or of truth to credence, will not be readily apparent.

Fox criticizes Saadiah for holding that reason is a source of knowledge that teaches us, for example, that we should approve of truth and reject falsehood. The basis of the criticism is that such a preference is not analytic: "There is no analysis that one can produce of the statement 'Truth is good and falsehood bad,' that can show it to be necessarily true, given Saadia's own definition of necessary truth."[38] Now this is certainly an odd procedure, first to fault a philosopher for using a term in a variety of senses and then to fault him again for not making one of those senses trivially reducible to another. When Fox uses the idea of analyticity to find "no element of rational necessity" in the predilection for truth that Saadiah ascribes to rationality, one can only wonder exactly who is equivocating.

Fox goes on to quote Nietszche's "shattering question" about why we should prefer truth to falsehood and to suggest that anyone who is "offended" by the suggestion that things might have been the other way around, that is, that "reason" might just as well have chosen falsehood over truth, is merely expressing arbitrary prejudices, since "There is nothing internally contradictory about the assertion that truth is bad and falsehood good" and Saadiah "offers us no ground" for treating a preference for the truth as on a par with the law of contradiction.[39] Now surely anyone who has read Aristotle's discussion in the *Metaphysics* on the law of contradiction will see the sense in which that law and our preference for truth are on a par. For both are so primary that they cannot be proved without a question-begging dependence on other thoughts, which will in turn depend on them. It is for this reason that they must be treated as truths of reason if they are to be assumed at all—not that they are innate knowledge, necessarily, but that they are a priori in the important epistemic sense that there is nothing that can be used to prove them. We might assume that we should dispense with them. But that would rest on an arbitrary preference for avoiding all claims rather than making any. And that preference would itself be groundless. Its specious appeal would rest on the incoherent assumption that everything can and must be proved. On the contrary, the demand that claims be grounded *presupposes* the pertinence of making truth claims and has no sphere of application if the question for truth is abandoned. Aristotle gave as good a dialectical argument as is possible in defense of the law of contradiction, when he shows how those who might like to dispense with it reduce themselves to silence. The same argument serves equally well for the case at hand: One can indeed be quite uninterested in the truth, but one certainly cannot *say so*—least of all while professing to discredit the views of some philosophers and to set aside others as irrelevant.

Turning to the *mitzvot*, Fox surveys Saadiah's applications of the concept of 'rationality,' and writes that "the difficulties increase dramatically." He finds in Saadiah "a variety of cases in which he asserts that something is required by reason, but none of them is a case that on examination meets the standards of rational necessity he himself has set."[40] In other words, Fox presses his equivocation. It might behoove us, in the interest of charity, to watch him when he pushes the concept of reason beyond the realm of the analytic. But Fox's charity runs out after he writes in a parenthetic preterition, "It is needless to add that we do not want to subject a tenth-century philosopher to criticisms concerning analyticity or essentiality that are familiar to contemporary philosophers." Since the rule of charity is a hermeneutic and heuristic principle rather than simply a matter of compassion, those who fail to extend it are themselves the real losers. Saadiah can no longer benefit from Fox's indulgence. But if we can learn from philosophers who are not Quine or Wittgenstein, we should be willing at least to entertain the possibility that we can learn from philosophers who are not Carnap, Ayer, Reichenbach, Locke, or Hume.

Fox observes that Saadiah assigns to reason the principle that earned benefits are better than those that come solely by grace or favor and without merit or desert. At best, Fox argues, since this is not a statement that it is contradictory to deny, "Saadiah labels as a rational judgment that which cannot qualify as such by any known standard, unless he uses the term 'rational' very loosely to mean something like 'reasonable' in the sense of 'based on wide-spread experience.'" But I wonder how many "known standards" of rationality Fox tried before he reached this global conclusion. Consider what we know about Saadiah: that he took creation itself to be an absolute act of grace, representing infinite generosity because it answered to no prior desert.[41] Why could he not re-gard the reward reserved to the righteous in the hereafter, which he took to be vouched for by God's justice,[42] as even greater, since it involves eternal bliss, whereas creation, which expresses infinite bounty, gives us only a finite existence, in which, by Saadiah's account, sufferings are never overbalanced by joys and pleasures?[43]

If infinitely enduring blessedness can be achieved by merit, then surely merit rises higher than grace or favor alone would bring us, and earned benefits are greater than those that are merely bestowed, quite apart from what common sense or common prac-tice or common experience have to say about the matter. Now all this may sound very mechanical and arithmetic, but the problem is not in Saadiah's concept of rationality, but only in reliance on arithmetic imagery to try to represent moral and spiritual truths. As Saadiah argues, glossing Isa. 55.9 ("High as the heavens are above the earth, so high are My ways above your ways and My thoughts above your thoughts"), "The Allwise says that His ways, in goodness and generosity, are higher and loftier than the benefi-cence and grace bestowed by creatures, as the heavens are above the earth—not to suggest that it ceases on reaching that limit. On the contrary, He symbolizes His generosity by reference to the heavens only because our senses can reach no higher."[44]

The sound basis of Saadiah's claim for the superiority of earned to merely bestowed deserts is the recognition (which he prefers to represent by the scriptural image of the light sown for the righteous) that the Torah and its *mitzvot* open a window on transcendence for us. Even God's act of creation, a pure expression of absolute grace, did not do that; it only made actual the subject and the arena of testing from which that higher reach can be attempted. Saadiah's point is that God not only created us, but also gave us the Torah, which is something more, as surely Fox would acknowledge.

Fox goes on to criticize Saadiah for saying that capital punishment, among other penalties, is a demand of reason. This seems to him to mean that Saadiah is (equivocating by) taking reason in a conventional, thus fallible, corrigible sense. He says this because he thinks that capital punishment is easily recognized as problematic, since in our own times it is controversial and since he finds Saadiah arguing for it by analogy: Just as we sacrifice a limb to save the body, so reason dictates that we sacrifice one member to save a whole society from corruption: "Analogical argument is the basic form of all probability claims, but it certainly cannot lead to conclusions that a rational man must affirm as necessarily true."[45]

Now, to begin with, Fox is mistaken. Analogical argument can lead to conclusions that any rational person must accept as true, *if that person accepts the aptness and relevance of the analogy.* Moreover, argument from analogy is often an effective teaching device, because it makes obvious the formal structure of a situation without reliance on too purely abstract a repertoire of formal concepts or schemata. But the most important point to make here is, not that Saadiah had a right to use analogy in bringing to the surface what he took to be the rationality of the Torah's use of capital punishment, but rather that we must distinguish our own sense of controversy about such issues as capital punishment from Saadiah's sense that, once understood, such principles would be uncontroversial. Saadiah, we might say, could be wrong about what reason requires in a given case, without being wrong about identifying the conclusions he has reached as those that reason in his view requires, that is, without having or using an untenable or inconsistent conception of reason itself. Note again, in the analogy, that the argument hinges on objective interests in the individual or the body politic, not on formal claims about consistency and inconsistency.

Saadiah does not think that disagreement about, say, capital punishment will survive an adequate understanding of what capital punishment involves. Surely if one knows that life is more precious than limb, as Saadiah held that any rational man *would* know,[46] *and* if one knows that to execute, say, a murderer for the capital crime of murder is no different in any relevant respect from sacrificing a member to preserve the life of an individual, then one does know *by reason* that capital punishment is justified. One who disagrees would have to differ with Saadiah over the values that are to be presumed or over the aptness of the analogy. In formal terms, the reasoning is impeccable, although clearly Saadiah is relying on reason to supply some concrete intuitions about the value of life here, just as he relied on reason materially to recognize the superiority or transcendence of some values beyond mere survival when he spoke of God's recompense as better than continued survival in the world. All analogical reasoning is based on likeness, and the weakness of such reasoning in generating formal paradigms and schemata is based on the possibility of human disagreements about what constitutes a relevant kind or pertinent degree of likeness. But the fact that differences of outlook may reflect different views of what constitutes an apt comparison in no way vitiates the soundness of an argument grounded in what is found to be an apt comparison.

Fox criticizes Saadiah for holding that requital of benefits, rejection of insult and abuse, and restraint of wrongdoing (or injury, in the rendering that Fox prefers) are dictates of reason, when these are plainly not "logically necessary or required by a correct metaphysical understanding of the essences of things, since their contraries are not self-contradictory."[47] But Saadiah in fact takes reason to be alive to these axioms of his because he does not share the radical empiricist assumption that reason can have no material content. In his thinking, reason can be attuned to theses about value because reason is, at bottom, an intuitive recognition of specific values or goods, the claim exemplified vividly in Saadiah's thesis about our immediate attachment to the truth.

Now it may be that Fox is so thoroughly imbued with the spirit of radical empiricism as to find the very idea that reason may have a material content foreign to his thinking. But to impose an alien view upon a philosopher is not to find a flaw in that thinker's execution of the philosophic project he pursued, nor is it to "try to see and understand" that thinker's views "in his own context." Still less is it to criticize a philosopher's conceptual coherence. It is merely to equivocate, as the schoolmen put it, to quibble over terms. The question whether rational judgments can have a material content is not settled by the bias of radical empiricists against that claim. The arguments of Leibniz, Kant, and Plato about the role of the a priori in our scientific thought and everyday experience remain unanswered. Philosophers of mathematics still dispute whether mathematical theories deal with objective facts and whether mathematical claims can be made without (substantive) rational intuitions or even ontological commitments. Saadiah plainly thought that reason does have a material and indeed valuative content. Perhaps Fox knows of some arguments that would refute that view and silence the Platonic legacy, but if he does, he has not included them in his dismissive remarks about Saadiah. And if he does, he must himself face the question of what it can mean for a theist to speak of the *mitzvot* as acquiring an absolute (transrational?) authority from their being commanded by an absolute God. Can a God who is absolute be anything other than an ideal? Can such a God be real in any other way than as a Platonic form is real or known by any other means than reason, material reason, of precisely the kind that Fox disavows? Fox may say that he knows God by faith or that he does not know God at all. I'm not sure what it means to speak of faith as if it were a way of knowing—making it, in effect, both the warrant and the content of a claim to truth, and making it impossible in principle, as Saadiah seeks to do, to discriminate critically among divergent claims upon our credence. I don't know exactly how Fox would claim that he knows God. But I do know that Saadiah had an answer to such questions; that it was not the answer of a radical empiricist[48] does not make it an incoherent one.

Fox evades the issue by attempting to associate Saadiah's views about rational knowledge of objective truths as to values with theories of moral sentiment and intuition. He argues that intuitionism would make moral standards "completely contingent," a position that Saadiah "regards as absurd." But the theory that we have moral knowledge is not coextensive with those theories of moral sentiment or intuition that regard our moral notions as mere opinions or feelings, and it in no way commits Saadiah to subjectivism. Nor, of course, are all moral intuitionists subjectivists or relativists. The most prominent form of moral intuitionism in Saadiah's time, as in the twentieth century, was realist and objectivist.[49]

After attempting to reduce Saadiah to sentimentalist or subjective intuitionism on no stronger warrant than his appeal to a notion of moral knowledge or rational apprehension of objective values, Fox attempts to reduce him to utilitarianism on the ground that Saadiah's equation of reason with wisdom leads him to offer justifications or explanations of various laws in terms of the benefits they afford. Does not Saadiah support the legitimacy of laws against murder and fornication on the grounds that murder is destructive of human life and fornication puts us on a par with the beasts, allowing no man to know his own father so as to honor him or receive his legacy? "What we have here," Fox announces, "is only a hypothetical imperative, whose necessity is simply rooted in the rule of reason that one who chooses an end is bound by reason to choose the means that are requisite for its realization. There is no necessity whatsoever in these ends, and hence they do not bind us categorically. A utilitarian view of rational morality is no stronger or more binding than the ends it recommends. Whoever finds these ends attractive will be constrained to choose these commandments as means, but no man qua rational must necessarily find these ends binding on him."[50]

But, to begin with, I thought it was notorious, at least since the nineteenth century, that the end does not always justify the means (especially if the means are such as to violate the principles or values necessary to give validity to the end). And the claim that certain means have value through the ends they serve is not at all tantamount to the reduction of those means to such ends. One can certainly believe that murder is wrong intrinsically and still argue that it is wrong consequentially as well. An appeal to harms and benefits is especially helpful in talking morals with persons who may not be conversant with or sympathetic to the notion of intrinsic rights or wrongs. It is useful, then, especially, in overcoming the kind of divergences of moral opinion that Fox professed to be concerned with just a page before his criticism of Saadiah's "utilitarianism," since it does not rest on supposedly controversial ideas about absolute and objective values.

But the argument *is* dialectical. That is how it can open grounds for discourse with, and potential for conviction of, persons who do not share all of Saadiah's premises. In no way does it commit Saadiah to reducing the commandments to their alleged "functions" or cashing out moral rules as prudential maxims. On the contrary, Saadiah argues extensively in the Tenth Treatise of *Sefer ha-Nivkhar ba-Emunot ve-De'ot* that no single prima facie good is adequate grounding for the good life and that choice of any one good in preference to all the rest leads to an obsessive, destructive, and radically incomplete existence, which only the Torah, with its divinely inspired arbitership among competing goods, can adequately overcome.[51] Saadiah's position here is compatible with a broad eudaimonism, but it is radically incompatible with utilitarianism or any other form of reductive teleology, because it finds no common denominator among the diverse goods that call for our attention and rejects (with arguments from individual experience and shared tradition, rather than from pure reason) the very possibility of such a single common aim.

One might suppose that the resultant pluralism of Saadiah's ethics differs from utilitarianism only in the complexity of its goal. If so, one might imagine that Saadiah's teleology remains a reductive naturalism, despite its pluralism as to goals. But when Saadiah holds that the disparate goods are incommensurate and that their disputes for our allegiance can be settled only by appeal to a transcendent standard, he has taken the matter of ethics away from any naturalism that appeals solely to the goods of this world. The higher standards that God employs and explicates for us in practical terms in the Torah are the ones to which, by Saadiah's claim, God-given reason grants us partial access. But the claim that the *mitzvot* serve such higher aims still does not make Saadiah a reducer of those commandments to the values they serve, since *these* means may be essential to their aims, or even constitutive among them: essential, in that they may be indispensable (for how do we respect human life and personhood without laws against murder and adultery, rape, and incest?); constitutive, in that the values served might be indistinguishable in some cases from the means by which we are to serve them, for example, in honoring God or recognizing reason's teaching of our obligation of gratitude, by the very means which in Saadiah's view God has specified through prophecy as appropriate and desirable.

Fox goes on to accuse Saadiah of reducing wisdom to the Greek idea of *techne* and omitting all reference to the speculative. The charge is of course untrue: Even in the two pages Fox cites from the Rosenblatt translation[52] Saadiah makes reference to "the speculative method," and he includes astronomy and cosmology along with the practical sciences that he argues distinguish man. But Saadiah's theme in mentioning these sciences and the arts that spring from them, which include the art of government, is not the reduction of reason to *techne* but the demonstration of the dignity of man in terms designed to be uncontroversial even with interlocutors who hold the achievements of speculative reason to be problematic. Saadiah takes his cue here from the sort of discussions that we find reflected in the writings of his younger contemporaries, the Ikhwân al-Safâ, where man's superiority to the animals rests not on his vaunted skills, intelligence, or cultural achievements but on his being subject to divinely imposed obligations and responsibilities.[53]

Rather than contrast the achievements of human practical and speculative intelligence with the special dignity of transcendent obligation, as the Ikhwân do, Saadiah makes human reason the mark of the appropriateness of revelation, arguing that human attainments make it only fitting that humanity alone should be "subject to the commandments and prohibitions and reward and punishment," since man is the cynosure of creation. The theme is an ancient one and is taken up in the Renaissance and Enlightenment by thinkers from Pico to Mendelssohn, to Kant, to Fichte, under the rubric of the dignity and vocation of man. It is a mainstay of the humanist tradition, and it is notable in Saadiah's treatment that he does not make the dignity of man rest on technical achievements, as Fox seems to want to suggest. Rather, he finds its basis in moral insight, responsibility, and accountability. Saadiah argues here in much the manner that Kant and Mendelssohn will use. He relies on a conception of reason and its access to higher values, which Fox ignores and rejects but which Kant, in the practical sphere, will make an exception to the empiricist bent of his account of the understanding, so as to give morals a clear grounding in pure reason through the concepts of human freedom, dignity, the moral law, and the pure ideal of reason.

Turning to the revealed commandments, Fox treats it as if it were an inconsistency for Saadiah to ascribe them to God and again as an inconsistency for him to find any practical value in them. But Saadiah's position is simply the rabbinic one that our insight into what is valuable is limited and that part of God's grace is to reveal to us more about what we ought to do than human reason unaided would ascertain. Fox ridicules Saadiah's rationales for the laws about incest, as though the purported inadequacy of his attempts to grasp the rationality of a wisdom that surpasses our own were somehow proof of the inadequacy of Saadiah's conception of reason. Scientists do not abandon the presumption that nature is intelligible merely because they have found, repeatedly, that particular models of its intelligibility prove inadequate or incomplete. Anthropologists and social theorists, specifically, have sought for centuries to express in commonly apprehensible terms the aim or end or wisdom behind the all but universal human prohibition of incest.[54] Their foundational disagreements and divergences of expression do not invalidate the inquiry. And the purported failure of Saadiah's particular effort to account for the biblical incest laws in terms of such humanly apprehensible values as the rejection of dissoluteness or the development of a workable mating system in no way undermines his larger thesis that there is a wisdom in such laws beyond what human beings could have devised. The irreducibility of such a conception of wisdom to a matter of analyticity is evidence not of Saadiah's incoherence but of the continued pressing of an irrelevancy.

In his most recent book, Fox advocates the view that we may *appreciate* the rationality of the commandments once we know them, but that we could never have anticipated them, namely, derived them a priori.[55] But even in science, when rationalists claim that the workings of the world are reasonable or intelligible, they rarely mean that *we* could have anticipated the laws of nature a priori, and I am not aware of any who believe that we could have anticipated the laws of nature without first being given *either* the first principles those laws instantiate or the concrete evidence from which they are intuited inductively.[56]

Fox accuses Saadiah of inconsistency for holding that God revealed to us through his prophets the manner in which it is appropriate for us to worship him, while seeming to imply that in such cases—perhaps in *all* cases—we see aspects of the rational basis of the Law only after it is revealed. This Fox pillories as an "appeal to the authority of revelation"[57]—as though Saadiah's allegiance to reason somehow commits him to a rejection of revelation. But the dichotomy between rational and revealed laws is of Fox's introduction here, not Saadiah's, and it is not inconsistent of Saadiah, as Fox proposes, to hold that the authority of the entire

Law is divine *and* that our human faculties are better attuned to the rationality of some *mitzvot* than others.

When Saadiah affirms that we know the Law in its fullness through revelation but accept the authenticity of revelation itself ultimately, not solely on the basis of miracles, but through our recognition of the veracity of its teaching,[58] Fox senses inconsistency once again. The doctrine is simply the biblical and rabbinic one of an obligation to reject false prophets, which, as Saadiah recognizes, depends on our possessing some critical and evaluative capabilities independent of what a self-proclaimed prophet proffers. If some supposed prophet commands us to commit adultery, Saadiah argues, then we should reject that claimant as decisively as if he had commanded us to accept falsehood and reject truth. Fox, still pressing his notion of the arbitrariness of human reason, takes this to mean "approval of lying" and "disapproval of truth," but Saadiah's sense is better captured in the modern idiom by the idea of calling black white and white black.

Maimonides says of Moses' hesitation in adopting his mission at the burning bush that Moses knew that the Israelites would question the authority and authenticity of one who claimed to come to them with a divine vocation, and (Maimonides suggests) *rightly so.* They would want some proof.[59] The rabbis propose the veracity of a purported prophet as the ultimate criterion here. Since prophets purport to be moral teachers, Saadiah relies on our God-given rational insight to provide us with an acid test: If a "prophet" were to promote fornication, incest, and human sacrifice, that would be sufficient proof of his imposture. If we discover wisdom in a system of laws, that is evidence of its divine authority. If we abdicate our responsibility to use our critical intelligence (another name for what Saadiah calls "reason"), we will not be closer to God's absolute will, as Fox seems to hope, but simply morally adrift.

As Saadiah explains, the manifestation of signs and wonders to vindicate a claim to prophecy becomes relevant only if the claim itself meets the test of reason: "If Reuben and Simon come before a judge, and Reuben claims, say, that Simon owes him a thousand dirhems, the judge will ask for evidence; if it holds up, the money is due. But if he claims something absurd, as though he had said: 'He owes me the Tigris river,' his claim is null and void, since no one has title to the Tigris, and the judge is not permitted to call for evidence on the matter." It is not an analytic truth that no one has title to the Tigris, just as it is not an analytic truth that permission of adultery and incest form no part of the divine Law. Yet Saadiah, who was himself a judge, knows that one cannot operate as a judge without the ability to discriminate rational from irrational claims; and one cannot understand the Torah unless one brings to it a basic human understanding of some of the differences between right and wrong—an understanding that is open to learning and growth, but not so open that it would take any law to be as acceptable as any other.

I do not wish to dwell longer on Fox's arguments, his attempts to make Saadiah's conception of the complementarity of reason and revelation appear an inconsistency. This is just an example of the fallacy, all too frequent in Jewish-studies scholarship, of uncritically assuming a sharp dichotomy between two terms and then charging with inconsistency or confusion any thinker who seems not to presume the same dichotomy. But I would be remiss not to observe that throughout Fox's discussions, where he professes to be mystified by Saadiah's meaning, he has stuck closely to the passage he is examining. A piece of hermeneutical advice that Saadiah offers and obeys might have led to a more sympathetic understanding: the advice to seek elsewhere in the canon that is glossed. That is the method behind the artful glosses of the rabbis, and Saadiah elevates it to a virtual science.

But Fox's aim seems to have been not sympathetic understanding but the expression of pique, directed ultimately not at Saadiah but at the phantom of reason. If we ask why and how reason becomes an enemy rather than an ally or a tool, the familiar answer from Jewish legal positivists is that if reasons are given for the commandments, the commandments are too readily reduced to their purported aims and then dismissed with the claim that the same ends can be achieved by other means.[60] I am somewhat dubious of the notion that the aims of the commandments can so readily be achieved by means alternative to their own, although in some cases that is clearly true. But, since the argument is so frequently repeated, one at least should mention that we do not bolster the position of the commandments of the Torah in the life of Israel by treating them as arbitrary dictates of authority. If the decision to hew to the life of the *mitzvot* is an arbitrary one and on that ground as sound as any other, so is the decision to reject them. We have seen many members of a generation, the American immigrant generation, who were given no more grounds for cleaving to the *mitzvot* than to the arbitrary authority of tradition, and many of them and their offspring rapidly found alternative lifestyles and traditions that were equally or more strongly appealing. Only the claims of rationality, problematic as they may sometimes seem to human beings of admittedly limited insight, can offer us grounds for preferring one way of life over another; and if that choice is not always as obvious as Saadiah hopes, neither is it ever quite as arbitrary as Fox fears. Thinkers who feel in themselves an allegiance to the life proposed by the Torah are well advised to seek the sense in which wisdom can be found in it in human terms, just as those who wonder whether there is wisdom in the life of the Torah are well advised to study the closely concatenated chain of tradition in which a conception of such wisdom is elaborated.

THE RATIONALITY OF THE COMMANDMENTS ACCORDING TO THE RABBIS

Clearly the ritual laws of the Torah represent a challenge to a rationalist philosopher, not an anomaly, but a matter worthy and deserving of explanation. But no one who is genuinely committed to the project of explanation believes that an explanation can replace what it explains. I would like to offer an explanation here, not of the ritual laws of the Torah, but of the relationship of the rational to the ritual as categories that the Torah deploys. Such an explanation requires an adequate understanding of the relationship of law to ritual in general. I think that one of the problems conventional thinkers have when they confront ritual laws is that they lack such an explanation. But before I attempt to offer one, it is useful, I think, to take a brief look back at the rabbinic discussions that Fox excludes from his discussion of Saadiah and then at the manner in which Maimonides refined on Saadiah's thinking on this subject.

The classic proof-text for the claim that there are rational commandments—and thus, indirectly, for the distinction of rational from ritual commandments is a remark in the Talmud apropos Lev. 18.4, "My ordinances shall ye perform, and My statutes shall ye keep and follow; I am the Lord your God." In accordance with the exegetical presumption that there is no redundancy in the Law, no merely rhetorical repetition, the sages sought distinct senses or nuances in the terms *mishpatai* and *chuqqotai,* traditionally rendered, "My ordinances" and "My statutes." They glossed *mishpatai* as "items which, had they not been written, it would be a religious obligation to write." They glossed *chuqqotai* as "items which Satan and the nations of the world malign" (*Yoma* 67b). Rationalists rejoice in this passage, because its rhetoric suggests that some commandments are so important that it would have been imperative to institute them, even if it meant altering the Torah! But Jewish legal positivists, rejecting a penchant for naturalism, which they find or fear might take comfort here, argue rightly that the passage in no way implies that human reason, working unaided, could have deduced the substance of the commandments. Marvin Fox points to another talmudic passage in which R. Yochanan is quoted as saying, "If the Torah had not been given, we might have learned modesty from the cat, not to rob from the ant, chastity from the dove, solicitude toward our wives from the cock" (*'Eruvin* 100b). Fox notes the parallel with the admonitions of Proverbs (6.6–8, 30.25–31), that we can learn from the behavior of animals, but adds: "Neither the biblical nor the talmudic statements suppose that man would by himself have known what is good. Rather, having been taught by the divine commandments to know good and evil, man can now look with admiration at certain animals which instinctively live in accordance with some of these divine patterns. By choosing to imitate these animals, natural man can make his life somewhat more decent and tolerable than it would be otherwise. By such imitation alone he could never arrive at ideas of obligation or commandment, certainly not at a theory of natural moral law. . . . If there were no antecedent standard, how would man have known which animals to imitate? How would he have been able to decide that the chastity of the dove rather than the sexual habits of the rabbit were the appropriate model?"[61]

All this I think is sound. Indeed one could, and should, go further. For *Yoma* 67b gives paradigm cases of the two classes of commandments it sees referred to in Leviticus. The paradigms for *ordinances* are, in the order given: the biblical laws against idolatry, incest, bloodshed, robbery, and blasphemy. Three of the five would be classed as *ritual* commandments by conventional standards. The paradigms for *statutes* are the prohibitions against eating pork or wearing fabrics of mixed linen and wool (*shaatnez;* Deut. 22.11, which specifies the "mixed gender" of Lev. 19.19), the laws of release from levirate marriage (*chalitzah*), the purifications of "leprosy" (*metzorah*), and the scapegoat (Lev. 16.7–10). At least one of the laws addressed here, that of levirate marriage, has a social purpose clearly identified in the Torah: that the name of the childless brother not be blotted out from Israel.[62]

What we see here is not a preoccupation with the disputes between legal positivism and natural law but the practical workings of a system of legislation. Obviously one cannot deduce a priori what the concrete requirements of the law will be. But that is as true of the laws against bloodshed and robbery as it is of the dietary or marriage laws. When laws are framed loosely or vaguely, it becomes impossible to interpret them in practice. Every law requires specificity, and few can be interpreted and applied in practice without resort to some authoritative grasp of their intentions and some authoritative, paradigmatic application of those intentions to concrete situations. Readers of the English Bible who imagine that the Ten Commandments include one that reads "Thou shalt not kill!" repeatedly, if vulgarly, face a quandary about war or even the right to life of animals, which surely has no basis in the text before them. Knowing that the Hebrew text is a commandment against murder, not "killing," alleviates some of the confusion. Knowing how to discriminate between murder and manslaughter and assigning differential treatment to these two acts, as Torah does (Num. 35.16–25), eliminates a good deal more confusion. But clearly, we are in no position to apply a law unless we can interpret it, and we are in no position to interpret it unless we have some means of access to the values the law intends, demarcates, and assigns pragmatic significances.

In the task of interpretation (let alone the legislative tasks that inevitably accompany it) we are hampered enough by the ambiguities of texts and the complexities of human situations that we need all the help we can get. To set tradition and reason, the authority of revelation and the counsel of understanding apart from one another, as rivals rather than allies in securing us the guidance we need, is simply poor strategy. Of course, a priori formalism could never simply *deduce* the objects, let alone the contents of any law. But neither could sheer positive fiats ever contain specifications enough that they could provide prescriptive guidance to one who simply refused to use human intelligence and responded to their precepts with sheerly mechanical literalism. As Saadiah's discussion of the "rational laws" makes clear, even with regard to "bloodshed" and "robbery," we need culture, authority, and the prescriptive force of tradition, to demarcate what is proscribed; and this no sheerly positive force or text or pronouncement can do, unless its reception is guided by some inkling of what in these areas is right, what is wrong, and why. Even revelation, no matter how positive and explicit, would be of no avail, unless we could evaluate the basis *and the tenor* of its claims.

When Fox says that we would not know whether to take our moral lessons from the bonding of doves to their mates or the promiscuity of rabbits, what makes his argument sound is the appeal to values: Mere imitation can never provide moral instruction. But neither can sheer fiat. We must know what the issues of concern are and what their absolute and relative importance is taken to be. Part of the function of any legal code or system of regulations is to make that clear—just as we cannot play a game if we do not know what is at stake, and the rules of a game are incomplete if they do not specify the object of the game and how we know when we have won or lost, or when we are playing better or doing worse.

Saadiah is helpful here, since his conception of reason and of the proper aims that it can find in the Law are not narrow and reductive but broad and inductively open to what the laws of the Torah themselves convey, not solely as prescriptions, but as precepts, that is, principles whose very enunciation defines and demarcates areas of normative concern. Having mentioned as examples of rational laws prohibitions against bloodshed, fornication, theft, and lying, he writes: "I observe that some people suppose that these four categories of depravity are not objectionable at all. They deem objectionable only what is painful or worrisome to them; and for them the good is confined to what is pleasant and reposeful to them. . . . But to slay an enemy is pleasure to the slayer but pain to the victim, and seizing another's property or spouse is pleasure to the taker but pain to the loser. So on this view the same act will be both wise and foolish at the same time."[63] Saadiah's point is that the seeming appeal to rationality of an egoistic hedonism, like that of the Epicurean,[64] is hopelessly incoherent because of the narrowness of its moral horizons.

The problem, as the ensuing discussion reveals, lies not just in egoism but in the narrowness of any utilitarian scheme of values: Saadiah can warrant what he takes to be a biblical abomination for lying in the claim that lies pervert or distort reality and thus introduce conflict and ugliness into the soul.[65] The appeal to conflict here seems to apply Plato's idea of justice as integration and to anticipate Kant's (ultimately Socratic) claim that lying embeds a self-contradiction, between the intent to communicate and the intent to deceive. But the reference to ugliness also suggests that lying is an insult to creation. The argument is an ingenious one, perhaps informed by the rabbinic, *midrashic* charge that when Job cursed his day he "defaced God's coinage"—that is, in wishing himself dead, he insulted the image of God, which he bore. Saadiah takes the whole of creation to bear God's stamp and thus regards any lie as an ugly affront to God.[66] Saadiah similarly offers rationales for each of the commandments he introduces in this context, not all as ingenious as this one, but none of them, in the nature of the case, simply or strictly utilitarian.

My purpose in citing this discussion is not to accept or reject Saadiah's *ta'amei ha-mitzvot* in their particularity, as if to blame or congratulate him for his insights or limitations as an exegete. My purpose, rather, is to point out that Saadiah can explain why (and when) lying is wrong, whereas a strictly utilitarian account cannot. Saadiah's general method is not to approach the text with an a priori notion of the goods a law might serve, whether utilitarian or otherwise, but to allow the text itself to inform and enlarge our ideas about the good. This is the inductive method of textual study that Saadiah learned from the practice of the Arab grammarians and Hebrew philologists who were the guides of his higher education.[67] It is a method far more receptive to the possibility of learning from a presumptively revealed text than can be provided by any reading that assumes in advance that we know exactly what the categories are that the text intends to address. Saadiah's openness does not, of course, require setting aside everything or *anything* we know before turning to the text. Indeed, such know-nothingism would be crippling to the exegetical encounter in general and to Saadiah's hermeneutical approach in particular; for his approach is founded on putting all that we know into dialogue with what we find written in the Torah.

What the sages highlight when they speak of what it would be obligatory to add to the Torah, had it been left out, are not laws that could have been prescribed a priori, as distinguished from laws that in our wildest dreams we could never have anticipated without positive revelation. For, indeed, no laws can ever be deduced a priori, and many can be legislated arbitrarily, without the least color of inspiration but simply to express particularity, peculiarity, mere authority, or belonging (like the secret handshake of some secret society). Surely no one can say that the objects of the laws against incest are evident a priori. Yet, equally surely, no one can say that the laws of *chalitzah* are so arcane in aim or method that no human mind could have anticipated their purposes, which plainly and explicitly include the release of the reluctant brother-in-law of a widow from an otherwise disruptive or potentially destructive marital obligation. It is quite clear that such laws could easily have been devised by human ingenuity and often are.

But if the distinction between *mishpatim* and *chuqqim* is not a matter of a priori deduction versus arbitrary fiat, still less is the distinction that the sages make a matter of discriminating laws that serve some utility from those that have none. Rather, the distinction is between laws whose aims are so central to the constitution of the biblical law that it would be impossible to conceive it as God's law without them (it would be a religious obligation to write them in) from those whose purposes are less obvious, far enough removed from the central thematic of the manifest purposes of the Torah or of human laws in general that one who was hostile to those purposes (the Satan, that is, the adversary or accuser[68]) or alien to them (the nations of the world) would fail to see the good in them and would subject them to criticism or even hold them up to ridicule. The biblical prohibitions of blasphemy, idolatry, and incest are all ritual commandments in that they seek to regulate our use of symbolism and assign cosmic significances to elemental human actions and relations. But, for that very reason, they are so central to the thematic purposes of biblical law in setting out its normative scheme that the Law would be inconceivable without them. The laws of levirate marriage and *chalitzah* serve purposes too. They too are constitutive of the fabric of biblical legislation. But, to the outside observer or the unsympathetic critic, their purposes readily seem (or can be made to seem) arcane or obscure and their means of pursuing those purposes, arbitrary and, so, irrational. The problem is not that no purposes are in play, but that the

Law itself is relied upon to define, delineate, and modulate those purposes relative to one another and relative to the universe of values that laws may serve. Those who regard the familiar as intelligible and the unfamiliar as absurd will naturally have difficulty with such laws, until acculturated to the language they speak, the categories they define, and the frame of reference they evoke.

The locus classicus for Jewish legal positivism is the remark of Rab quoted in *Genesis Rabbah* (44.1), "What difference does it make to the Holy One, blessed be He, whether a man kills an animal by cutting its throat or chopping off its head? The point is to refine man." The remark is quoted apropos of the use of the word *refine* in 2 Samuel 22.31, where the concept is applied to God's word and hence to the Torah at large. Jewish legal positivists seize the passage to show that the commandments are arbitrary fiats on the part of God. But in making such a claim, these interpreters twist the language and ignore the background of the remark, violating both text and context. Textually, the aim ascribed to the paradigmatic ritual commandment is not an arbitrary discipline, the mere assumption of the burden of authority, but a purifying or refining discipline, one that makes us better as human beings by refining our sensibilities in ways that Maimonides explains. Contextually, as the late Ephraim Urbach points out, Rab's formulation finds its archetype in the remark of Rabbi Akiba to the Roman Rufus Turnus, "As for your question: 'Why is not the infant born circumcised?' it is because the Holy One, blessed be He, gave the commandments to Israel only in order to refine us by this means." The formulation ascribed to Rab generalizes and thus thematizes the point.[69] But the background shows us that the purifying discipline of the commandments to which the biblical term *tzerufah* is applied is intended to represent not an arbitrary but an improving discipline.

The image, as the commentators make clear, is drawn from the assaying and refining of silver or other precious metals, where each trial or proof removes more dross and yields a purer and more precious sample. The image was particularly appropriate in a context where Jews were made to suffer for their allegiance to the commandments and the rabbis could represent those commandments as a purifying discipline imposed by God.[70] To represent this discipline not as an assay or proof or process of improvement or refinement but as an arbitrary imposition would have seemed not only a cruel twisting of the knife, but also an irrelevancy in terms of the problematic that the argument (an argument from analogy) was meant to address. Note further the reliance on the premise of God's transcendence: "What difference does it make to the Holy One, blessed be He." The inference is not that it does not matter, for ex hypothesi the commandments *were* given. So there must have been some good reason. The most general reason: to perfect their recipients, who are made better by the life of allegiance to the commandments than they were made by the mere fact of creation.[71]

Those who admire authority sometimes forget that the concept is generic rather than specific and that much depends on what kind of authority one questions or respects. By the same token, those who admire discipline sometimes forget that discipline is a means to an end rather than an end in itself. When discipline is recommended, one must always ask, "discipline for what, or against what?" The authoritative answer of the rabbis to this question is: "against lapses and in behalf of holiness." Thus Rabbi Eliezer ben Jacob said, "Whoever has tefillin on his head and arm, fringes on his garment, a mezuzah at his door, is secure against lapse, as it is said, 'A threefold cord is not soon broken'" (*Menachot* 43b, citing Eccles. 4.12). And *Mekhilta de-R. Ishmael* glosses the text calling Sabbath, "a holiness to you," as teaching us that the Sabbath enhances Israel's holiness. The early Amora, R. Chama B. Chanina elicits the thesis that the ritual laws of Israel, the *chuqqim*, were given to refine our moral character, from a fanciful gloss on the etymology of the word, saying, "they are graven (*chaqquqim*) on the inclination."[72]

Urbach finds two thematic streams with regard to the sense or savor of the *mitzvot:* (1) that they were given so that our obedience to them might enhance our reward, and (2) that they were given to refine us.[73] It is clear that Saadiah's account of the rationality of the commandments, and particularly of the rationality of the ritual commandments, is intended to promote a confluence of these two streams. For he argues *both* that observance of the commandments enhances our reward *and* that such observance enhances our standing in the order of reality, lightening and brightening the substance of the soul. Saadiah's synthesis is effectuated conceptually through the recognition that our reward is not an extrinsic response to arbitrarily selected behaviors or busywork but the very purification that observance of the commandments itself brings about. This idea is no radical invention of Saadiah's, but the clear thrust of the biblical legislation itself, discernible through Saadiah's inductive surveys of the commandments and their biblical rationales, and made explicit as a theme in the biblical promise that *by* observance of the commandments we shall become holy and Godlike. The same theme is made explicit once again by the rabbis, for example, in the claim that the reward of fulfilling the commandments is enhanced power to fulfill further commandments. The notion of the compactness of commandments with their rewards depends upon the recognition that the commandments are not arbitrary behaviors but intrinsic goods constituent in the good life as laid out by the Torah.[74] If the content of the *mitzvot* were arbitrary, a *mitzvah* as the consequence of a *mitzvah* would be at best a token reward. But Saadiah can say not only that the *mitzvot* strengthen the soul in the Aristotelian sense of fostering its virtues, but also that they enhance it in the Platonic sense, of purifying and clarifying its *substance,* enhancing its *capabilities* (as well as its deserts) for everlasting bliss.

MAIMONIDES' DEVELOPMENT OF SAADIAH'S POSITION

Critical appropriation of the insights of tradition, I have suggested, is more appropriate and more useful than either blind rejection or blanket appropriation. For no idiom can be penetrated without sympathy to its intensionalities and without sensitivity to its usages; and no category can be deployed effectively without critical awareness of its limitations. Despite the discomfort that philosophy may produce in some of our scholars, as mysticism did a few generations ago, the same heuristic principle applies to the philosophic expressions of the tradition as to its mystical, juridical, or ethical manifestations. In fact, these sister disciplines frequently express the same themes and values in their own distinctive idioms.

Maimonides is often critical of Saadiah but usually avoids naming him when he is most critical,[75] just as Saadiah himself avoids naming the *midrashic* source he castigates for assuming that angels once cohabited with mortal women.[76] In the sixth of his *Eight Chapters,* introductory to his commentary on *Mishnah Avot,* Maimonides criticizes "certain of our modern scholars who were infected with the illness of the *Mutakallimûn*" for applying the term *rational* to the commandments that the ancient sages said it would have been a religious obligation to write, had they not already been included in the Torah. The ancient sages, Maimonides insists, preferred the word *mitzvot*, "commandments," to distinguish this category from God's statutes, *chuqqotai* (Lev. 18.4), which the Satan and the nations of the world denounce. The criticism, it has long been noted, is directed to Saadiah. But the critique is verbal and semantic: Maimonides objects to calling certain of the commandments "rational" because it suggests that the rest are not, a doctrine that, as we have seen, Saadiah never held and never supported but that Maimonides is right to be concerned over, since it is the view that most readers of Saadiah have derived from his text.

As for the division Saadiah actually makes, far from rejecting it, Maimonides uses it in the very passage where he criticizes Saadiah's terminology. He refers it back to the original distinction of *Yoma* 67b, now offering as paradigms the laws of the red heifer and the scapegoat in the one case, the laws against bloodshed, robbery, larceny, fraud, and bodily injury in the other. He applies the distinction, which he accepts, to the dissolution of an aporia between the Aristotelian view that virtue is superior to self-restraint and the rabbinic view that there is greater merit conquering a powerful inclination to sin than in simply feeling unattracted to sin. The Aristotelian view, Maimonides argues, applies to vices that are universally, socially recognized as such (here using Saadiah's definition, although discarding his misleading designation). The rabbinic view applies to the positive laws (*ha-torot ha-shmi'iot*, Saadiah's term for the prophetically revealed laws). It is here that the creaturely merit of the sense of duty as against inclination has its proper place, Maimonides argues, citing a famous rabbinic dictum: "One should not say, 'I do not desire to eat milk and meat together' or 'I do not care to wear clothes of mixed wool and linen,' or 'I find no attraction in a consanguineous union,' but rather one should say, 'I do want it, but my Father in heaven has forbidden it.'"[77] But when it comes to the broadly acknowledged virtues and vices, Maimonides writes, "There is no doubt that a soul which longs and clamors for any of these is deficient." So, "Both views are correct, and there is no contradiction between them."[78] As for the distinction among the commandments: "Those commandments whose utility is plain to the masses are called ordinances (*mishpatim*), whereas those whose benefits are unclear to the masses are called statutes (*chuqqim*)."[79] The definition is Saadiah's.

Specifically addressing the issue of legal positivism, Maimonides writes:

> There are among mankind certain people who regard the giving of grounds for any of the laws as something dreadful. What they would like best is that no intelligible sense be found in any injunction or prohibition. What compels them to take this position is a malaise they discover in themselves but which they are unable to articulate or adequately to express. They suppose that if these laws afford any benefit in this existence of ours or were legislated for the sake of this or that purpose, then they might as well have originated from the insights and opinions of any intelligent being. Whereas, if they are something which has no intelligible significance and which is not conducive to any utility whatever, then they must certainly derive from God—for none of them would be the outcome of any human process of thought. It is as though for these feeble intellects man were higher than his Creator, for it is man who speaks and acts purposively while the deity does not but simply orders us to do things of no benefit to us and forbids us to do things of no harm to us. Exalted be He, and exalted further still above such notions! In point of fact, just the opposite is the case, as we have shown [*Guide* 3.25, 27, 28] and as is made clear by the words, "As a good for us each day, to give us life as we have today" (Deuteronomy 6.24), and "who shall hear all these statutes and say, 'Surely this great people is a wise and discerning nation'" (Deuteronomy 4.6). It states explicitly that even the statutes (*chuqqim*), all of them, will manifest to all nations the wisdom and discernment in which they are conceived. And if the laws have no knowable, rational ground and afford no benefit and forestall no harm, then wherefore is it said of him who professes or performs them that he is wise and discerning and so manifestly worthy that the nations will think it remarkable? Rather, as we said, each of the 613 commandments most certainly does serve either to instill a sound opinion or remove an unsound one or impart a rule of equity or eliminate inequity, inculcate good traits of character or guard against those traits of character which are vicious.[80]

Thus, even when Maimonides is most critical of Saadiah's prior construction, he builds upon and improves Saadiah's work and strengthens his claims. Typically, Maimonides criticizes Saadiah, not by name, for his concessions to the Epicurean-influenced view of Muhammad ibn Zakariyâ' al-Râzî regarding the preponderance of pain and suffering over pleasure, normality, and accomplishment in this world. But, even as Maimonides pinions the hedonistic underpinnings of the Epicurean dilemma, he builds on Saadiah's own rejection of hedonism and development of the theme of the intrinsic worth of this life.[81] Maimonides follows and expands on Saadiah's approach as to the rationality of the commandments by developing three distinctions that are present in Saadiah's work only in embryo: (1) the distinction between the general or thematic purpose of a law and its particular and detailed means,[82] (2) the distinction between acts and virtues, which Saadiah's account tends to blur, and (3) the distinction between God's ultimate purposes, which are beyond our ken, and God's aims for humanity, aims we *can* understand, ones that it is in no way erroneous to find served in the Torah.

The Distinction between a Law's Purpose and Its Means

Where Saadiah argues that human reason captures only a smattering of the rational purposes of the ritual commandments, Maimonides follows Saadiah's qualitative rather than his quantitative differentiation, grounding the distinction between what we can and cannot understand in the Law in Aristotle's central distinction between means and ends. The *mitzvot*, as the Rambam shows, both in his legal writings and in his *Guide to the Perplexed,* are readily grouped under the large aims they serve. In this broad claim he agrees with Saadiah. Indeed Maimonides relies on Saadiah's thought that we can *recognize* the wisdom in God's law, even when we can never predict the form it will take.[83] But he is much more pointed about the ends served by God's laws. In terms of the broadest classification, according to Maimonides, the *mitzvot* seek (1) to establish safe, secure, and prosperous relations among men, (2) to improve human character by promoting the moral virtues, and (3) to foster our intellectual and spiritual perfection, the attainment of higher insight, which is our loftiest (but never our only) goal. The three goals are not in competition. The first is a minimal requirement of the civil foundations on which Maimonides, like Aristotle, rests the humanity of human life. The second promotes the first and is an absolute prerequisite of the third. The third requires special skills and efforts but is the goal around which all our other human activities should be organized, the one that the rest all serve, regardless of their varying degrees of intrinsic worth.[84] The scheme plainly derives from Saadiah. One who wants to question whether such goals as these are indeed recommended by reason probably needs a richer conception of reason rather than a further investigation of Maimonides.[85]

There are many ways in which these three aims can be achieved. Maimonides argues explicitly that the Torah achieves them consummately and is unrivalled as a system of law in that regard. All other schemes, he claims, are either derivative or degenerate forms of the approach found in the Torah, if indeed they go beyond the merely human (sc., secular) concerns of providing for civil security and basic economic cooperation. But the insight that the Rambam develops here is Saadiah's recognition that the *means* by which laws seek to achieve such broad ends as the three he lists are underdetermined by the ends. Thus, when the ends are construed broadly, the means will necessarily appear arbitrary, relative to those broadly stated ends. That is a fact about all systems of law. The problem is compounded when the general aims are very broad and the means proposed are very particular. It is compounded further when the general aims are in any way obscure to us, seem shrouded in mystery, or in history, and the means appear radically *over*determined relative to the aims they serve. Such is the case quite regularly with ritual obligations.

Maimonides offers a paradigm case: Accepting from Saadiah the premise that worship is due to God, Maimonides agrees that this general theme does not determine the form or even the mode of worship. In ancient times, when sacrifice was the only known mode of worship, it would have been too jarring and dislocating to expect the Israelites not only to accept the new Mosaic conceptualization of the Divine, but also to change their conception of the mode and aims of worship. So sacrifice, and even the idea of propitiation were retained.[86] But the sacrificial cult was refined, regulated as to time and place and manner, restricted, and modulated, to remove even the merest hint or reminiscence of pagan religious practice. As a result, the contingencies of history became determinants of the content of the Law. The stage of Israel's spiritual development was respected, even coddled, as an embryo is cossetted in the womb, or a newborn mammal is given milk before it is ready for solid food.[87] But the pagan practices of the surrounding nations became determinants of what would and would not be instituted among the practices of Israel.

We can readily understand the general purposes of all the laws of the Torah, the Rambam argues. But when it comes to the proximate details—why these particular means are used to achieve this general aim—human reason rapidly swims out of its depth. Even so, a kind of anthropology, the study of pagan literature and customs, can be most informative in filling in the mediate categories between broad themes and specifics of practice.[88] What we understand about the ritual laws, then, is not simply "a little" but their general aims. What we fail to understand and what it would be a fool's errand to seek to understand comprehensively, the Rambam writes, is the full particularity of means.[89]

The Distinction between Acts and Virtues

Saadiah tends to fuse actions with the corresponding virtues, and virtues with their consequential and constitutive rewards. The trend is not unusual, and I think I have shown that it can have its benefits. But Maimonides sharply distinguishes actions from virtues even as he presses further the biblical theme of the compactness of virtues with their rewards. In a famous passage in the *Guide,* for example, he differentiates the virtue of justice, which enhances our character, from the mere practice of justice in conformity to the Law.[90] The intended distinction, as I have shown elsewhere,[91] is not between supererogatory expectations and minimal requirements but between the dispositions that underlie our choices and the actions that effectuate them. Either term in this relation may be considered instrumental to the other: Right actions facilitate right choices through the mediation of habit; virtues of character facilitate right actions through the exercise of the corresponding dispositions. The commandments aim at promoting certain kinds of choices, both for the life those choices will produce for the individual and the community and for the ethos those actions will produce, again, in the individual and the community.[92] Neither virtuous actions nor the corresponding individual and communal virtues are chosen solely for their intrinsic worth. Both contribute to the good life on all three levels, material, moral, and intellectual/spiritual.[93]

Maimonides' distinction of actions from the associated virtues enables him to make much clearer than Saadiah does what sort of benefits the ritual laws can be expected to provide or promote. The issue here is not one of seeing why reason would commend the pursuit of holiness, as though that were an arbitrary goal and we might just as well have been ordered by God to become an *unholy* people and a nation of mountebanks, catamites, bullies, or buffoons, instead of a nation of priests. Rather the issue is one of understanding *how* specific moral and ritual practices can foster our becoming a nation of priests and a holy people. Maimonides' explicit introduction of the concepts of ethos, virtue, vice, moral disposition, and other conceptual tools from the Aristotelian repertoire, his substitution of those technical terms for the poetic and Platonizing remarks of Saadiah about the substance of the soul and the ways in which it is clarified and brightened or sullied and darkened, allows him to connect his moral psychology and ethology with his anthropology, through the idea of symbols and symbolism (e.g., what is reminiscent of pagan worship) and thereby to show in *generic* terms how specific sorts of ritual might affect our character, just as he can show, using al-Fârâbî's Platonic account of imagination, how specific sorts of ritual, mythic, and poetic symbols can be conceptually fruitful and suggestive.[94]

The Distinction between God's Purposes and His Aims for Humanity

Saadiah argues strenuously that life is not a joke, a tasteless hoax at man's expense, a cheap or empty or pointless charade. His argument hinges on his claims about man's reward and the earnestness or authenticity of our engagement in our situation.[95] Maimonides is much less certain than Saadiah of the aptness and appropriateness of our gauging of God's purposes.[96] If God is perfect, he has no needs. If God is absolute, one action of his is as much to his purpose as another and no creature exists solely for another's sake. To say that God created all things for his glory is to recognize (despite the hierarchy of the great chain of being) that in some measure each thing is created for its own sake. One cannot believe, Maimonides argues, that the heavens exist to serve mankind, and we must overcome the hybris of supposing ourselves to be the noblest of God's creations, for whom (as in Saadiah's world) all else was created.[97]

Yet, by the same token, man is as much an end or purpose of God's plan as any other creature is, and if there are things on which our existence depends (since we are finite beings), they do exist for our sakes as well as for their own. To say that God acts *without* purpose is to make God's actions futile, idle, or vain. To say that God might have achieved his plan without the particular means he used is to impugn his wisdom, as though we had said that something otiose was created.[98] The complex nexus of causes that is nature allows its denizens to achieve their goals and fulfill their natures by the means and in the manners that are appropriate to their natures—at their own speeds, as it were.[99] That is the beauty and the grace of God's act of creation.

Saadiah touches on the theme when he speaks of the imparting of natures as one of the three basic modes of creation.[100] But again Maimonides richly develops it. Its application to our purposes goes beyond Maimonides' bold theme of the evolution of ritual and symbolism in step with the development of our cultural capacity.[101] It extends more broadly to the cosmological issue of the legitimacy of our continued application of the idea of purpose in a world whose ultimate purpose is beyond our ken and cannot be learned by extrapolating our own values and experiences. God concealed his face from Moses, the most perfect of all prophets, and a fortiori will he conceal his inner identity from mankind at large. But human life does not require us to see God's face, to know his inmost purpose or the absoluteness of his wisdom as *he* knows it. In the language of the Torah, as Maimonides reads it, what man needs to know is "God's back," the relevant facts about God's absolute goodness discoverable in nature and applicable to the governance of human actions.[102] These give us the foundations of the scientific quest for understanding in the world and of the legislative quest for governance of ourselves. When we are told to be holy, to become like God, we do not need to know in absolute terms what God is in himself; we need to know only what is most perfect in ourselves as human beings. This is what we must cultivate. For just as we assign to God no attributes that do not represent perfections, insofar as we can understand perfection, so we do not pursue in our quest for human perfection any divine attributes that do not represent what humanity can be at its best.[103]

What this means for our understanding of ritual law is that we have access to a powerful source of guidance in the interpretation and elaboration of such laws. Not that the idea of human perfection is so wholly unproblematic and uncontroversial that we need only turn to it like an icon for ready reference. On the contrary, our penchant for projecting spurious goals and specious values on the image of a perfected humanity must be constantly controlled and disciplined. It must be enriched and enlightened with the aid of every rational, critical, experiential, intuitive, and traditional resource we can find, to crosscheck our readings and counteract our idle projections. But the fact remains that we are not without a paddle if we know that the overall governing aim of our ritual laws is to foster the perfection of our natures, and to do so by specific sorts of means. We can regulate and modulate our application of the principles and practices of the Law by that knowledge, as Maimonides does when he cautions against excessive asceticism and extends Saadiah's medical conceit by exposing the vulgar fallacy of supposing that if a little medicine is good for us a lot will be all the better[104] (and as Saadiah himself did, when he argued to the same effect, relying on psychology rather than analogy, to show that the life of the anchorite is melancholic, bitter, unfriendly, and ultimately self-indulgent and unholy[105]). For no matter how powerful and sophisticated a car one drives, one cannot steer it unless one knows where one is going.

TOWARD A PHILOSOPHY OF RITUAL

Having said these things and perhaps cleared a little of the rubble from the ground and discerned at least the outlines of a few of the mighty structures that once stood on this site, I feel ready to say a word or two about ritual and law. My thesis, announced at the outset, is that all laws have a ritual aspect and that all sound laws are rational. Let me explain first what I mean by 'ritual,' for I think it is obvious from what has been said up to now that I take a law to be rational if it faithfully serves some human good. By ritual I understand symbolically freighted action that bears part of its significance in the modalities of its performance, and that, as a matter of primary intention, uses those modalities themselves symbolically to express certain attitudes toward specific values that the ritual symbolically intends.

Since human beings are symbol-making, symbol-finding, symbol-reading creatures, and since much of our symbolism is self-conscious or mannered, and most of it is value-freighted, the realm of ritual will be broad on this account. I do not think it will be all-encompassing. Much of our behavior is not action in the classic sense, that is, it is not intentional, it does not pursue a consciously chosen purpose. Much of our intentional behavior is not symbolic; or, if it is taken as symbolic, it does not bear its symbolism as a matter of primary intention. When we signify, we are always in some measure aware of what we mean to signify and of the fact that we are signifying something. But in ritual, self-consciousness goes further; the reflexivity is of a higher order. For in ritual we are not just using actions to signify a value but expressing a stance, a posture, an attitude, toward that value, by the very manner in which we act.

I'd like to say a word here about the effort to define a notion like ritual. This will consist of three appeals on behalf of logic and semantics addressed to anyone who wants to define words like *ritual,* whether or not they find my definition useful in the end.

1. A definition of *ritual* should be based on the recognition that ritual is a genus, not a species. There are different sorts of rituals. We should not equate the realm of ritual with that of religion. Not every ritual act is religious, and not every religious act is a ritual. We should not define *ritual* so as to make the phrase "religious ritual" redundant.

2. We should not resort to persuasive definitions.[106] Ritual should not be *defined* so as to render impossible the judgment that someone's participation in a ritual is improper or insincere. Ritual may be an achievement word, as are words like *poetry* and *art* or *culture;* but it is a mistake to define *ritual* so as to include only rituals one favors or admires, rendering "good ritual" or "effective ritual" or "successful ritual" redundant and "bad ritual," "unsucessful ritual," or even "empty ritual" sheer contradictions in terms. We should not define the extension of the class of rituals such that we must understand what rituals *are* by no other notion than the one in which we express what we hope rituals can be or what we wish they were. If there is to be good poetry and bad

poetry, then the criteria by which poetry is identified cannot be the same as those by which poetry is judged, and the sense of "poetry" in which we say, "the Chrysler building is sheer poetry," must be different from that in which we say, "doggerel is bad poetry." People who say that rituals are "confirming" or "integrating" or that they bring people together are not only being too general; they are also being too wishful, forgetting that rituals also rend people and groups asunder. They are forgetting that the Nuremberg rallies were also rituals.

3. Finally, we must avoid a vice particularly common to philosophers that I call "typifying the paradigm" or "false abstraction." We begin from an experience, event, or object that means a lot to us and then try to speak about a broad species of things by addressing just this one, but in pseudo-abstract terms, as though we were characterizing a whole species or, indeed, a genus. Philosophy without attention to countercases will never go beyond stereotyping and rather unreflective autobiography.

The conditions I have set out as definitional to ritual are not met in all intentionally symbolic acts, but a great deal of human behavior is symbolic in the way described. Taking a walk or having a conversation can be rituals on my account, although just walking or just speaking generally will not be. Baseball surely has a ritual aspect. So does cricket, and the ritual aspect of such activities becomes clearest if we compare baseball and cricket, not so much by their athletic differences or the explicit differences in the rules of play as by the differences in the modalities of performance and participation—the dress and demeanor of the players, the use and abuse, presence or absence of backchat and catcalls from the stands. Most symbolically significant actions carry room for added overtones that are expressive of who or what we are or think we are or would like others to think we are. Consider the different ways that different people dance or walk or write a letter or a note. Most organized activities establish modalities of manner and detail that readily acquire expressive significance vis-à-vis the values that the acts involved can (thereby) intend. If someone says that my definition of ritual would make recitation of a poem or displaying of a painting in some respects a ritual act, I would agree. Recitation of a poem and displaying of a painting *are* rituals. It is *because* they are rituals that we can so readily discriminate between recitation of a

poem and other forms of verbal behavior or between, say, displaying a painting and just hanging it out to dry or shelving it in a
storeroom, acts that *generally* do not have symbolic aims as a
matter of primary intention.

Poets often recite their poems in a particular timbre or tone of
voice or slowly or with particular sonority, resonance, volume,
emphasis, or inflection. The fashion in recent years in English is
sometimes to use a rather dead and prosy tone. But that too is an
intonation and carries a message, just as the poem does. The
rhythms, rhymes, assonances, and alliterations that may lend their
art to poetic compositions serve to set *these* words apart as objects
of special interest, calling attention not just to the *senses* of the
words, but also to the special function they are called upon to play
in *this* composition or recitation, the value that is assigned to the
poem *as* a poem, quite beyond the normal function of simply
communicating or communicating simply. Paintings are similarly
framed, literally or situationally, by their placement, for example.
So are sculptures and stories and theater pieces, each in their own
specific, or individual ways. To make an utterance or expression
into an artwork is to ritualize it, that is, to assign a significance to
the act of expression itself by the very manner in which it is presented or performed.

Etymologically, rituals are said to be actions that are done in a
certain *manner* (thus, "property," *ritu*). Often there is an element
of repetition or stylization. I do not take these characteristics alone
as a basis for a definition, because I think they are secondary to
what actually constitutes the heart of ritual intent, and because I
think the coverage they give us of the class of ritual acts is somewhat crude: Many things are done in a certain manner. There is a
proper way of building a house, making a bed, or fixing a leaky
pipe. Yet these are not rituals. There can be a manner in, say,
scanning the horizon or calling hogs, without these actions being
rituals. But when actions are done in a certain manner *in order* to
express an attitude toward some value, I take them to have a ritual
aspect. When these expressive dimensions of the action are underscored by mannerism, style, repetition, or other modalities that
arise out of the mode of action itself, the ritual aspect becomes
more prominent or explicit.

Rituals often become institutions. That is, they are *made* institutions, because human groups have social interests in the values

they intend and in promulgating and regularizing specific attitudes vis-à-vis those values. But we should not confuse rituals with institutions. Not every institution is a ritual: The IRS is not. And not every ritual is an institution. Some are performed only once, as when David danced before the ark of the Lord. The prophet who tells the story seems to approve of David's spontaneity, but liturgically it is the disapproving Michal who wins the day: David's songs become an institution. His dance does not. And even some prayers are uttered only once. What would become of sincerity without spontaneity, or of spontaneity if *all* rituals involved repetition or tradition or the normative intentions of the group.

One cannot say that counting cars, or bird watching, or fishing is a ritual, although these may become rituals in certain circumstances. One cannot say, I stress, that all rituals are religious. Birthday parties, swim meets, and letter writing are rituals, but usually not religious in any central way. The Japanese tea ceremony and the old Chinese custom of gazing at the moon with friends are rituals, but not generally religious rituals. Prayer is a religious ritual, but "celebration" is religious only sometimes. Repetition is a modality capable of quite a range of expressive nuance, and so it is widely used in rituals. It marks the rhythms of time and the seasons, not only of the year but of the moment, and of life, voicing analogies and recurrences that are not to pass unmarked, lending intensity along with a sense of regularity. But repetition is not of the essence in ritual. One might pray only once in one's life, and then in a form of one's own devising. Manner is essential, but only as a marker, to make more explicit the primacy and focus of expressive intent. Had Hannah prayed with less spontaneous immediacy, Eli would not have mistaken her for a drunken woman.

Is kissing a ritual? It is when it is done to express an attitude vis-à-vis some value. The symbolism need not be portentous or profound. People kiss hello, goodbye, goodnight, or thank you. The values involved have to do with meeting, parting, generosity, or kindness. The attitudes expressed might be gladness, sadness, or gratitude. The corresponding emotions might be heartfelt, shallow, perfunctory, or insincere. It is possible to be false in nonverbal as in verbal expression, since what is outwardly expressed does not always correspond to inner intention. The range of our expressive capabilities is potentially as broad as the spectra of our attitudes themselves. And those spectra in turn are differentiated by the objects (specific values) to which they attach, as well as by the postures we adopt towards those values. Kissing is a ritual when it is part of a symbolically significant sequence of overtures and responses, as in courtship, but not when (or insofar as) it is done solely to gratify our osculatory impulses. In such a case people say, "I didn't mean anything by it," or "It didn't mean a thing." Sometimes a kiss doesn't mean what it is taken to mean, and sometimes it is taken to mean what it does not. Symbols can be misappropriated, given or taken incorrectly or in bad faith.

I say that having a conversation is a ritual, because there are definite conventions and expectations about such an event that create a subtext to what is more overtly said, a subtext expressive of attitudes toward the value of the participants and the interest and worth of what they are saying. Normally, there should be pauses for replies, for example, and some common focus of interest, not just a welter of words or even a barrage of statements uttered at cross-purposes or without reference or relevance to each other. The values intended in the manner in which a conversation is conducted might include the dignity or desert of the other to be heard; the worthiness, seriousness, or casualness of the subject being discussed; the friendship, fellowship, or professional relationship of the participants. Attitudes toward such values are expressed through signs of attentiveness, boredom, disagreement, respect, concern or unconcern, impatience or rapt fascination, among many other possibilities. In a conversation, a sidelong glance at the clock can be more telling than anything that is said out loud. Generally there are ways of marking when a conversation is entered, who the participants are and are not, and when the conversation is ending or over. The conventions may be subtle, nonexplicit, and the regularities informal rather than rigid; but they are as necessary as the ability of the speakers to hear and comprehend one another. For without the accompanying cues and signs, much the symbolic work of a conversation, including much of what is unspoken but transacted, as it were between the lines, would remain unaccomplished. The formalism (at whatever level of formality or informality it occurs) is not what makes the conversation a ritual. Rather, it is a condition of communication of this kind, a symptom of the presence of unspoken interactions that are given expression symbolically. It is the attitudinal intensionality behind the symbolism that is the source of the visible formalism and the real basis of the ritual character of a conversation.

Rituals have intentions, that is, they make reference beyond themselves. All symbols intend objects, acts, values, or ideas; but rituals universally express attitudes as well, toward values associated with the objects they intend. A word may intend a thing; a sentence will intend a state of affairs. Some rituals, like some sentences, are performative. They accomplish the very acts they symbolically address. A marriage does that; so does a prison sentence. But when a ritual is performative, it always intends more than it merely pronounces. Kenneth Seeskin asks (in discussion) whether a ritual act can have intrinsic value. I think the simple answer is yes. But it depends on what the act is. No act has intrinsic value simply by being a ritual. If a parish priest blesses the animals of his parishioners, that may be wise or foolish, expressive of goodwill or of cynical calculations about the locus and focus of the religious interests of his own flock. If a member of the Ku Klux Klan burns a cross on a mixed couple's lawn, he is expressing attitudes that he harbors or wants to express concerning miscegenation. The act, like any other, must be judged on its merits or lack of merits. Ritual is its genre and its vehicle, its medium. To ask if rituals have intrinsic worth seems to me like asking if books are any good, or if paintings are worth much. Some are, of course. But I wouldn't commit too much to any of these sight unseen.

What I find interesting here is that rituals vary in illocutionary force and carry as wide a range of connotative senses and intensionalities as speech acts do. A marriage ceremony, unlike the simple words "I now pronounce you man and wife," and the act of passing sentence, unlike the mere words "I sentence you to twenty years in the state penitentiary," necessarily intend an attitude that accompanies each act, toward the act itself, toward the parties, and quite likely toward others as well. The marriage ceremony (and the larger festivities surrounding it) may express joy or honor. Or, if the ceremony itself is performed perfunctorily, its subtext may lean in quite another direction. But there is always an attitude expressed toward certain values, the expression of which is a primary intension of the ritual, insofar as it is a ritual, and the means of its expressing is always in the modalities of the performance.

As a ritual (which it normally is in our society), sentencing typically expresses the gravity and authority of the court, the seriousness of the offense, the displeasure of society, the responsibility of the offender. A judge may assert some of these values explicitly, verbally; but the symbolism of sentencing as a ritual is distinct from the explanation of the values that a sentence is intended to affirm. It is an expression of certain attitudes *toward* those values: Normally, in our system, the party to be sentenced is expected to be present, to hear the sentence, and to stand while hearing it. The symbolism affirms the court's legitimate jurisdiction, expresses society's demand for accountability, avows the offender's responsibility for actions or omissions deemed that offender's responsibility, and acknowledges to the public, who are represented among those present, the dignity of the offender as a moral agent expected to accept such responsibility. The ritual symbolizes not only values, but also the attitudes socially deemed appropriate and made normative with regard to those values. Since these are normative attitudes, the symbols employed are matters of convention. Even though the law does not require the judge to speak in a grave voice when passing sentence, judges generally know that this is what to do. There will also be rules about the matter: Judges are elevated, wear robes, enter the courtroom after others are seated, and are met on entering by the rising of those present. In British courtrooms, they wear a wig.

But the norms about a ritual, conceived as an institution, whether those norms are formal or informal, do not determine the minds of the participants. Nor do conventional symbols, despite their prominence in all areas where symbolism is employed, determine the thinking or even the usage of those who may employ them. It is possible to use conventional symbols with unconventional or unexpected intentions, as when the trappings of a courtroom are used for purposes of satire or ridicule in a play or movie. The Talmud (*Yevamot* 104a) remarks of a certain rabbi that he performed *chalitzah*, ritual release from levirate marriage, "with a slipper [rather than a shoe], alone [rather than in the public square], and at night [rather than in broad daylight]." But rather than simply declare the act void, the rabbis marveled at its boldness.[107] Just as a poet who well understands the usages of a language can play with meanings and intensions, so can a ritualist who knows the limits and potentialities of the language of ritual. And this is true not only for iconoclasts, but also for traditionalists specifically. I remember being asked by an elderly Yemenite patriarch in Rehovot whether I didn't think it unseemly to intersperse long strings of *mi-sheberakhs* between the *'aliyot* of the Sabbath Torah reading, and how did we handle such things in Honolulu. He felt that the practice of his congregation was undignified, and was sure I would agree. He decided (partly by observing the worship of his fellow congregants through what he assumed were my eyes) to initiate a change, and later proudly told me he had done so, concentrating all the petitionary *mi-sheberakhs* at the end of the sequence of *'aliyot,* before the *maftir,* as I told him was our custom.

It is because rituals intend values and express attitudes toward the values they intend that rituals can be misappropriated, burlesqued, profaned, or vitiated. Objects of value, after all, have an existence outside the attitudes a given individual may assign to them. Particular groups and human society at large have interests of their own in such objects and in the usages and symbolisms in which they are intended, not to mention in the attitudes that are expressed toward those values. Part of the care that is invested in the proper manner of performance in rituals that are social institutions is an expression of social concerns that the values intended by a ritual not be misconstrued; part shows a concern that the attitudes expressed toward the values so carefully delineated be the appropriate attitudes toward those values. Just as affirmative sentences can be used to assert lies or affirm errors, the symbols of ritual and the attitudinal responses they express (and thereby evoke[108]) can be misappropriated. Moral and metaphysical errors about what is of value or about what attitudes are appropriate toward specific values can lead to the misapplication of the symbolisms that rituals deploy. A judge who cannot distinguish gravity from abusiveness in sentencing, a justice of the peace whose demeanor at a wedding suggests that marriage is a farce, a military officer who issues orders in a tone that leaves his subordinates in doubt whether he expects or intends to be obeyed, fails in the ritual dimensions of his task. His symbolisms are wrong because they are inappropriate, ambiguous. They convey the wrong message. They are miscues. There can be norms about rituals because rituals convey a message, and it can be a matter of moment that the right message be conveyed.

Religions use rituals to express spiritual values. That is, the values intended in religious symbolisms are those that are taken to be holy. Such values, if they are to be expressed, can only be expressed symbolically. The transcendence of the holy (even when it is taken to be immanent or immediately present with us) does not allow such values to be expressed more directly. In a sense, of course, all expression is symbolic. Even when I point directly at your cap, the tip of my finger is not your cap, although it designates your cap. But what has a fingertip to do with a cap? Context, convention, and intention are all necessary conditions even in so simple an act of designation as this.[109] Words certainly have only the most tenuous linkage to what we hope to indicate by means of them. Words are significant sounds, or graphic representations, of such spoken words, but rarely is the object that words represent a sound. Even onomatopoeic words are conventionalized, somewhat self-consciously, to make it clear that they *are* representing a sound and not just *making* a sound. When words represent *things* (always, I would argue, by way of a concept or idea, unless they are proper names), they are clearly not related to the things they represent or the concepts through which they represent them, except through a convention that is largely arbitrary—*wholly* arbitrary if we look for any *intrinsic* connection between word and object or expect in any way to predict, without knowing the usages of a language, what objects a given word will represent, or vice versa. It is because there is no *intrinsic* and necessary connection between a symbol and its object that exotic rituals so often appear bizarre to those unfamiliar with their usages.

In ordinary language and symbolization we signify objects that are transcendental, that is, separate or *separable* from the mind. In religious language and symbolism, we intend objects and values that we take to be transcendent, that is, beyond the ordinary or empiric.[110] The attitudes that our rituals express in such a case are extraordinary as well. They express reverence, awe, sometimes terror. When they express gratitude, it is not (or normatively should not be) of the perfunctory kind that might be expressed in a bread-and-butter note. The excesses that we find associated with religious ritual are symbolizations of the enormity ascribed to the objects and values intended: When Shiite devotees flagellated and slashed themselves, the frenzied devotees of Attis castrated themselves, the Christian *penitentes* nailed themselves to crosses, or ancient pagans offered human sacrifice, it was because they took the holiness intended in their ritual acts to be of such enormity that no ordinary sacrifice would suffice, no mere ascetic exercise would be commensurate, no mere enthusiasm would reach, no mere discipline could express the passion of Hasan and Husayn, the madness of Attis, the suffering of Christ, the terror of the unseen god.

The symbols chosen are not deducible from a knowledge of the objects or values they intend; nor are the rituals that articulate these symbolisms deducible from the attitudes they are intended to express. But, as with the red rose, there is a *structural* correspondence: Great things are represented by great things, pure by pure, impure by impure; extraordinary awe by extraordinary manifestations of the ordinary signs of awe. All the potentials for structural mapping are present, even that most perverse of mechanisms, transvaluation, that is, structural reversal, representation of the pure by the impure and of impassivity by violence and violation.

Rituals require discipline just as theology requires dispassion, and the parallel is not merely accidental. Because religious rituals express religious passions, they can not only map, but also excite or cool those passions. The modulation of ritual can not only express it, it can also guide and channel theology, cool and soothe the fevered brow of metaphysics. It did so, for example, when ethics affirmed its sway in metaphysics and, in the enormity of human sacrifice, discovered the radical inauthenticity of the teleological suspension of the ethical. That is, ethics tempered metaphysics (whose chief vehicle in ancient times was ritual) in the world-transforming change of thought that comes down to us iconographically, as the episode of the binding of Isaac.[111]

It is true that religious rituals, like other rituals, serve functions beyond the symbolic. Prayer may be a way of communicating with God, of cementing a community, of causing rainfall and of blessing the crops or the animals brought together on the steps before a church. Marriage is a way of uniting couples and formalizing the bond between them. Sports events are certainly a way of making money, and so are faith healing sessions, whether or not they are a way of treating illnesses. Taken at face value, the liturgy of *Kabbalat Shabbat* is a way of reconciling God with his *Shekhinah*, assuring them a conjugal visit on the Sabbath, overcoming the estrangement of the *Shekhinah*'s exile. But, beyond the real or notional *pragmatic* impact of a ritual as a performative act, it still and always intends values, and in the modalities of its performance expresses attitudes with regard to the values it expresses. The same pragmatic act without the symbolism and expression would not be a ritual.

We can read a book sitting and holding it in our laps, or we can read from a Torah scroll, written on specially prepared parchment by a trained scribe with special ink and in a special hand, reading only when the scroll is spread out on a table after being carefully removed from an ark devoted to housing just such scrolls. The reading can be silent or spoken, or it can be cantillated in musically ornamented phrasings that parse each sentence and give artful emphasis to key words. No intimate knowledge of what is going on is needed for any human outsider to discern that this reading is a ritual. Nor is it hard to make out—as the scroll is lifted on high, displayed, bound up, rolled, wrapped in lavish clothing, and carried through the room—that the scroll is being honored. Now *why* would a *scroll* be honored? What we celebrate in triumphal procession, singing verses from the Psalms in march-like cadences, is the values, norms, and precepts that we find recorded within. We symbolize what we do not state directly. Any reading relies on symbols. But if the message of this reading is the content of the text, then the manner of the reading is symbolic too, and what it symbolizes is the glory and dignity, the transcendent value—in a word, the holiness of the Torah.

Not every symbolism is so plain. Systems of symbolism are complex, multifarious, and open ended, as diverse and multifaceted as language, which brings symbolism to its most explicit. Symbols are anchored in convention but reach into the heavens like a paradigm of creativity, spontaneity, and originality, by way of poetry and other creative modes of expression and of thought. Religious rituals are often communal and share a base of common intentions or historic associations. But, like the usages of language, the public symbolisms of ritual depend ultimately on current custom; and customs may shift and diverge widely from epoch to epoch, community to community, individual to individual, and moment to moment.[112] Ritual reaches a high form in prayer, where poetry and language make its symbolism explicit and in some measure self-transparent, self-explanatory, or at least self-regulatory. But even here meaning is never fixed and absolute. Where there is a text there is a subtext; and where there is symbolism arises the occasion and the opportunity for appropriation, misappropriation, evolution, growth, and loss.

Ritual is not merely form and repetition; nor is its authenticity confined to the unrecorded and ineffable experience of ages past or locales exotic and remote. It is not merely an encrustation, fossilization, ossification of what was otherwise unique, living, original, inimitable, individual, and spontaneous. For it is also, as Mary Douglas argues, the structuring mode that gives content and direction, categorial interpretation, to the otherwise inchoate matter of social and personal experience, religious or otherwise.[113] Seeking the ancient roots of Hebrew prayer, Moshe Greenberg finds that such prayer is both structured *and* individual. It finds its voice and form in the common stock of human language, the language of petition, thanksgiving, confession, acknowledgement, praise, and blessing. Its roots are not adequately discerned by those who dichotomize it "into spontaneous, free invention on the one hand, and preformulated, prescribed prayers on the other." Neither form is "degenerate" or original. Rather each is in-arched into the other, strengthening the prayer itself, shaping its language, bearing aloft its thematics and sustaining the direction of their flight.[114]

Opposing the dismissal of ritual as mere rote and combating the romantic notion that only what is unique and spontaneous is authentic, Mary Douglas writes[115] of the efforts of sophisticated theologians to dissolve the prescriptive hold upon "the Bog Irish" of the traditional Catholic abstinence from meat on Fridays:

> The Catholic hierarchy in England today are under pressure to underestimate the expressive function of ritual. Catholics are exhorted to invent individual acts of almsgiving as a more meaningful celebration of Friday. But why Friday? Why celebrate at all? Why not be good and generous all the time? As soon as symbolic action is denied value in its own right, the floodgates of confusion are opened. Symbols are the only means of communication. They are the only means of expressing value, the main instruments of thought, the only regulators of experience. For any communication to take place, the symbols must be structured. For communication about religion to take place, the structure of the symbols must be able to express something relevant to the social order. If a people takes a symbol that originally meant one thing, and twists it to mean something else, and energetically

holds on to that subverted symbol, its meanings for their personal life must be very profound. Who would dare to despise the cult
of Friday abstinence who has not himself endured the life of the
Irish labourer in London? Friday abstinence must be interpreted
under the same rubric as Jewish abstinence from pork . . . Pork
avoidance and Friday abstinence gain significance as symbols of
allegiance simply by their lack of meaning for other cultures . . . [Against the backdrop of Hellenistic persecution], eating pork came to be abhorred as an act of betrayal as well as of
defilement.[116]

The authentic meaning of a ritual is not its meaning at its point
of origin. Although that may be interesting, it becomes important
in religions only because they seek continually to capture the transcendent and often seek to recapture it from the past, when its
appearance has been recollected or projected there. Rather, the
authentic meaning of a ritual is the meaning given it by its practitioners, severally or collectively. Thus the momentousness of their
responsibility: *their* intentions are the meaning of their ritual acts.
If they misappropriate a symbol, alienate it from the sacred, and
assign it to the realm, say, of competitive emulation, social bonding, ethnic pride, or personal prejudice, the ritual immediately
acquires the significance that each actor gives it; for it is their act.
This does not mean, however, that they can make it what they
want: The actors are still acting expressively, and to do so they
must use a repertoire of symbols that (like the symbols of language) cannot fail to have a range of socially familiar and accepted
senses, connotations, and associations. Whatever an individual intends in his or her own action will be the the very intention of that
act. That intention need not correspond to the ancient or normative or socially legitimated object or intention(s) of the act. But by
that very token, the act may fail in its socially normative aims, miss
or fall short of or surpass the traditional or conventional symbolism that is its familiar milieu.

That there are facts about rituals does not imply that there are
no values about them, that there cannot be a right and wrong in
ritual beyond the relative and technical question of whether behaviors have been executed as prescribed. Like any symbolic system,
systems of rituals establish constitutive norms, norms that are laid
down and significant *within* the system. But because ritual symbolisms intend values beyond themselves and express attitudes toward

those values, rituals can be appropriate or inappropriate to a circumstance, appropriate or inappropriate in the symbols they invoke. A priori, language has only an arbitrary relation to the objects it intends. Yet it can be rightly or wrongly, truthfully, erroneously, or mendaciously applied, once significances are assigned. In the same way, rituals, although symbolically constructed, can be rightly or wrongly applied.

In the Iatmul society of New Guinea a mother's brother (*wau*) traditionally responded to a serious offense against a third party by his sister's son (*laua*) with the ritual of *naven:* "The *wau* dresses in a tattered and filthy version of the costume worn by widows, and hobbles about the village, exposing his genitals, pretending pregnancy, and generally making a spectacle of himself. The show delights everyone except the *laua* and his close kin, and the *laua*, especially, responds to the performance with expressive signs of shame. The *wau* finally brings this portion of the proceedings to a conclusion by running the cleft of his buttocks down the shin of his *laua*, to the mortification of the latter. A ceremonial exchange of goods then takes place, the *wau* offering a dead chicken to the *laua* for a spear and strings of shells. Feasting follows, and often a delayed exchange of pigs and other valuables between *waus*, *lauas* and members of their clans."[117] These actions appear bizarre and disgusting to most outsiders and quite possibly to the participants too, for that matter, since part of the significance of this act of self-abasement derives from the emotive force of the symbolism it employs. External accounts of such behavior might easily get stuck in fascination with its exoticism or might hastily reach a relativistic conclusion about the practices that "we" and "they" consider acceptable or unacceptable. But we should not ignore the functional value of the ceremony in a society where violence is frequent, formal rules are widely regarded as made to be broken, and symbols, especially those connected with status, are prominent in the lives of the members—a society, indeed, not radically different from our own.

What is genuinely important, if our interest is in norms, is that in any society where grave offense or injury has been given, amends *are* appropriate, and part of amends is the symbolic expression of grief or shame or regret. Societies and cultures differ in the modes of symbolism they assign to diverse intentions, in the degree of intensity they deem symbolically appropriate in diverse circumstances, in the extent to which shame and responsibility for amends are transferred or shared, and in the extent to which the symbolic character of the expression is stylized or underscored. They differ too in the precise occasions when they treat formal and informal amends as adequate, appropriate, or obligatory. But they do not differ in regarding amends that are in part symbolic as an appropriate sequel to an offense, just as they do not differ in regarding expressions of gratitude as an appropriate response to generosity. Every society has some means of expressing gratitude.

Rituals have their own distinctive sets of ailments—scrupulosity for example, where the niceties of performance become obsessive. Many such problems can be traced to a structural difficulty about symbols in general. Because symbols intend a referent, they are naturally associated with that referent and easily confused with it or taken as a surrogate for it. Magic is one such surrogacy, the substitution of symbols for facts and acts, the assignment to symbols of power over things, with no greater warrant than the presumptive sanctity of the symbols. It is quite understandable that the gestures and items by which holiness is intended should themselves be invested with a borrowed sense of holiness, especially because the manner in which those gestures are performed and those objects handled is itself freighted with the attitudinal symbolism that we find to be of the essence in ritual. Thus there are ritual objects, that is, objects that acquire significance within the context of a ritual, and to mishandle such objects is to mishandle symbols. For it is as symbols that these objects acquire a determinate, contextual significance.

Let me give an example. Despite the rarefied usage of certain rather bohemian or romantic Zen practitioners and Sufis, one cannot readily express reverence irreverently—as many a folk mass reveals. I once spoke in a synagogue where the rabbi wanted to teach his confirmands the joy of religious spontaneity, naturalism, and self-expression by having each one make a Torah-reading *yad*, or pointer. But many, ultimately most of the students, taking the line of least resistance, brought increasingly crude items for this task (or homework chore, as it was seen). By late spring all were bringing twigs bound up with string or rubber bands. The message conveyed was quite the contrary of what the rabbi had hoped, or what the traditional intensionality of using a *yad* might have suggested. We can certainly see, in the response to such crude expressions of "spontaneity," how ritual acts and objects would legitimately be vested with a borrowed sanctity, to protect the symbolism that is their aim.

Yet it is critical to remember that such sanctity is borrowed and not to forget what it is borrowed from. When a symbol stands between us and its object, its function is to intend that object; but its very position and role risk transforming it into a surrogate of its object. That is the core of the difficulty we Jews have with idolatry. The objection is expressed with dramatic irony on the occasion of liberated Israel's earliest first hand experience with idolatry, when Aaron fashioned a golden calf for the people out of their own jewelry, and they proclaimed: "This is thy God, O Israel, which brought thee up out of the land of Egypt." Symbols can be an avenue *or an obstacle* to what they intend, and rituals, when elevated to the status of an end in themselves, can block the very pathways they were meant to open up.

The modern day religious positivists of Judaism provide a valuable object lesson in that regard, and before one follows them into a dogma of the pure positivity of the *mitzvot,* one might profitably learn from the extreme case of the ritual positivists of the Mimamsa school of Hinduism. The members of this sect reached the point of claiming that the rituals they found prescribed in the sacred texts were so demanding of concentration for their correct performance that any thought of the divine would distract the mind and vitiate the operation altogether. The only solution was not greater *kavvanah,* to use our own term, but banishing all thoughts of God. The only true piety was found in the atheist officiant. Such an extreme, with its Orwellian overtones, contradicts, violates, and reverses the very values that were meant to justify a ritual. It entails, in my view, a perfect reductio ad absurdum of what I have called "religious positivism," an attitude that is more widespread in Jewish orthodox circles and far more characteristic of Jewish orthodox intellectuals than any such notion as fundamentalism.

RITUAL AND LAW

But enough about ritual for the moment. Let us speak about laws. Laws are prescriptions and proscriptions of behavior that are important enough that we are willing to accept their imposition on ourselves because we expect to see them imposed upon others. It is because of this importance and the accompanying expectation of sanctions that the scope of law is always minimal in crucial respects. Few laws attempt to regulate thought, because we know that thoughts are hard to regulate and because we are not so eager to see each other's thoughts regulated that we would willingly submit to the attempts of others to regulate our own. All laws pursue some good, since no one would accept the imposition of a regulation without some reason. All sound laws honestly serve some genuine good and on balance tend to promote its achievement. That is what makes them rational. To say that a law is just, I think that we would need to know that the good it serves can be met without too severely compromising other goods. That is what makes legislation such an interesting and dialectical process. But our present task is not to legislate but to discern the basis of legislation; and that, I submit, is always the service of some prima facie good.

Where ritual enters the picture is in the fact that the goods laws serve will, invariably and necessarily, underdetermine legislation. The legislator wants to specify the "doable good" or, more often (in view of the minimalist bias even in the most invasive schemes of law), the *un*doable evil, that is, wrong, injustice, and injury. He wants to demarcate the *fas* from the *nefas*, the *ma'rûf* from the *munkar*. But the principles he draws upon for guidance are always generalities—values, themes, concerns—the sanctity of life or property, the dignity of art or security of national boundaries. What he wants to *set down*, as a legislator, are specificities. And what a judge must evaluate are particularities: If we want to protect the dignity of life, we must legislate against murder, and if we want to distinguish wickedness from negligence or mere accident, then we must differentiate murder from manslaughter and distinguish both in turn from accident. That means that intentions must enter into law, and since intentions are invisible, we need objectifying tests for them, an entryway for convention, if principle is ever to be transformed to norms of practice.

If we want to protect property, we must decide at what level. We must decide what property is and is not, what kinds of property to protect, and by what means to do it. We must determine our criteria of ownership and what entitlements ownership does and does not involve. In the United States, for example, most salaried workers would be guilty of a crime if they attempted to keep all of their wages; a public figure has little power to control the noncommercial use that is made of his or her words or face or image but can restrict commercial use of his or her name, likeness, or creative expressions. In ancient Israel, wayfarers could take produce from a stranger's field without guilt of criminal trespass, but not more than they could carry without use of a container. Acts that would be punishable by law on the little island I live on were not a crime biblically—not because morals are relative, or because some cultures deem theft perfectly acceptable, but because laws invariably must *construct* such ideas as property and theft, as Saadiah (among others) teaches us, if they are to give formal expression to the rather widespread human desire to protect some form of property and preserve the values of life, personal security, prosperity, and order that generally depend upon the institution of an idea of property.

Every society must decide what sort of sanctions to impose in the interest of the security of property, how serious and of what kind. Are property crimes to be treated as gravely as crimes against persons, major and violent thefts in the same way as petty larcenies? Where do we draw the lines that separate such classes? Here, in the issue of sanctions, if not earlier, conventions become communicative, that is, they become symbolic. They order and differentiate, convey a message about who is in charge and why, about what a society stands for and what it will not stand for. The gap between the abstraction of principle and the particularity of praxis is mediated (but only in specified respects) by the symbolic ordering of a legislative fiat, directing behavior and guiding action into approved pathways and away from proscribed extremes by the use of symbolic boundaries.

Laws in general are not symbolic in the first intention. Symbolism is not their primary purpose; it is not what they are about. But all laws use symbolism. All have a symbolic dimension, and all express attitudes toward specific values that they intend rather discretely. Plato (*Laws* 719–736) differentiates rational from positive systems of law on the basis of whether a sanction or an explanation (appeal to some good) is offered as an answer to the human question *Why?* But even the most rational of rational laws generally have sanctions, and in the Anglo-American tradition a law without a sanction is legally deemed a dead letter.[118] Yet, despite the biblical *measure for measure,* the relationship of a sanction to the principle a law serves is always underdetermined by that principle, and the function of a sanction is always partly symbolic in character.

No punishment can undo a murder or a rape or restore what has been violated in a mugging or a robbery or even in a burglary. Punishments may seek to deter or reform, but they are also, always, a matter of "sending a message," expressing a norm in a uniquely coded symbolism, a symbolism reserved for those occasions when the precisely articulated, minimal standards of a society have been clearly overstepped. Whether or not the imposition of a sentence effectually deters some future crime, it clearly and rather unequivocally expresses an attitude on behalf of society about the values that lie behind the laws that societies enact or institute or are willing to enforce. Punishments do not restore a balance or repay a debt. But they ritually undo a wrong, demarcate and underscore a convention. The hierarchy of punishments sets out a socially instituted, or official, order in the severity of offenses, and punishments are exacted accordingly. But by that very fact, they limit retribution, so that once a punishment has been executed, an offender's presumptive deserts (which punishment curtails) can be restored.[119]

It is not part of the definition of a law that it should also be a ritual. But all laws are rituals nonetheless. Because all laws are underdetermined by the purposes they serve, all laws are given a degree of slack, in which arbitrary determinations can and must be made, specifying, say, the modes and kinds of sanctions, the precise boundary conditions of various terms and categories, the objectifications of such notions as intention, privacy, personality, interest, and concern. These determinations are not made arbitrarily *simpliciter*. Their arbitrariness is strictly with regard to the primary and general *pragmatic* interest of a law. But since laws always address values and always have something to say about values, the mode and manner in which the slack is taken up to make a norm operative and operable as a law, itself becomes a vehicle of symbolic communication about values that the law intends, thus making the law a ritual, whatever else it may be. It is here that the characteristic *overdetermination* of rituals becomes visible and prominent in laws. Rituals specify a great deal more detail than is necessary on a minimal, utilitarian account of the function of the behaviors they invest. Yet that overspecification is functional symbolically, as a matter of primary intention. When laws are written, enacted, and enforced, they invariably acquire such a symbolic significance and intensionality vis-à-vis the values they address. It is an inevitable accompaniment of their being given the degree of specificity necessary to transform general values into enforceable norms.

Laws, as norms, set up a system of virtualities by which they delineate societal expectations in critical or sensitive terrain. Thus their ritual function is essential, not tangential or incidental. When Saadiah says that legislation can transform what is neutral in itself into an obligation or the opposite, he does not mean, as we have seen, that duty is a matter of arbitrary fiat. What he does mean is that behavior that is neutral in the abstract acquires or can be assigned a significance in context that makes it anything but neutral. We all know this. Signing my name to a piece of paper can appear a neutral act, but only in the abstract. In the concrete it may be an act of fraud or generosity, a crime, a display of moral weakness, an act of heroic courage, a blasphemy, or a jest.

When Maimonides says that the most general ends served by a law do not set forth its means, we can think very clearly of the rule of the road: There is no intrinsic right or wrong in driving on the left or right side of the road, and there is little that reason can say about the grounds for preferring the one side or the other. But reason can speak decisively (although not analytically) in favor of the need for a society where people drive cars to choose a side for all the road users to stay with. The means that all laws employ are arbitrary in the sense of being radically underdetermined by the aims or goods that laws pursue. Convention steps in to fill the vacuum, and with it come symbolism and subtexts. Surely not in trivial realms like rules of the road, one might object. But I fear that the answer is that symbolism is most active in what seem to be the most trivial realms. The symbolic associations and ritual assignments of the left and right hands are well known, but one who doubts that individuals, communities, and societies say much about themselves in the way they drive and keep or fail to keep, enforce, or fail to enforce the rules of the road, does not do much driving, or has not done much "comparative driving" in diverse constituencies and jurisdictions.[120]

Convention itself is never arbitrary, pure and simple. It has its own agenda of values and messages to convey. In secular laws these may be quite simple and directly signaled. They may be as simple as the affirmation of authority, communal solidarity, national or local, to which allegiance is expected and by which, in the extreme but critically marginal case, sanctions (specified in manner and thereby in message) will be exacted. But consider, by contrast, a law like that of the Torah. There is a subtext in all Jewish ritual, probably in all social ritual, that identifies the *we,* spoken of explicitly when we say "our God and God of our fathers," or "our God, King of the universe," as we do in every ritual blessing. But the focus of each blessing is not the *we* but God and the bounties, beauties, and marvels he provides—not least the commandments, our paramount blessings in much the way that the *ayât* or verses (literally, portents) of the Qur'ân are the paramount miracles for Muslims. It would be a mistake of the kind I have labeled the "generic fallacy" to call group cohesion the "underlying" aim of ritual, merely because it seems to form a lowest common denominator among widely disparate ritual practices. What is at issue in ritual practice is not always the uniting of disparate individuals, families, and random bands of persons, but it is always the expression of specific attitudes toward specific values. We can never capture what is intended in the elevation of the Host if we simply focus our eyes on the congregation, when all their eyes are focused on the Host, and all their minds are striving to rise into it and beyond it.

Yet, if we do focus on the congregation, we must focus on their eyes and what they intend. If religious ritual unites a community, it is not by mere or minimilist affirmation of the community as such, without reference to the basis of its bonds in history or destiny or sacred realities (although there is a form of secularist or functionalist ritual that tries to do just that), but through the shared expression of shared attitudes toward shared values, values that are both real and emotively powerful for the participants. Such a focus is what gives definition, social energy, normative authority, material content, and direction to a communal identity, not just as a group in the abstract or even as a people or community, but as this group, this nation, with this culture and these values. Such definition is a prime concern of the Torah, addressed in all three of Saadiah's scriptural modes: history, destiny, and the prescriptive, ritual, moral, and properly legal content, the *mitzvot* that in the Torah bind history to destiny and assign a meaning and a mission to the corporate identity of Israel.

The Torah's entire contents, both as initially revealed and as subsequently elaborated, are understood to stem from God, not only as its legislator, but also as its justifying source and aim. God is here the fountain of the goodness that the Law intends, invokes, prescribes, and serves. And, as a result, the constant message behind every symbolism in the Law will be divine goodness and the human values of kindness, holiness, truth, justice, and mercy, which alone can instantiate such goodness in human terms. As in any law, the specification and particularization of obligations and their attendant (but often normative) symbolisms will rest on conventions. And, although convention is not arbitrary, the particularities of its means are radically arbitrary relative to the larger purposes it serves and the higher themes it exemplifies. Knowing those purposes or themes in a purely general or abstract way would not suffice as a basis for deducing *any* of the means of their expression or fulfillment, let alone for differentiating among those values and prioritizing their requirements. Even this fact does not imply, however, that such means are *ever* wholly arbitrary in their specification and selection. Even in their particularity they must and will serve purposes, both pragmatic and expressive. And often in laws the pragmatic and the expressive intertwine, and the pragmatic becomes expressive, or the expressive pragmatic.

Some laws have symbolism as their primary intention. These are ritual laws in the strict and proper sense. It is a convention in American society, with its heritage of secularizing legislation and Enlightenment abstraction, at least politely to ignore them, or more strenuously to deny that they exist or have any legitimate scope of application. Ritual is thought of as a matter of religious faith and worship; and faith is thought of as a matter of internal conscience, worship as a matter of personal style and aesthetics, neither of which can be legitimate subjects of legislation. But at a time when worship could include human sacrifice, ritual law was necessary, not merely marginally, but certainly, to the very project of legislation. And what we must recognize now is that the time when worship could involve human sacrifice is not past. Cults that draw their spiritual energy from the frisson of violence and violation continue to follow denatured passions into such excess. The demand of artfully depraved imagination for domination of our spiritual lives is by no means confined solely and safely to the past. Superstition too is not a mere artifact from the past; and the time when faith means not just a credo or a catechism but the right to withhold surgery or blood or antibiotics from a dying child is not past. In such circumstances, the law does and still must become involved; preservation of its calming influence, even in regard to the extremes of symbolism, is no mere matter of inertia or the mortmain of tradition.

The birth of Christianity and its vast campaign to spread the message of monotheism to the peoples of the world led to the dismissal of Jewish "ceremonial" law, which once had been the banner of monotheism. Now it was an archaic and obsolete convention, a rag rather than a banner, sharply set apart, somehow, from the still operative prescriptive force of what were taken to be quite separate and separable moral commandments. Even legislative provisions that were not strictly or solely ceremonial in character could be bracketed in this fashion. The biblical prophets had made the charge of ritualism against ancient Israel, the rabbis raised it against the Sadducees, and now the charge was turned against the work of the rabbis and the prophets themselves. As Mary Douglas writes, "The belittlement of ritual is nothing new . . . Paul's thunderings against the judaisers have been basic texts of the Reformation: 'For Jesus Christ neither circumcision availeth anything, nor uncircumcision: but a new creature' (Galatians 6.15); 'Let no man therefore judge you in meat or in drink or in respect of a festival day or of the new moon or of the Sabbaths, which are a shadow of things to come' (Corinthians 2.16–17)."[121] Here the rhetoric of Paul reverses the rabbinic image of the Sabbath as a foretaste of the world-to-come, emptying the symbol of its meaning by insisting on the inadequacy of the lesser to the greater, which it represents, and ignoring what Douglas, inspired by the work of Lienhardt with the Dinka,[122] rightly sees as the true efficacy of symbols: Granted they cannot replace what they represent, but they can structure our very reality by the representations they give us of it and of the values they portend.

Ironically, but predictably, the same charge of ritualism becomes the cannon of schism and reform within the Church itself: "The Papists, in the eyes of Calvin, had gone after the shadow, after superstition and empty ritual."[123] And when secularity and humanism, appalled at the religious wars that marked the birth of modern culture (which seemed to render medieval intolerance only more efficient, national, and systematic), took up the mantle of

Christianity as the arbiter of humane values, modernity did not abandon but only generalized the Christian polemic against the archaic Hebraisms of biblical ceremonial, even in the very act of laying claim to all that was thought purest and most precious in the Torah.

The outcome was the notion that biblical (and a fortiori talmudic) law overregulates human life, a natural result of losing touch with the intensionalities of its symbolism, while polemically denying the practical relevance of all symbolic norms. In the West at least (and here I must exclude both the Islamic nations and Japan from the West, not to mention the newly reviving religious ethnicities emergent in the ruins of the former Soviet empire), I think we have reached a stage of sufficient distance now from the fanatical demand that ceremonial symbolisms be enforced with whip and sword that we can look back upon the idea of ritual laws in general and of our Jewish religious symbolisms in particular, not simply with a romantic nostalgia, but with a certain respect and appreciation. We can understand and reappropriate their celebratory and other attitudinal functions. Above all, we can begin to recognize that laws operating in the symbolic sphere are vitally important in setting the tone, modulating the ethos, orienting the aspirations that will determine our worth, not merely our success, but the very terms in which we appraise our failure or success.

Our Enlightenment heritage can be narrowing, and the still more iconoclastic romantic heritage, itself a secularization, *soi disant* universalization, of the ancient Christian polemical claim to universality can be parochial. We have something to learn from, say, the Confucian sympathetic understanding of ritual (*li*) as a chief means of cultivating human character. Properly attuned ritual, as Plato and Confucius recognized, like music, can be a principal, not marginal, means of cultivating that virtue of character which the Chinese call "human heartedness" (*jen*) and which in Hebrew is called "loving kindness, piety, or humanity" (*chesed*).[124]

It is here that we see the usefulness and value, even wisdom, of Saadiah's recognition that actions which might be neutral or meaningless "in themselves" can become morally significant in the context of a system, and of Maimonides' clear differentiation between the principles that motivate and justify a norm (but cannot determine its specificity) and the means of implementation that effectuate and instantiate, even *institute* those principles (but can never exhaustively or sufficiently represent or designate them). These two insights, that of Saadiah, with his characteristic sensitivity to the subtle interactions of psyche with society, and that of Maimonides, with his Aristotelian sensitivity to the organic (rather than deductive) relation of means to ends, go a long way toward explaining how rituals can become normative, even obligatory.

The two principles are not confined, in their explanatory or justificatory power, to those norms whose *central,* dominant, or overriding aim is ritual; they apply equally to all laws. For no law finds in the mere general principle of its legitimation the operational specificity that any law requires. And all laws contain an arbitrary aspect, necessitated by the valuative biases of the law (consider the presumption of innocence), the need to read intentions from behaviors (consider the *reversal* of presumptions in the case of the *rodef,* for example), the need to devise a system of sanctions (treating offenses as though they were commensurate with tangible impairments of privilege, as though symbolism or even suffering could undo a wrong). As Edna Ullman-Margalit writes, specifically addressing the frequent recourse of the law to presumptions: "Presumptions operate as corrective devices which regulate in advance the direction of error, where errors are believed to be inevitable. A presumption, on this view, reflects a social decision as to which sort of error is least acceptable on grounds of moral values and social attitudes and goals."[125] In other words, presumptions, besides establishing a tilt or bias in the law, make a statement, express, *and institute* an attitude toward specific values intended in our laws.

The presumptions we make in law (and whenever we make rules we make presumptions[126]) express and establish our attitudes about the fundamental divisions and distinctions, choices and determinations that the law must make. The law itself is concerned with justice, but in the very manner in which we enforce and interpret, refine, and relax the law we express and institute determinate conceptions about the constituent material values that we take to constitute justice and to coexist or compete with it. The presumption of innocence is not a way of maximizing material justice. Nor is it a way of maximizing formal justice or uniformity, for its impact will vary from case to case. Rather, it is a ritual that sets a boundary of inviolability around the deserts of personhood, when those deserts are most severely challenged by the threat of criminal sanctions. Similarly, the priority of persons to property, which is so central, so structural a theme in biblical and talmudic law[127]—or the presumption of death in the English common law of missing persons, or the resistance to the presumption of death in the rabbinic law of the *agunah,* or the biblical insistence on a formal bill of divorcement (lest the biblical odium for adultery become a means of oppressing cast-off but undivorced wives)—all these are rituals that enshrine particular values and schemes of priority among values. All of them represent the ritual side of law, drawing boundaries, setting out categories, establishing (rather than merely *finding*) categories, and thereby, inevitably, expressing attitudes toward the values that the laws in their material application intend.

The arbitrary dimensions that we find so frequently in law, but notice most often in the places where laws chafe, are features of law as a symbol system. Humanistic rules of evidence, and the prohibition (in rabbinic law) of self-incrimination, are not derivable from the pragmatics of legislative efficiency. They serve rather to enshrine and protect specific values (the sanctity of personhood, dignity, and desert, for example) and, by so doing, to define and delineate the values they intend—which would not fully emerge as values if laws and institutions did not give them positive, prescriptive, and *detailed* social articulation; which is to say that those features of a law, of *any* law, that arise from its expressive, as distinguished from its pragmatic function, are expressions of the ritual aspect that is found in all laws. These will appear arbitrary or "irrational" only if one expects a closer fit than is conceptually possible between value or principle and practice or usage. In other words, they will appear irrational only to one who is alien (or hostile) to the aims and methods of a particular system of law, or to one who fails to grasp the logic of the relationship between laws and the values they serve.

Much of what is involved when we legislate against rape is a symbolic issue, not a matter of injury or the assessment of material or psychological damages, but the maintenance of the symbolic boundaries of personhood. The same can be said of incest.[128] Laws against incest are not just marginal or vestigial taboos, as utilitarian schemes of legislation tend to represent them. Rather, they are central and constitutive protections of the integrity of the human personality and identity. And their authority does not cease where the presumptive boundaries of damage to the psyche stop. Rather, the symbolic boundaries they establish are enforced (and need to be enforced) wherever the bonds of close kinship are found. For these boundaries are the boundaries of human personhood and individuality, and the society that fails to protect them has not merely sacrificed the interests of some of its members but has opened its own veins.

Facing the old antirationalist canard that once we know the aims of laws (if indeed they can be known) we can achieve the same ends by other means and so (the old charge goes) dispense with the *mitzvot,* we can now respond more confidently that to achieve the end without the means is not always quite so easy as it sounds. If rituals are symbols and serve simply to convey or express a message, so the charge would be, why can't we just *say it,* just speak the message, without resort to one particular symbolism or mode of expression? The answer I would give is threefold. First, in most rituals we are doing other things besides expressing by the modalities of our actions certain attitudes toward certain values: We are marrying or divorcing, punishing or rewarding, regardless of the symbols that we use to underscore, celebrate, define, or assign significances to these acts. The symbols, be it noted, are not so readily changed without systemic changes in the acts they help to constitute. To "punish" privately or in secret is not to punish; to punish hastily, without trial and deliberation, is not punishment either. It fails to serve the social function of punishment, even if the agent of this act announces as he executes it "I am punishing you for your wrongdoing."

Second, the symbols that we choose can bear both intrinsic and consequential (or associative) value. They have worth in their poetry and in the association of tradition they draw with them. Their subtexts are manifold and rich, embodying insights and truths about values that go far beyond the reductively pragmatic significance of the actions they embellish or impregnate with significance. To act "naturally" and "without ritual or symbolism" would be like trying to speak without connotations, overtones, or evaluations. Such a language would be the most artificial of all, and its subtext, if it were translated into words, would be angry, alienated, nihilistic. For the complete denial of affect is not the transcendence of affect. There is no expression without sign and symbol, and there is no signifying without valuation and the subtle or not so subtle discontinuity between what is subjectively intended and what is objectively or socially apprehended. To abolish that would be to abolish the difference between minds and things, that is, it would be to abolish privacy and personhood.

Third, and perhaps most importantly for us here, rituals can and do become a vehicle and language of our values, a means not only of their celebration, but also of their expression, criticism, and evolution. Ritual symbolism provides a table, as it were, on which the logic and dynamic of the values themselves, which are intended in our symbolisms, can be explored, developed, tested, compared, and worked out, in the very act of their expression and symbolic elaboration. Religions and cultures need rituals in the same way and for the same reasons that mathematicians need diagrams, poets need words, or painters need canvas. And although it is true that a picture can be painted on paper instead of canvas, no painter would pretend that the same painting can be made on paper as on canvas, or that crayons are as adequate to every subject as oils, acrylics, tempera paints, or watercolors.

Kierkegaard's Climacus in the *Concluding Unscientific Post-script*[129] conducts a thought experiment to gauge the impact of religion on men's lives. He imagines that the pastor has preached a sermon on the theme "A man can do nothing of himself, but with God he can do everything." All the people nod their heads and seem to understand and appreciate the burden of the message. But on Monday Climacus sends to the Copenhagen city Deer Park a spy, who finds the same people who listened attentively to the sermon now getting along quite well without God, pursuing their various pleasures and interests. They seem to have no notion of the "everything" that they can do "with" God. Should they have? Should hearing the parson's word's have transformed them? Should it have given them supernatural powers, or robbed them of their natural powers? Or is there another sense of self-transformation, a spiritual sense?

Clearly, Jewish ritual observance is a way of living "with" God in the sense that "ordinary" actions—eating, sleeping, dressing, doing business—are endowed with symbolic significance and by the modalities of their performance express attitudes toward the holy. Of course, such symbolisms do not literally remove us from the realm of nature any more than they remove us from the realm

of moral responsibility. Nor should they. But they invest our daily
actions with an intention toward the holy and in that sense put us
into relation with the transcendent.

I am not inventing this theme and applying it to Jewish ritual
usage. The point is made by Halevi when he speaks of the Jew in
his fable as never being far from the presence of God, and not
requiring the thought or imminence of death to place his actions in
the light of the transcendent. When a traveler who is an intimate of
the king, in Halevi's frametale, is chided by his fellow courtiers for
not seeking the king's protection when about to depart on a dangerous journey, he replies: "Madmen! Is not one who relied on him
in time of safety more entitled to expect his aid in time of danger,
even without voicing his request . . . All my doings have been at
his command and instruction, while you have honored him according to your own estimate and conjecture—yet he fails you not.
How then will he abandon me on my journey, since I did not speak
out as you did but trusted to his justice."[130] The thought is very
much that of the Psalms: One who lives in the presence of God
need not regard God as some mere *mysterium tremendum* to be
called upon (or dreaded) only in emergencies. The same point is
made in the *Shulchan Arukh*, the authoritative code of Jewish
ritualism, when the author, Joseph Karo, takes as his unifying
theme the motto *Sheviti ha-Shem kenegdi tamid*; for the whole
object of the *Shulchan Arukh* is to make every action a ritual
expression of devotion.

But, of course, rituals lose the value they acquire in this way, as
expressions of devotion to God and recognitions of his holiness, if
they are deprived of their symbolic significance or assigned some
rival significance. The normative significance is the assignment of a
dimension of sanctity to every ordinary action (*a fortiori* to those
actions that directly address the holy, where the task of ritual is to
focus, define, and regulate our approach to the holy). The object of
the Torah is to modulate our lives so that the whole life of Israel
becomes the symbol of God's holiness. Again, I am not making this
up. The Torah commands us to become a nation of priests and a
holy people, to seal God's covenant in our flesh, to bind God's
words as a sign upon our hands and for a frontlet between our
eyes, to write them upon the doorposts of our house and on our
gates, to speak of them when we sit at home, when we go out,
when we lie down, and when we rise up. The whole life of Israel

becomes a symbol of God's holiness, by which Israel itself is made holy and Godlike—but only if the conceptual significance and thematic coherence of the symbol is retained, only if the symbol is not allowed to become an end in itself.

CONCLUSION

We have come a long way, so let me sum up. By a ritual I understand a symbolic action that has values among the objects of its intension and that expresses attitudes toward those values through the modalities of its performance. What I wanted to show in this paper is that rituals can be rational actions in spite of the apparent irrationality that is a manifestation of their extreme particularity. That particularity, I have argued, is an artifact of the expressive, symbolic character of rituals. When rituals are made law, that particularity may chafe and become a subject of complaint. But I argue that all laws have a ritual aspect, in that the broad moral purposes of law as law *underdetermine* the precise behavioral prescriptions needed if a law is ever to prescribe or proscribe concrete particular actions. Since all laws draw conventional but pragmatically significant boundaries to discriminate natural or artificial categories (e.g., between intentional or unintentional acts, important and unimportant affronts, major and minor infractions, relevant and irrelevant distinctions, persons and property, persons and other persons, etc.), all laws have a ritual aspect. Laws assign an "official" pragmatic significance to the various categories of action they identify and discriminate, and they could not function as laws or secure the purposes they pursue if they did not do so. But since those purposes in their generality underdetermine the exact boundaries that a law will establish, those boundaries must be drawn by reference to other standards, which are in some measure arbitrary relative to the primary intention of the law. That fact does not make the introduction of specifications itself arbitrary or irrational. For the purposes of a law could not have been achieved without some appropriate specification, even though those purposes themselves do not dictate a unique choice among a wide range of possible, workable, even acceptable specifications.

It is characteristic of all systems of law that the specifications that institute or implement the underlying values carry a symbolic load. They express and perpetuate significances. And since these significances intend values and express attitudes towards those values by the very manner in which the laws are promulgated, enforced, interpreted, modified, obeyed, or disobeyed, all laws are ritual institutions. That is, all have a ritual aspect. But we call a law a "ritual" or "ceremonial" law when the symbolic or expressive aspect is dominant, that is, when it is itself a matter of primary intention. Similarly we call a pan "hot," not when it has a temperature above absolute zero, but when it is hotter than most pots that have been just standing on the shelf, when it is more like a pot that has been baking in the oven, when it is hot relative to the tolerances of the human body.

The initial goad to action of this paper was the work of Marvin Fox, a distinguished scholar who has argued that Saadiah Gaon was unable to define and defend a coherent conception of a rational law. Part of my purpose was to show that Saadiah, his ideas ably seconded and developed by Maimonides, not only has such a notion, but also does not ever discriminate a class of ritual laws that is *not* rational. But although this issue is its point of departure, my purpose here is broader than the defense of Saadiah and Maimonides, who seem to survive through the centuries despite the many unsympathetic responses to their ideas. Fox finds Saadiah calling self-contradictions "irrational" and attempts on that ground to hold Saadiah to a purely formal conception of rationality, as though the term *rationality* had no sense unless it was defined so as to apply only to propositions, and then such that a proposition P shall be rational if and only if it is self-contradictory to deny P. I think I have shown that such a reading can be imposed on Saadiah only by ignoring most of what he said on the subject of rationality in regard to God, and the relation between them, which is the central interest of the Torah.

The concept of rationality that emerges here is that a practice will be rational if (and to the extent that) it serves some human good. One of the things we can learn from Saadiah is that we should not define the human good so narrowly as to exclude the expression of thanks to God for our existence and the bounties by which that existence is ornamented and blessed. One of the things we can learn from Maimonides is that while the determinants of the exact manner in which we express such gratitude are radically underdetermined by the general value they serve, they are not for that reason morally neutral or prescriptively arbitrary. They have significances in history, in our lives as individuals, and in the array of human cultures and associations. They have linkages that form them into systems and give them meanings in relation to each other and to a host of values that we cannot rightfully ignore. An action that might seem arbitrary or even irrational "in itself" is rarely without meaning in its context. Indeed, human actions are never found in isolation and can be evaluated "in themselves" only by abstraction.

Some philosophers imagine that an act or expression, belief or strategy cannot be rational unless those who contemplate it are prepared to specify the grounds on which it alone and no other action should be performed. This, I think, is excessive. There are sure to be many worthy and worthwhile human aims and many appropriate and effective ways of pursuing them. The idea that there is only one rational aim is constrictive and misleading, unless that aim itself is construed very broadly and pluralistically. But, even given a worthy aim, there may well be a variety of alternative means of achieving or pursuing it, and to say this does not imply that none of these will be any better or more appropriate than any others. Nor does it imply that none are worth adopting on the grounds that to choose the best would involve the pondering of imponderables.

I think that many people tend to confuse rationality with utility, in some rather reductive sense, and correspondingly to ignore the extreme importance, even from the most pragmatic point of view, of the symbolic and expressive dimensions of human life, action, and experience. Similarly, a kind of artificial behavioral atomism leads many people in our society to imagine that they can isolate an action from the context in which it acquires significance and that they can abandon, alter, or reverse it without systemic impact on their other actions and on their social milieu. Our Enlightenment and even our Romantic ideologies make us too ready to imagine ourselves as isolated, asocial, ahistorical, and acultural beings and to overlook the intermeshing of our acts and choices with those of everyone around us. The functionalism that is so symptomatic of the "sexual revolution," the individualistic attitude toward divorce in our society, even the prevalence among us of rather reductive, needs-based, and consumerist ideas of religion are all cases in point. But to explore these issues would have made an already long paper much longer—would have turned it into a book.

What I wanted to focus on here, instead of presenting such a book, is the old fallacy that Plato exposes at the root of the perversity of the tyrannical mind, the fallacy of supposing that one cannot demonstrate that one is really in charge unless one does something truly outrageous. One unwholesome outcome of such illogic is the human demand for the supernatural: We readily overlook the universal governance of God in nature and look for invasions, disruptions, violent and spectacular lightshow, and moral arbitrariness before we are prepared to see the hand of God. The same illogic is at work in morals too: For God merely to demand of us what is reasonable and in our interest does not seem to the seeker of arbitrary disruptions and violent interventions to be imposing enough as an affirmation of God's power and authority. There must be something outré, impossible, bizarre, immoral, violative, or at least counterintuitive. God's commands must go beyond the moral, into the teleological suspension of the ethical, into human sacrifice, ritual incest, antinomian excess, or Dionysiac frenzy, before we will admit that they are God's—as if the demands of human decency and self-respect, aid to others, love of nature, and pursuit of our own perfection and that of one another were not enough responsibility, were not a human project worthy of divine command. To find a purpose for a ritual, to see it as a symbolic act, as action made poetry and made affirmative, expressive, *definitive* of values, seems somehow insufficient—as though it were ennobling of God to issue commands that have no reasons, as though ritual acts were purer if they were done for the sake of ritual itself, and as though religious acts would be more pristine and holy if they had no material content such as devotions, celebrations, acts of thanksgiving, individual or communal articulations (and definitions) of our aspirations and the directions in which those aspirations bear us. If an act is not bizarre, we seem to be saying, quite superstitiously and projectively, if it is not arbitrary and pointless, how are we to know its prescription came from God, and how are we to claim that we can worship God by its performance?

Maimonides gives us a good answer to that question: We know a norm comes from God if it leads us toward our perfection as human beings. Not toward service of our "needs"—not even of our need to revel in the irrational as such, but toward fulfillment of our identities, as individuals, as members of a culture and a community, and as members of the human race. We become like God, the Torah teaches, by becoming holy. We become holy, Maimonides explains, by perfecting what is most Godlike in ourselves, our minds and spirits, and the character that sustains those minds and spirits as the body sustains the actions on which our character depends. Those of us who have an appetite for mystery will find ample mystery in plumbing the meaning of such fulfillment of our human nature and identity. But they will not find mystery for its own sake in the life devoted to such a quest, any more than they will find a single, simple, one-word answer as the outcome of that quest. And they will not find mysteries that are in principle insoluble.

All laws involve ritual, but what are called "ritual" or "ceremonial" laws are those in which the ritual aspect becomes prominent or dominant. Here the symbolic expression of a normative attitude toward some specific values becomes a paramount concern. To legislate in such an area (as all societies do, in areas that they regard as important enough, whether they acknowledge or conceal the fact) is a legitimate and vital social function, if for no other reason than the reason that certain crucial values cannot be articulated or given social form at all without such expression. If we say that tolerance forbids the imposition of social symbolisms by one group upon another, or by any group upon an individual, we are uttering an important partial truth. Clearly the realm of thought and the related realm of expression deserve to remain free. But the less readily announced other half of the same important truth is that tolerance, the privacy of thought, freedom of consciousness, and internality of allegiance, are sustainable only by the maintenance of the invisible boundaries of personhood which only rituals can demarcate and therefore which only rituals can defend.

For every person who tends not to take ritual laws too seriously there are three others in the world who take them very much too seriously, in every culture. The irony is that often these two attitudes coexist in the same individuals. For people find it much easier to disparage the significance of the rituals of others than even to notice that they have ritual commitments of their own. What is needed, rather, is a critical reexamination and, in some cases, reappropriation of ritual norms that serve the human good, even if only very indirectly and, as Maimonides puts it, by numerous intermediate steps. Surely no one wants to revert to the religious wars of Swift's Big- and Little-Endians. But neither should we presume that even ceremonies are always purely a personal matter. A society that tolerates polygamy (as America has begun to do) has sacrificed real interests, violated real boundaries, and will, if the biblical account is right, pay a real price. A society that values tolerance so highly that it will sacrifice a million lives to AIDS rather than restrict the sexual liberties of its members, or respects the "right" of medical personnel to practice when HIV-positive, or protects the "privacy" and livelihood of AIDS-infected prostitutes, has paid and will continue to pay a price in human tragedy. And when the AIDS vaccine is finally found and those whose lifestyles demand large numbers of sexual partners revert to the behaviors that the AIDS epidemic, with its tragic toll of infected partners and infants, has only partially restrained, the reversion will be an invitation to the next opportunistic infection. Ritual makes a difference here, and can make a larger difference. For ritual is a matter of tact, of privacy and boundaries, implicit symbolisms, spoken and unspoken commitments to life, to truth, to the highest Good, to personhood—margins, dignities preserved or violated. And culture can outpace the ceaseless mutation and the evolution of viruses only by constant and continuous thought and thoughtfulness.

NOTES

Special thanks to Roger Ames, Mary Douglas, Martin Golding, Roy Mottahedeh, Cassandra Pinnick and the members of the Academy for Jewish Philosophy, Josef Stern and Daniel Frank, in particular, for their helpful comments and suggestions, made in writing and in conversation.

1. See Altmann 1943, 1944; Elstein 1969; Ben-Shammai 1972.

2. Saadiah 1970 (henceforth *ED*), 3, Exordium.

3. In the previous verse of David's exhortation, he makes reference to all of God's commandments. The context strengthens and confirms Saadiah's reading.

4. The following two verses make it clear that the lying in question here is conceived in the first instance as an effort to conceal the evidence of theft or fraud, as Rashi, Ibn Ezra, and Rashbam explain.

5. See Goodman 1991a, esp. chap. 1; 1976a, pp. 357–62.

6. *ED* 3.1: 119–20 (Kafah).

7. *ED* 140–41 (Rosenblatt); the square brackets are Rosenblatt's.

8. See Goodman 1986.

9. See *ED* 3, Exordium, 1; 9.1, 7–9; *The Book of Theodicy*, 357 (Goodman).

10. See *The Book of Theodicy*, 224 n. 1; 409 n. 7; etc. (Goodman).

11. *ED* 3.6: 130 (Kafah); 155 (Rosenblatt).

12. See *The Book of Theodicy*, 128; cf. 82 n. 181, 94, 103–4, etc.

13. Thus Saadiah argues, as the Torah does, that we can detect a false prophet if he commands us to do immoral things.

14. *ED* 3.6: 130 (Kafah); 155 (Rosenblatt).

15. Norbert Samuelson wonders how a rationalist like Saadiah can apply to God notions like that of desire, purpose, or intention. The classic answer, developed at some length by Maimonides, is that the underlying theme or purpose of creation is that all beings, to the extent possible, should express and perfect their natures. Thus man fulfills his divine mandate of approaching or becoming like God insofar as this is possible by perfecting his humanity. See Maimonides, *Guide* 1.53, 3.13, with Leviticus 19.2 and Plato, *Theaetetus* 176.

16. Saadiah's view departs widely from what is often called "the" natural law position.

17. *ED* 3.3: 120–21 (Kafah); 145–46 (Rosenblatt).

18. *ED* 3.3: 120–21 (Kafah); 145–46 (Rosenblatt).

19. Cf. Kant's similarly pietist treatment of autonomy and reverence for the moral law.

20. *ED* 4.5: 192 (Rosenblatt); cf. Maimonides, *Eight Chapters* 8:92 (Gorfinkle): We should never deem ourselves so perfect or imperfect morally as to assume that we cannot still improve or lapse.

21. See *ED* 9.5; *The Book of Theodicy*, 129 (Goodman) and on Job 33.28–30, 15.34, 20.26, 22.20.

22. *ED* 5.1: 169 (Kafah); 205 (Rosenblatt). I translate the biblical passages in keeping with Saadiah's rendering. For example, he translates Lev. 5.1, "If any person sin by hearing the sound of a voice that crieth for help, of which he is a witness, or seeth such a thing, or knoweth of it, and doth not report it, he shall bear his iniquity." Saadiah understands "they set their soul on their iniquity" (Hos. 4.8) as an idiomatic transposition; cf. his glosses of Lev. 14.3, and Job 6.7, 15.22, 18.7, 19.20. Just as Saadiah glosses the trope of God's searching the heart and trying the kidneys by reference to the impact of our actions upon our ethos, Maimonides takes "a seeing eye and hearing ear" in terms of accountability.

This moral reading of providence is corroborated in the Psalms: When "the fool saith in his heart there is no God," it is his actions that speak, and what they deny is accountability.

23. See Saadiah on Job 21.19, glossing Lev. 26.39, and following *Sanhedrin* 27b in *The Book of Theodicy;* cf. Prov. 11.3, 11, and Goodman 1991a, pp. 137–38.

24. *ED* 6.4: 203 (Kafah); 246 (Rosenblatt).

25. See Goodman 1991a, esp. chaps. 3–4.

26. See *ED* 9.5; *The Book of Theodicy,* 129, 353–54, on Job 33.28.

27. *ED* 7.5 (variant), 424–26 (Rosenblatt).

28. See Goodman 1990.

29. *The Book of Theodicy,* 359–60.

30. Fox 1975, p. 174.

31. Fox 1975, p. 175.

32. Fox 1975, p. 175.

33. *The Book of Theodicy,* 127 (Goodman).

34. *The Book of Theodicy,* 129.

35. *The Book of Theodicy,* 126–27.

36. Fox 1975, p. 176.

37. Spinoza, *Ethics* IV P. 18 S.

38. Fox 1975, p. 176.

39. Fox 1975, p. 176.

40. Fox 1975, p. 177.

41. *The Book of Theodicy,* 123–24.

42. See Goodman 1976b.

43. *ED* 9.1: 262 (Kafah); 324 (Rosenblatt). Saadiah goes on to argue that the anxiety and insecurity of all human beings express an underlying awareness of the inadequacy of this life and the superiority of the life of perfection reserved to us in the hereafter.

44. *The Book of Theodicy,* 123.

45. Fox 1975, p. 178.

46. See Saadiah on Job 2.4, in *The Book of Theodicy,* 173.

47. Fox 1975, p. 178.

48. Saadiah argues for the legitimacy and necessity of rational theorizing in his distinctive and deservedly famous epistemological Introduction to *The Book of Critically Chosen Beliefs and Convictions.* Saadiah's epistemology has been studied rather thoroughly; see Heschel 1944; Vajda 1967; Efros 1974.

49. For the objectivist intuitionism of the Mu'tazila, see Hourani 1971. As Hourani makes clear, the position, widely championed in Saadiah's time, has plenty of modern counterparts. G. E. Moore is a celebrated case in point.

50. Fox 1975, p. 180.

51. See Goodman 1980. By making the Torah the arbiter among irreducibly diverse values, Saadiah assigns it the same role Plato, in the *Republic,* gave to reason in the establishment of justice—or, more precisely, the same role Plato assigned to a rationally devised law.

52. *ED* 181–82 (Rosenblatt).

53. See Ikhwân al-Safâ', 200–202 (Goodman).

54. For my own attempt, see Goodman 1986.

55. Fox 1990, chap. 6, originally published in *Dinei Yisrael* 3 (1972). In republishing this essay Fox seems to reaffirm its theses; he cites his 1975 critique of Saadiah, reprinted in 1977, as "an extended discussion of this topic," remarking, "Critics have disagreed with my views on this subject, but I have seen no counterarguments that are persuasive" (p. 129 n. 12).

56. Even arch-rationalists like Leibniz, Spinoza, and Descartes held no such view: Leibniz used the principle of sufficient reason to discriminate sharply between the demands of logic and the determinants of reality. Descartes made similar use of divine volition. And Spinoza, the most rationalist of the three, despite his belief that all facts were in principle deducible from knowledge of the nature of God, warranted that thesis in the insistence that knowledge of the nature of God in the relevant sense cannot be distinguished from adequate ideas of the natures of the particulars in question—ultimately, of all things.

57. Fox 1975, pp. 182–83.

58. *ED* 3.8.

59. Maimonides, *Guide* 1.63.

60. Martin Golding remarks that the legal positivists in question here are not utilitarians like Austin. Emphatically not. As David Novak says, they have more in common with Kelsen. But I find a comment by Mary Douglas particularly sage here: The *motivations* of these positivists are anything but positivistic. To which I would add that the same is true of Kelsen, and even of the Vienna Circle: The motives behind positivism in none of these cases were positivistic. But the outcome was unequal to the motives. Key texts of the natural law, legal positivist, and legal realist traditions are collected in Golding 1966.

61. Fox 1990, pp. 127–28.

62. Deuteronomy 25.5–10. The reason is repeated three times in these five verses and assigned almost cosmic significance in the story of Onan (Genesis 38.8–9, with 46.12). It is also given articulate social significance in the parallel legislation occasioned by the case of Zelophehad's daughters (Numbers 27.1–11, with 36.1–12).

63. *ED* 3.2:120 (Kafah); 142 (Rosenblatt).

64. That Saadiah's reference is to Epicureans is clear from the

allusion to *ataraxia,* optimal pleasure construed as repose or undisturbedness.

65. *ED* 3.2:123 (Kafah); 142 (Rosenblatt).

66. See *Exodus Rabbah* 30.11 and Saadiah's discussion in *The Book of Theodicy,* pp. 178–79, with my note p. 182 n. 1.

67. See my introduction to *The Book of Theodicy,* 5–16, and Goodman 1991b.

68. So Saadiah understands the term, since he categorically rejects the mythic notion of fallen angels; see *The Book of Theodicy,* on Job 1.6, pp. 154–57.

69. Urbach 1975, vol. 2, p. 846 n. 90.

70. Cf. the (Stoic influenced) *midrashic* images of a potter who fires only the best wares, a farmer who yokes his strongest ox, or improves his flax by beating, or one who harvests the ripe figs before they breed worms: *Gen. Rabbah* 32.3, 34.2, 55.1–2; *Song of Songs Rabbah* 2.16.2.

71. See Maimonides, *Guide* 3.26; 2.6, 10, 12; Goodman 1991a, pp. 107–10, 247 n. 50, 249 n. 67.

72. See Urbach 1975, vol. 1, p. 366.

73. Urbach 1975, vol. 1, pp. 366–67.

74. Cf. Goodman 1991a, esp. chap. 3.

75. See Goodman 1980.

76. See *The Book of Theodicy,* pp. 155–59, 168 n. 31; the glosses Saadiah criticizes are found in *Pirke De R. Eliezer* 22.

77. See *Sifra* to Leviticus 20.26.

78. Maimonides, *Eight Chapters* 6:36–37 (Gorfinkle, Hebrew), 75–78 (English).

79. Maimonides, *Guide* 3.26.

80. Maimonides, *Guide* 3.31.

81. See Maimonides, *Guide* 3.13, which introduces the critique of Saadiah with the sentence, "Often perfect minds grow perplexed inquiring after the object of existence"; see Goodman 1976, pp. 262–77; *The Book of Theodicy,* 41–42, 91–92, 114–116, 303–4, 362–63, etc.

82. Cf. *ED* 3.3.

83. Cf. Maimonides, *Guide* 3.21.

84. *Eight Chapters* 5.

85. See Goodman 1989.

86. *Guide* 3.29, 30.

87. The image is the Rambam's; see *Guide* 3.32.

88. See Maimonides, *Guide* 3.29, esp.: "The meaning of many of our laws became clear to me and their grounds became known to me only when I studied the schools, views, practices, and forms of worship of the pagans . . . The greatest book on this subject is *The Nabatean Agricul-*

ture, translated by Ibn Wahshiyya" (Munk, 3.64b; Pines, 518). Pines explains (518 n. 25): "Abû Bakr Ibn ʿAlî Ibn Wahshiyya seems to have been the author of this work, which he passed off as a translation from the Chaldean. The work appeared in 904." Maimonides finds the pagan world view philosophically primitive, even at its best. But he highly values the insights into biblical law to be derived from the comparative study of pagan ideas and institutions.

89.   *Guide* 3.26. Josef Stern (1986) rightly connects Maimonides' rejection of the quest for the reasons of the detailed particularities of the Law with his Ghazali-influenced voluntarism: We do not know the full explanations of these requirements; in a way we cannot, and certainly we need not know all such reasons. But that does not mean there are none. What seems arbitrary at a given stage of knowledge or civilizational development proves rational in a broader historical perspective. The very distinction between will and reason, Maimonides insists, is a human one, ultimately resolved in the absolute unity of God.

90.   *Guide* 3.53.

91.   See Goodman 1991a, pp. 2 and 235 n. 1.

92.   See Goodman 1978.

93.   Cf. *Guide* 3.35: "Every command and prohibition whose purpose is to inculcate a certain oral trait, instill an idea or improve behavior exclusively with reference to the individual's personal development is classed as between-man-and-God by the Sages, even if it actually does affect relations between man and man—for this may result only after numerous intermediate stages."

94.   It is in the spirit of this approach that I proposed the exegetical analyses of *kashrut* and *gilui arayot* in Goodman 1986.

95.   See *The Book of Theodicy,* p. 383, and my discussions at pp. 41–42, 114–16, 139, 143, 254, 362–63.

96.   See *Guide* 3.13 and 1.2.

97.   *Guide* 3.13.

98.   *Guide* 3.31.

99.   *Guide* 3.32; cf. Ikhwân al-Safâ 1978, pp. 108–15 (Goodman).

100.   *The Book of Theodicy,* 393–96.

101.   *Guide* 3.32.

102.   *Guide* 1.54.

103.   See Maimonides, *Guide* 1.53; and cf. Goodman 1991b.

104.   *Eight Chapters* 4.

105.   See *ED* 10.4, and Goodman 1989, p. 409.

106.   Are there philosophers now unfamiliar with this concept? It appears there may be. See Stevenson 1944, chap. 9.

107.   For the glossing of *greatness* as "boldness," see Maimonides, *Guide* 1.46.

108. I think David Shatz makes good sense in calling attention to the evocative, or even evocational power of rituals.

109. See Goodman 1988a.

110. See Goodman 1988b.

111. See Goodman 1981, pp. 12–19.

112. Much that Levi-Strauss says in *The Raw and the Cooked* about the shifting symbolisms of mythic motifs applies equally to rituals, which are, after all, as the anthropologists have long taught, the visible, social, and expressive counterpart of mythic motifs.

113. See Douglas 1982, pp. 34–38.

114. See Greenberg 1983, pp. 38–39, 55–57. The thematic of these early prayers, stated in the most general terms, is ethical, nonmagical, intimate, social, and personal.

115. Douglas 1973, pp. 21–76.

116. Douglas 1973, pp. 60–62.

117. D'Amato 1979, p. 62; see Bateson 1958, pp. 1–33, 38–39, 98, 107, 123–41, 161–77, 229–30, 286–89.

118. Herbert Fingarette, 1977, argues that laws seek to control the will and so must use force and suffering to humble the recalcitrant will. He distinguishes as "ceremonial," laws that have no penal sanctions. But ritual laws often bear grave penal sanctions; and other modes than the threat of sanction, including persuasion, incentive, and social pressure, are commonly relied upon by civil laws. Theologically, Fingarette argues that the role of God as law-giver is inconsistent with the ascription of divine mercy (personal communication, November 12, 1979); he represents song as the antithesis of law (1978). But in Jewish theology the giving of the Law *is* an act of mercy, and the Torah (Deuteronomy 31) speaks of itself not simply in terms of sanctions but vividly in terms of song. Answering my claim that biblical law rests on a synthesis of poetry with precept, of aggadah, or narrative, with halakhah, prescription, Fingarette writes: "When you say the Torah fuses law and song . . . what I'm saying is that the *concept* of law excludes song, and so to the extent there is 'song' the rule of law is undermined or ignored. Sure one may 'temper' justice with charity, but it's still the case that justice is not charity, charity not justice; they are different and incompatible concepts." To this I reply that I think one begins to come to grips with the biblical idea of justice when one recognizes that biblically there are not two concepts here but one, bearing the same name, *tzedakah*. Justice demands mercy, and charity is justice to the poor and to all claimants in keeping with their deserts. See Goodman 1991a. As to the incompatibility of law with song, I think any hybrid proves its vitality by its survival and fecundity. The great fear that the fusion of law and song engenders in the minds of jurists who are not inured to rabbinic exegesis (and here I do have in

mind the European tradition of legal positivism, as represented by Bentham, Austin, Hart, Kelsen, and Ronald Moore) is that of vast and uncontrollable vagueness. But it is precisely here that the rabbis exercise the characteristic specifying and particularizing, restraining and expanding, adjusting and reshaping methods of the jurist with the greatest skill, delimiting and determining what is and what is not required by justice conceived as charity. Their characteristic method of attaining specificity is that of ritual, where the Torah, most characteristically, constructs its *rationales* by way of myth; for the last point, see Carmichael 1979 and Goodman 1986.

119.   See Goodman 1991a, chap. 2.

120.   Woody Allen said in a film once that the only cultural amenity of Los Angeles was that California makes it legal to turn right on a red light. But even this convention is determined by the ethos of drivers: Only where the right-of-way of pedestrians is respected is it safe (where traffic keeps to the right) to legalize a right turn on a red light.

121.   Douglas 1982, pp. 34–35.

122.   See Lienhardt 1961. Douglas (1982, p. 36) calls this, "The most important book in anthropological studies of religion, because it broke the impasse foisted on anthropology by the confusion of ritual with religion and the rigid separation of religion from ordinary life."

123.   Douglas 1982, p. 35.

124.   See Skaja 1984.

125.   See Ullmann-Margalit 1990, 1983.

126.   Cf. Maimonides, *Guide* 3.34.

127.   See Greenberg 1976; and compare the poignant framing of the value in question in Chaim Grade's novel, *My Mother's Sabbath Days*.

128.   See Goodman 1986 and May 1991.

129.   Climacus 1941, pp. 417–49. Cf. the discussion in Burgess 1975, pp. 46–47.

130.   Halevi, *Kuzari* 3.20–21:158–60 (Hirschfeld).

REFERENCES

Altmann, Alexander. 1943. "Halukat ha-Mitzvot le-Rasag." In *Rasag: Kovetz Torani*, edited by J. L. Fishman. Jerusalem.

———. 1944. "Saadya's Conception of the Law." *Bulletin of the John Rylands Library* 28:320–39.

Bateson, Gregory. [1936] 1958. *Naven: A Survey of the Problems Suggested by a Composite Picture of the Culture of a New Guinea Tribe Drawn from Three Points of View.* 2d ed. Stanford: Stanford University Press.

Ben-Shammai, Haggai. 1972. "Halukat ha-Mitzvot u-Musag ha-Hokhmah be-Mishnat Rasag." *Tarbitz* 41.

Burgess, Andrew. 1975. *Passion, "Knowing How," and Understanding: An Essay on the Concept of Faith.* Missoula: Scholars Press.

Carmichael, Calum. 1979. *Women, Law, and the Genesis Traditions.* Edinburgh: Edinburgh University Press.

Climacus, Johannes [pseud.]. 1941. *Concluding Unscientific Postscript to the Philosophical Fragments.* Translated by David F. Swenson and Walter Lowrie. Princeton: Princeton University Press.

D'Amato, John. 1979. "The Wind and the Amber: Notes on Headhunting and the Interpretation of Accounts." *Journal of Anthropological Research* 35.

Douglas, Mary. 1973. *Natural Symbols.* London: Barrie and Jenkins.

———. 1982. *In the Active Voice.* London: Routledge.

Efros, Israel. 1974. "Saadiah's Theory of Knowledge." In *Studies in Medieval Jewish Philosophy,* pp. 7–36. New York: Columbia University Press.

Elstein, Joab. 1969. "Torat ha-Mitzvot be-Mishnat R. Saadiah." *Tarbitz* 38.

Fingarette, Herbert. 1977. Presidential Address. *Proceedings and Addresses of the American Philosophical Association* 50(6):499–525.

———. 1978. "The Meaning of Law in the Book of Job." *Hastings Law Journal* 29(6):1581–1617.

Fox, Marvin. 1975. "On the Rational Commandments in Saadiah's Philosophy." In *Modern Jewish Ethics: Theory and Practice,* edited by M. Fox, pp. 174–87. Columbus: Ohio State University Press.

———. 1990. *Interpreting Maimonides: Studies in Methodology, Metaphysics, and Moral Philosophy.* Chicago: University of Chicago Press.

Golding, Martin. 1966. *The Nature of Law.* New York: Random House.

Goodman, L. E. 1976a. "Equality and Human Rights: The Lockean and the Judaic Views." *Judaism* 25:357–62.

———. 1976b. "Saadya on the Human Condition." *Jewish Quarterly Review* n.s. 67:23–29.

———. 1976c. *Rambam.* New York: Viking.

———. 1978. "Maimonides' Philosophy of Law." *Jewish Law Annual* 1:72–107.

———. 1980. "Saadiah's Ethical Pluralism." *Journal of the American Oriental Society* 100:407–19.

———. 1981. *Monotheism.* Totowa, N.J.: Allenheld Osmun.

———. 1986. "The Biblical Laws of Diet and Sex." *Jewish Law Association Studies* 2:17–57.

———. 1988a. "Context." *Philosophy East and West* 38:307–33.

————. 1988b. "Ordinary and Extraordinary Language in Medieval Jewish and Islamic Philosophy." *Manuscrito* 11:57–83.

————. 1989. "The Rational and Irrational in Medieval Jewish and Islamic Philosophy." In *Rationality in Question: On Eastern and Western Views of Rationality,* edited by Shlomo Biderman and Ben-Ami Scharfstein, pp. 93–118. Leiden: Brill.

————. 1990. "Saadiah's Interpretive Technique in Translating the Book of Job." In *Translation of Scripture (Jewish Quarterly Review* supplement), edited by D. Goldberg, pp. 47–76.

————. 1991a. *On Justice: An Essay in Jewish Philosophy.* New Haven: Yale University Press.

————. 1991b. "Crosspollinations: Philosophically Fruitful Exchanges between Jewish and Islamic Thought." In *The Jews of Islamic Lands,* edited by Jacob Lassner. Detroit: Wayne State University Press.

Greenberg, Moshe. 1976. "Some Postulates of Biblical Criminal Law." In *The Jewish Expression,* edited by Judah Goldin, pp. 18–37. New Haven: Yale University Press.

————. 1983. *Biblical Prose Prayer as a Window to the Popular Religion of Ancient Israel.* Berkeley and Los Angeles: University of California Press.

Halevi, Judah. [1905] 1977. *Kitâb al-Radd wa-'l-Dalîl fî Dîn al Dhalîl (The Book of Rebuttal and Evidence in behalf of the Scorned Faith,* known as the *Kuzari).* Edited by David H. Baneth. Jerusalem: Magnes Press. (Translated by Hartwig Hirschfeld. New York: Schocken, 1964).

Heschel, Abraham Joshua. 1944. *The Quest for Certainty in Saadiah's Philosophy.* New York: Feldheim. (Reprinted from *Jewish Quarterly Review* 33–34 [1942/43, 1943/44].).

Hourani, George. 1971. *Islamic Rationalism: The Ethics of 'Abd al-Jabbâr.* Oxford: Clarendon Press.

Ikhwân al-Safâ'. 1978. *The Case of the Animals vs. Man.* Translated by L. E. Goodman. Boston: Twayne.

Lienhardt, R. G. 1961. *Divinity and Experience: The Religion of the Dinka.* Oxford: Clarendon Press.

Maimonides. [1912] 1966. *The Eight Chapters.* Edited and translated by Joseph Gorfinkle. New York: Columbia University Press, 1912. (Reprint, New York: AMS, 1966.)

————. [1856–66] 1964. *Le Guide des Égarés (Guide to the Perplexed).* Edited and translated by S. Munk. 3 vols. Paris, 1856–66. (Reprint, Osnabrück, 1964.)

May, William. 1991. "The Molested." *Hastings Center Report* 21 (May–June):9–17.

Saadiah Gaon al-Fayyûmî. 1970. *K. al-Mukhtâr fî 'l-Amânât wa-'l-'I'ti-*

qâdât (*The Book of Critically Chosen Beliefs and Convictions,* known in Hebrew as *Sefer ha-Nivkhar ba-Emunot ve-De'ot* [here abbreviated *ED*]). Edited by J. Kafah. Jerusalem: Sura. (Compare the translation of S. Rosenblatt [New Haven: Yale University Press, 1948]. Translations here are my own.)

―――. 1988. *The Book of Theodicy (Commentary on the Book of Job).* Translated by L. E. Goodman. New Haven: Yale University Press.

Skaja, Henry. 1984. "*Li* (Ceremonial) as a Primal Concept in Confucian Spiritual-Humanism." *Chinese Culture* 25:1–26.

Spinoza, Benedict de. [1677] 1925. *Ethica Ordine Geometrico Demonstrata.* Edited by Carl Gebhardt. In *Spinoza Opera.* 4 vols. Heidelberg: Carl Winter.

―――. [1677] 1985. *Ethica Ordine Geometrico Demonstrata.* Translated by Edwin Curley. In *The Collected Works of Spinoza,* vol. 1. Princeton: Princeton University Press.

Stern, Josef. 1986. "The Idea of a *Hoq* in Maimonides' Explanation of the Law." In *Maimonides and Philosophy,* edited by S. Pines and Y. Yovel, pp. 92–130. The Hague: Nijhoff.

Stevenson, Charles. [1944] 1950. *Ethics and Language.* New Haven: Yale University Press. Reprint.

Ullmann-Margalit, Edna. 1990. "Revision of Norms." *Ethics* 100:756–67; cf. *Iyyun* 39:139–50.

―――. 1983. "On Presumption." *Journal of Philosophy* 80:143–63.

Urbach, Ephraim. 1975. *The Sages: Their Concepts and Beliefs.* Translated by Israel Abrahams. 2 vols. Jerusalem: Magnes Press.

Vajda, Georges. 1967. "Autour de la Théorie de la Connaissance chez Saadia." *Revue des Études Juives* 126:135–89, 375–97.

CHAPTER 5

Mitzvah as Metaphor

Moshe Sokol

1

The inquiry into *ta'amei ha-mitzvot* is a long and distinguished one, extending back to the classical period and continuing into the twentieth century.[1] I. Heinemann distinguishes four different approaches that the sources have taken over the years to account for, as he puts it, the "value" of the *mitzvot:*[2]

1. *Utilitarian:* This approach maintains that the value of at least some *mitzvot* is that they improve the lot of the Jew in this world and the next. For example, Yehuda Halevi suggests that reciting *birkot ha-nehenin* enhances Jewish pleasure and joy in life.[3]

2. *Intellectualist:* This rationalist view, whose leading medieval and modern exponents are, respectively, Maimonides and Mendelssohn, maintains that the purpose of many, if not most or all of the *mitzvot,* is to teach and embed in the Jew correct theological beliefs. Thus, for example, observing Shabbat, it has long been maintained (following the verses in the Torah itself), serves to remind the Jew that God created the world and is its master.

3. *Moralist:* This approach emphasizes the moral purpose of many *mitzvot.* A thinker such as Shmuel David Luzzatto, for example, claimed that one of the characteristic features of the Torah is its desire to inculcate the virtues of mercy and compassion.[4]

4. *Nationalist:* This more typically modern thesis maintains

that the value of many *mitzvot*, such as the holidays, resides in their ability to reinforce the national bonds of the Jewish people.[5]

Even a cursory review of the overall body of *mitzvot* makes it hard to deny that each one of the considerations underlying these accounts plays a role in at least some *mitzvot*. Surely *some mitzvot* have, among several possible ends, at least a nationalist end (e.g., the rituals associated with *pesach*) or a moral, theological, or perhaps utilitarian one. In effect, then, each account starts from a perfectly reasonable beginning (except, perhaps, for the utilitarian thesis, but more about that later), and all too often seeks to extend the account beyond its natural borders. In search of a comprehensive theory of *ta'amei ha-mitzvot*, proponents of the moral, theological, national, or utilitarian approaches seem to discover their favorite value lurking unexpectedly beneath many a ritual rock, as it were. This tends to lend the various theories a somewhat forced quality.

But the project of developing such a comprehensive theory is surely a desideratum. After all, we intuitively sense that some common assumptions, tasks, or methods underlie the *mitzvot*. This is especially so in the case of *mitzvot* we might call "rituals." By "rituals" I mean religiously mandated rites, or patterns of behavior, such as the *haggadah* service, recitation of *kiddush* on Saturdays and holidays, the sounding of the shofar, and so on. Some involve the use of ritual objects, others involve the recitation of set verses or prayers, and yet others involve physical motions, such as shaking the *lulav* and *etrog*. Many involve combinations of all these elements. We tend to lump all these activities under the common (English) term *ritual*. But what precisely is common to all of them, particularly if there are different values attached to each? After all, some may have primarily a nationalist value, others a theological one.

Other questions call out for answers as well. What accounts for the immense power that rituals exercise over religious devotees, and what accounts for the lasting power of so many rituals? Is there any general way to account for the particular details of ritual performance? Perhaps most important of all, what 'purely religious reasons' are there for performing or originating religious rituals? I believe that an ideal philosophico-theological, as opposed to social scientific, theory of ritual would account for ritual in purely religious categories. But what counts as a purely religious category?

My aim in this paper is to briefly sketch out a theory of religious ritual that seeks to answer these questions. This paper is drawn from a larger work, and in this context I shall need to treat only cursorily certain issues that are more fully addressed therein.

2

Rituals are often spoken of as symbols of a certain sort. Within the Jewish tradition, Samson Raphael Hirsch has perhaps made the most systematic use of a theory of symbols to explain a large class of *mitzvot,* which he calls the "*edot,*" in all their detail. Indeed, he wrote a 235-page treatise exploring the topic.[6] While there is much to be said for Hirsch's approach, it is hard to deny that there is a certain artificial, almost rigid, quality to his use of the theory, in at least some instances. After all, how can one really know just what God intended in originating the *mitzvot* in all their particulars?

More recently Clifford Geertz defines religion as a "system of symbols which acts to establish powerful, pervasive and long-lasting moods and motivations in men by formulating conceptions of a general order of existence and clothing these conceptions with such an aura of factuality that the moods and motivations seem uniquely realistic."[7] Geertz maintains that rituals, which are enacted symbols, relate *ethos,* "the tone, character and quality of life, its moral and aesthetic style and mood," with *worldview,* "the picture of the way things in sheer actuality are, their concept of nature, self and society . . . their comprehensive ideas of order."[8] As he puts it elsewhere, "In ritual, the world as lived and the world as imagined, fused under the agency of a single set of symbolic forms, turns out to be the same world."[9]

Geertz seems to be making an important point about ritual, stressing its capacity to shape the ritualist's way of experiencing the world.[10] Nevertheless, he does not spell out precisely *how* or *why* ritual functions in this way, nor does he apply his basic insight into tackling the questions I raised earlier in this essay. We have here the seed of an idea, but a theory of ritual requires more. In a sense, the theory I shall soon outline is an attempt to explore just how ritual *mitzvot* might perform the role Geertz ascribes to them.

3

My basic thesis, as the title of this essay suggests, is that religious rituals can be usefully thought of as a species of metaphor. But that is to say very little, or to say it poorly, unless we have some idea of what metaphor is. This of course has been the subject of a vast literature. Here I can do no more than summarize my own theory of what metaphor is, so as to justify its application to religious ritual. On the face of it, this claim seems at worst nonsensical, and at best metaphorical itself. Metaphors are usually taken to be figures of speech, the stuff of linguists and semanticists. How then can behavior be metaphorical?

Simply put, the basic idea I should like to advocate is that what makes a word or expression metaphorical is (1) its function and (2) the mechanism whereby it realizes that function.

Metaphorical Function

Theoreticians of metaphor have long sought to account for certain problems in the use of metaphor. For example, it is often thought that for an expression to be metaphorical it must be literally false, or couldn't have been intended by the speaker as literally true. But then why is the expression "Smith took the shirt off Jones's back" metaphorical, if the speaker intended to assert not only that Smith is a mean-spirited creditor, but that he actually stripped Jones of his shirt in collecting his debt. Similarly, we all have intuitions about which metaphors are banal and which are fresh. But what criteria are there for distinguishing between them? Most importantly, how do we go about interpreting metaphors? Some metaphors are extremely complex and quite difficult to interpret, especially those used in poetry. Indeed, many are embedded in larger contexts that are themselves metaphorical, for example, a metaphor that appears in a book by Kafka. A theory of metaphor should provide guidelines that aid in explicating metaphors, as well as criteria for determining what is and what isn't a correct interpretation. A metaphor's context is obviously crucial here in solving many of these problems, since by examining a metaphor's context we may learn a great deal about what it means. But what exactly is a metaphor's context, and how exactly do we appeal to it in interpreting metaphor?[11]

One way of approaching these problems is to analyze a metaphor by way of its function. If we want to know what the context does to a metaphor, we should inquire as to what a metaphor does to its context, that is, what its function is. In other words we need to examine how the metaphor contributes to the author's or reader's goals in writing (or speaking) or reading (or listening to) the metaphor in question.[12] No doubt, of course, the author or reader can have many different goals, and a metaphor can perform many different speech acts, such as asserting, commanding, and so on. But what exactly is the *characteristically metaphorical* way in which the metaphorical expression, as against literal expression, contributes to the realization of these goals? In short, what exactly is the metaphor's characteristic function?

Max Black, in a classic treatment of the metaphor phenomenon, maintains that metaphor "selects, emphasizes, suppresses and organizes features of the principal subject [the object of the metaphorical expression] by implying statements about it that normally apply to the subsidiary subject [the metaphorical expression itself]."[13] But which properties of the principal subject may be "selected, emphasized," and so on, such that the selection is metaphorical and effective? To say that "this bachelor is a male" is to emphasize a feature of the bachelor, namely, his sex, but it is surely not to speak metaphorically. Similarly, to say "the smiling sun" is also to emphasize certain features of the sun, but to do so only banally. How are we to account for these observations? And how are we to account for the jolt, the tension that an effective metaphor seems to set off in the reader? Speaking of "selection" or "emphasis" of certain features of the principal subject doesn't go quite far enough to explain this phenomenon.

Perhaps the best way to begin answering this question is to consider a picture puzzle. As children, we were presented with, for example, what appeared to be an elaborately leafy picture of a tree, and then we were asked to find the elephant pictures concealed therein. After examining the picture of the tree from all sorts of angles, we finally "saw" the elephants. Here we encounter a determinate structure that can be experienced under different aspects, as pictures of different things. Wittgenstein calls this phenomenon "seeing-as."[14]

While Wittgenstein limited his discussion of this phenomenon to picture puzzles and the like, discoveries in cognitive psychology suggest that human beings always experience everything in the world in precisely this way, that all human experience is in reality only "experience-as." Even if the world itself is determinate, a question philosophers have long debated, human experience is not. Since we human beings bring to the perceptual and experiential encounter all sorts of mental baggage, our experiences and percepts are in part determined by that baggage. There is no naked eye or virgin experience in the human encounter with the world. What we experience depends upon our beliefs, desires, emotions, percepts, wishes, hopes, and so on, what we might call an "experiential set," the sum total of mental states that determine the character of our experience. As R. L. Gregory says in regard to visual perception:

> The seeing of objects involves many sources of information beyond those meeting the eye when we look at an object. It generally involves knowledge of the object derived from previous experience, and this experience is not limited to vision but may include other senses . . . Objects are far more than patterns of stimulation; objects have pasts and futures. When we know its past or can guess its future an object transcends experience and becomes an embodiment of knowledge and expectation without which life of even the simplest kind is impossible.[15]

Consider, as an example, the different experiences of the artist and the radiologist, who both observe an x-ray. The artist, because of his interest in beauty and in the aesthetic experience, because of his desires for an aesthetic experience, because of his knowledge of the play of light and shadow and the possibilities of perspective, will have one experience of the x-ray, with distinctive emotional, cognitive, desiderative, attitudinal, and other elements. He may experience the x-ray *as an object of art*. The radiologist, on the other hand, because of his knowledge of and interest in radiology, will experience it *as a diagnostic tool* and have an entirely different experience, with quite different constitutive elements.

Now consider an artist who examines a particular x-ray, then studies medicine, abandons his art, becomes a radiologist, and happens upon the same old x-ray once again. His initial experience of the x-ray will be entirely restructured. He will no longer experience the x-ray as a work of art but as a diagnostic tool. The content of his experiential set, whose object is the x-ray, will undergo a transformation: new beliefs, desires, wishes, percepts, and so on will displace the old ones. There is a certain dynamic and fluidity to the change as well, in that each member of the experiential set has an impact on the other, setting off a kind of experiential chain reaction. A change in desire can have an impact on belief, which in turn can have an impact on percept, which in turn can have an impact on the original desire, and so on and on, until an equilibrium is reached.

This model of experiential structuring and restructuring illuminates the metaphor phenomenon. Metaphor's function, I would suggest, is to set off precisely this kind of restructuring of the reader's experiential set, whose object is the principal subject of the metaphor. Consider an example: suppose you are at the beach on a calm, sunny afternoon, relaxing, taking in the sun, the seagulls, and the rhythmic waves. You experience the sea as a vast, tranquil, free place in the world, your experiential set consisting of beliefs about the sea and its relaxing qualities, the desire to rest after a difficult semester, a yearning to explore its vast, liberating reaches. Next you pick up the volume of Tennyson you've taken along, flip open the pages until you come upon the following passage, asserted of a corpse and the sea to which it is flung, that it (the corpse) drops into its "vast and wandering grave." You reflect upon that line, and your experiential set undergoes a change and now consists of the following: a set of beliefs about the great depth and opacity of the sea and its consequent ability to hide and cover, its incessant wearing and eroding movements, its ability to swallow up everything not fit to stay on top, feelings of vague anxiety and foreboding, perceptions of the darkness that lurks beneath the sea's shining surface. The sea no longer *is* for you "a vast, tranquil free place in the world." It has now *become* "a great and forbidding place." This clearly involves more than a mere change of belief, which is merely cognitive. We have here a change in the reader's entire experiential set, his emotions, desires, and attitudes, a change in each element, which in turn triggers changes in other elements. Moreover, such change may in fact not even start with a change of belief; an emotional or attitudinal change may take place first; this in turn leads to cognitive change. Where this *systemic* change does takes place it can be so extensive that, at least in the maximally effective metaphor, the reader's *concept* of the metaphor's subject is no longer the same.

Statements such as "that bachelor is a male" or "the smiling sun" fail as metaphors on this account, because our experience of a bachelor or the sun is not restructured by the assertion, since our experiential set whose object is bachelor or sun *already contains* those elements the expression seeks to emphasize. The jolt or tension characteristic of a good metaphor, on the other hand, results from the mental battle that takes place between the shadow of our old experiential set and the force of the new one. Our avenues into the world do not give psychological ground easily, and we are torn between our entrenched earlier experience of the object and the power of the new one. Elements of the old experiential set mingle uneasily with inconsistent elements of the new one, until a new, internally consistent equilibrium is established. Once established, however, after maximal restructuring, we have a new object before us. The subject of an effective metaphor can never be quite the same again.

The Mechanism of Metaphor

I have argued that metaphorical function is a necessary condition for metaphoricality. Nevertheless, it cannot be a sufficient condition as well, since there are many media for the restructuring of experience, metaphor only one among them. A second condition, conjoined with metaphorical function, is necessary and sufficient for metaphoricality. That second condition is the mechanism of metaphor.

To get at what this mechanism might be, consider a visual paradigm. Rudolf Arnheim describes an experiment in which observers were asked to describe their impressions of two paintings of very different style, which were placed one next to the other. Then one of the pair of pictures was replaced by another picture and the changes in impressions resulting from the new combination were recorded. Arnheim summarizes the results of the experiments by stating that "an arbitrary confrontation deformed the two components of the pair . . . *The pairing of two images throws into relief a common quality*"[16] (my emphasis).

The characteristic mechanism whereby a metaphor realizes its function seems to be a linguistic analogue to precisely this visual phenomenon. Metaphor "interacts" the experiential set whose object is the principal subject ("men" in "men are wolves") with the experiential set whose object is the principal subject of the metaphor ("wolves" in "men are wolves").[17] I experience men, with all the components of my experiential set whose objects are men, and I experience wolves, with all the components of my experiential set whose objects are wolves. The pairing of the two experiential sets causes me to occurrently experience both simultaneously, which highlights characteristics of men's features that they share with wolves; this causes me to experience men quite differently. My experiential set whose objects are men now contains elements that were once only part of my experiential set whose objects were wolves. It should be added here that any metaphor is invertable; that is, whether men or wolves are the principal subjects is an arbitrary matter of focus, since asserting "wolves are men" results in the interaction and restructuring characteristic of metaphor as well, except that here the subjects are wolves. I shall call this phenomenon *bilaterality*. Its importance is especially relevant to ritual, so I shall not dwell on this point just yet.

In any case, if metaphor's function is to restructure the reader's experience, to recreate, as it were, the metaphor's object, it achieves that function through the distinctive interaction mechanism described above. Both these features are jointly necessary and sufficient for an expression to be metaphorical.

If this account of metaphor is correct, then one of its consequences is that nonlinguistic communication can be metaphorical as well. If, upon observing some outrageous, comical, and crude behavior by an acquaintance at a party, you look at a friend, grimace, and make a monkey-like face, you are metaphorically, if nonlinguistically, asserting of the acquaintance that he is a monkey. Both conditions for metaphoricality are met: the experience of the acquaintance has been restructured, as has that (by giving rise to an interaction between two occurrent experiences) of the principal and subsidiary subjects of the communicative act. Whether this counts as an instance of metaphor (as I am inclined to believe), or an instance of *metaphor-like* behavior, is for my purposes here not at all significant.

The stage has now been set to make good on my original claim, that religious ritual can be understood as a species of metaphor, since, on the analysis just presented here, nonlinguistic behavior can be quite as metaphorical as linguistic behavior.

4

Early on in this paper I suggested that a key issue that must be addressed in developing a philosophico-theological theory of ritual *mitzvot* is explicating what would count as a purely religious end in performing *mitzvot*. A maximally effective philosophico-theological theory for ritual *mitzvot* should explain *mitzvot,* such that their performance is justified on purely religious grounds. But what can we mean by "purely religious" end?

I would suggest here that for an end to be "purely religious" it must meet two conditions: (1) it must be *unique* to the religious life-plan, and (2) it must be *indispensable* to it. If an end in performing a *mitzvah* is not unique to the religious life-plan, say it is performed for health reasons and so could just as well be performed by a health-conscious secularist, then it should hardly count as a purely religious end. Similarly, if the end is not indispensable to achieving the highest goals of religious life, then it fails to account for ritual by the most serious categories the religion itself puts forward. This failure would make the theory a less than maximal account of the significance of ritual.

Applying this test to the four classes of classical explanations of *ta'amei ha-mitzvot* formulated by Heinemann would yield the conclusion that explanations that are either exclusively utilitarian, exclusively moral, or exclusively nationalist fail to meet the purely religious end desideratum, because achieving any one of these ends is not unique to the religious life-plan. Behaving morally or healthily, for example, are of course ends in many a nonreligious life-plan as well. Moreover, depending upon one's conception of the highest ends of religious life, any one of these ends may not be indispensable either. If achieving mystical union with God is the ultimate end of one's religious life-plan, it is far from clear that national unity is indispensable to achieving that goal. While it may more plausibly be argued that it is *helpful* in achieving the goal, it is far less plausible to claim that for any particular individual it is *indispensable.* Thus most of these theories, insofar as they are exclusivist, fail to account for at least some *mitzvot* in purely religious terms, at least as I've unpacked the notion of "purely religious." While this of course does not make the theories false, it does mean that they are not maximal.

If the ultimate end of performing *mitzvot* is linked in some way to the transformation of human experience, however, then it does not seem difficult to account for the performance of *mitzvot* in purely religious terms. This is so because it is hard to imagine any religious end the achievement of which involves no change in human experience. Whether one's conception of the ultimate aims of the religious life are, for example, union with God, or knowledge of him, these aims can hardly be achieved without some change in the experience of the ritualist, change of a more than purely cognitive sort. It thus turns out that the desideratum of accounting for ritual *mitzvot* in "purely religious" terms, as unpacked above, naturally leads to a theory of ritual *mitzvot*, which seeks to account for them by appeal to their broad impact on human experience. This in turn leads naturally to a theory of ritual *mitzvot* grounded in metaphor, since, on the account of metaphor summarized here, metaphor functions precisely to structure and restructure the reader's experience of the metaphor's object.

5

Before I proceed any further with an analysis of ritual *mitzvah* as metaphor, it might be best to examine a particular ritual observance as an example. Consider, then, the traditional performance of the *kiddush* ritual. On Friday night the head of the family, typically upon return from synagogue services, fills a silver cup with wine, and, with the family gathered around, he or she recites aloud, over a set dinner table, which includes covered *challot*, the *kiddush*. This consists of a series of verses depicting God as resting from his creative labors on the seventh day of creation and sanctifying the day, a blessing over the wine, and a blessing of God for sanctifying Shabbat in memory of creation and for sanctifying the Jewish people by commanding them to observe the Shabbat.

We have here a series of behaviors, call them R, performed by the head of the household. The ritualists, the head of the household and the family, depending upon their religious sensitivities and background, will experience both R and, on account of the performance of the ritual in its context (special setting, special time, etc.) will experience some other state of affairs, call it R*. This might be any number of things, such as God's presence in the world, the sanctity of the Sabbath day, God's omnipotence as creator of the cosmos, and so on. For the purpose of this analysis, I shall arbitrarily select one, God's presence in the world. The simultaneous experience of R and R* causes the ritualist to experience R and R*—God's presence in the world—as sharing certain properties. And it is experiencing R and R* as sharing these properties that causes the ritualist's experience of God's presence in the world to be restructured. For example, he or she might experience both God and the ritual as being bound up with human needs and desires, time-bound, family-bound, evocable by human activity, warm and secure, tranquil. This in turn causes the ritualist to experience God differently, restructured with emphasis on God as evocable by a special set of activities or state of mind, as bound to human activity and inactivity (the seventh day of rest), as time-sensitive, as immanent, as part of human needs and pleasures, as warm and nurturing, like the family around him.

It should be apparent that the precise nature of the interaction between R and R*, and the experiential restructuring that takes place, depends upon the exact nature of the ritual, the context in which it is performed, the particular background of the ritualist. The application of the *mitzvah*-as-metaphor theory to *kiddush*, as sketched above, is meant only to serve as a model for the application of metaphor to ritual in general. Indeed, even within the *kiddush* ceremony itself, what the principal subject is (note the range of choices listed above), what gets interacted, which properties are experienced as shared by the principal and subsidiary subjects, and the resultant restructuring all depend upon the particulars of the ritualist. What counts as a metaphor and how the metaphor is to be interpreted, how it *functions*, depends upon the reader; thus, in the case of ritual, which we are claiming is a species of metaphor, determining the actual end that results from the performance of some ritual depends upon the individual ritualist and the circumstances. The theory of *mitzvah*-as-metaphor is no more than a model for the analysis of ritual; the application of the model requires special insights into the particular conditions of an actual ritual performance.

All this is not to say, of course, that the metaphoricality of *mitzvot* is random. Linguistic metaphors themselves, while radically context- and individual reader-dependent, both in regard to whether they are metaphorical and in regard to their interpretation and success, nevertheless typically function as metaphors in somewhat similar ways for different readers. This is because most readers have similar experiential sets and therefore respond to language in similar ways. Otherwise, communication would be impossible. So too in the case of ritual *mitzvot*. By virtue of the historical, religious, and literary knowledge and emotional associations that the typical ritualist brings to the ritual, certain common experiences are generated by the performance, which in turn interact with the ritual itself. The metaphoricality of *mitzvot* can be as commonplace as the commonest of religious experiences or as fresh as the rich imagination of the creative ritualist. But more about this later.

Taking these points together we can see how the *mitzvah*-as-metaphor theory differs from the usual symbolist interpretations of *mitzvot*. At the heart of all theory construction is the attempt to subsume the phenomenon in question under a well-understood, theoretically articulate system. The symbolists seek to account for *mitzvot* by subsuming, and thereby explaining, them within the framework of a theory of symbols, according to which there exists a referential relation between most ritual objects or performance and a certain idea or attitude.[18] Certainly I do not wish to deny that such a relation exists in the case of some *mitzvot*, that is, those *mitzvot* in which the relation is explicit in the Torah or other original sources for the *mitzvah*, such as Shabbat and God as creator of the cosmos. Rather, in order to avoid the kind of artificiality and rigidity that comes of *over-extending* symbolist interpretations so as to provide for a comprehensive account of ritual *mitzvot*, the *mitzvah*-as-metaphor theory subsumes *mitzvah* under a different explanatory framework, the now theoretically articulate phenomenon of metaphor.

The metaphor phenomenon, on the account sketched here, does not require the existence of referential relations for its application (although of course it does not *deny* their existence or importance). Instead, it requires the existence of a certain function (experiential restructuring) and mechanism (interaction of experiential sets), which, it is claimed, indeed obtain in the case of ritual. This means, however, that there is a certain fluidity to the role of ritual, in that ritual can function metaphorically for different ritualists in quite different ways. There is no single "correct" metaphoricality for the ritualist, just as there is no single "correct" metaphoricality for the speaker of metaphor. What may function for you as a metaphor may, for me, be quite literal. If you have never heard of the expression "a high note," you may find it metaphorical; most of us will not experience it as metaphorical at all. So too in the case of ritual. You may experience *kiddush* in one way, with a primary subject and interactions quite your own, and I may experience it very differently.

Certainly both our experiences are likely to be shaped in one way or another by the particular details of the ceremony, the words uttered therein, the biblical texts alluded to, the laws governing the ceremony, the laws governing Shabbat generally, and so on. Nevertheless, the experience is also likely to be shaped by the personal background, history, desires, wishes, and knowledge of the ritualist. One of the important aims of the *mitzvah*-as-metaphor theory is indeed to provide theoretically for the personalization of ritual performance, that is, to provide an explanatory framework for *mitzvot,* such that personalization of *mitzvot* is part of their religious value. According to the symbolist school, for example, *mitzvot* relate referentially to certain subjects. If I absorb that referential relation, then I have successfully performed the *mitzvah.* Success thus depends upon absorption of a static relation. For the *mitzvah*-as-metaphor theory, on the other hand, no such static referential relation need exist, such that it must be satisfactorily absorbed. Successful performance of a *mitzvah,* that is, one that helps achieve the highest ends of the religious life-plan, requires a highly personal encounter: the encounter between my individual experience of the ritual and my individual experience of that to which the ritual gives rise. And it also requires that, as a result of the live interaction between these two occurrent experiences, my experience of that to which the ritual gives rise, for example, God (we shall see other examples later), is transformed, recreated after the image of the ritual itself. Ritual, like metaphor, is a highly pesonal experience indeed.[19]

Another consequence of the personalization of ritual, its context sensitivity, is that not all performances of *mitzvah* are metaphorical; only *successful* performances are. The insensitive or ignorant ritualist may derive no religious benefit at all of the sort described here from the performance of the ritual, in just the same way that an insensitive or ignorant reader may not even realize that some expression is metaphorical. In both cases neither the expression nor the performance is metaphorical for the reader or performer in question. The theory of ritual proposed here is intended to account for ritual by the highest of religious categories, by proposing how the performance of ritual can achieve a "purely religious" end. If not all ritualists perform ritual for the purest of motives, the problem resides more with the ritualist than the ritual theorist. Of course, to say that a *mitzvah* has not functioned metaphorically in circumstance C is not to assert that it is not a *mitzvah*, but only to assert that it has not functioned as such in context C. The deontic status of the *mitzvah* does not depend upon its metaphorical function. If one believes that *mitzvot* are binding, then even if the ritualist's experience is unlikely to be restructured for whatever reason, the *mitzvah* must still be performed.

In light of this discussion, however, it should not be hard to see how the account of the *kiddush* ceremony outlined here does indeed satisfy the "purely religious" end desideratum for a theory of ritual. First, the end in performing the ceremony is *unique* to the religious life-plan: the atheist would have no need to restructure his experience of God's presence in the world. Second, the end can also be seen as *indispensable* to achieving the highest ends of some religious life-plan, for the religious person, it would seem, can never apprehend God, or become one with him, if the experience of God is not as he truly is, namely, according to this tradition, evocable, immanent, and so forth. For example, I can't experience you as you truly are, if my experience of you is distorted by past prejudices. Likewise, I can't apprehend God, if what I experience is not him but some misconstrual of him. Ritual seeks to evoke God as he truly is, or, more accurately, to evoke those aspects of him that would have remained hidden, that we would not have experienced, if not for the performance of the ritual. Ritual seeks to recreate the religious experience by jolting it out of its complacency through the metaphorical oddities of the twin experiences it generates. Experiential transformation of key religious categories is central to the ritual enterprise. Thus, the theory of ritual *mitzvot* proposed here accounts for the performance of *mitzvot* by the standard of "purely religious end."

Before proceeding to discuss other aspects of the *mitzvah*-as-metaphor theory, we need to consider briefly two points. First, the question of communication. In a typical metaphor, the writer (or speaker) communicates some message, C, to the reader (or listener). But in the case of ritual, who is communicating to whom? Is the performer communicating to the observers of the ritual? To himself? To God? Or is it the originator of the ritual who is communicating to the performer and the participants of the ritual? Or is it all or none of the above? These questions raise several others: Can I be said to communicate C to R if I don't know that I am communicating C, or if R doesn't know that I am communicating C to him? Can I communicate C to R, not by doing or saying something myself, but by having R do or say something?

Answering all these questions in the context of this essay would take me far afield. Two points, however, can be made. First, if ritual is only metaphor-like rather than genuine metaphor, then it is not necessary that ritual be communicative. What is necessary is that ritual share the same function and mechanism as metaphor, which I believe it does. Second, it is not at all unreasonable to maintain that ritualists typically do intend to communicate by means of the ritual, most notably to God, that, for example, they care enough about him to perform his ritual; or that they wish him to respond kindly to their needs, spiritual or material; or that they wish him to be, say in the case of the *kiddush* ceremony (and *mutatis mutandis* in the case of other rituals), immanent, loving, evocable, and so on. They may not consciously intend to communicate the entire array of experiences evoked by the ritual performance, but, just as in the case of linguistic metaphors, the writer rarely intends consciously the full array of experiences evoked by the metaphor. Moreover, some ritualists may well intend to communicate to themselves and to other participants in their performance of the ritual, to evoke in themselves and others the experiences the ritual gives rise to. It is not counterintuitive to maintain that the originator(s) of the ritual may himself (themselves) be communicating to the ritualist and participants of the ritual. Surely I can communicate a secret message to you by asking you to engage in certain activities that I know will evoke specific beliefs or attitudes in you, precisely those I wish to communicate. On the face of it, then, it seems reasonable to maintain that ritual can be communicative and that it can be communicative in any or all the senses mentioned above. When the Jew performs a *mitzvah* he or she may be communicating to God, to himself, or to others around him, as indeed the originator of the ritual, whoever that was, may be communicating to the ritualist. Most critically, however, the means of communication is metaphorical.

Finally, we need to return briefly to the notion of *bilaterality* introduced earlier in regard to metaphor. I noted above that metaphorical focus is arbitrary: the principal and subsidiary subjects can always be reversed to produce (with appropriate changes) an apt metaphor. By this I mean *not* that, where inversion takes place, the interpretation of the inverted metaphor will be the same as the interpretation of the non-inverted metaphor, since this is patently false. What I mean is that, where inversion takes place, the inverted metaphor will be an apt one, by virtue of the interactive mechanism characteristic of metaphor. I also mean to suggest that in some circumstances the experiencer of metaphor may be empirically likely to (unconsciously) perform this inversion, since he experiences the occurrence as metaphorical and metaphor works by juxtaposing two experiential sets. Nonlinguistic metaphors seem especially likely to encourage such inversion, since they are nonsyntactic and therefore, to the experiencer, more open ended.

The key advantage to this observation, not surprisingly, is in ritual. Since ritual, as I am claiming, restructures the ritualist's experience of the principal subject by means of the mechanism of interaction, that interaction too is bilateral. In other words, in the case of ritual at least, the restructured experience of the principal subject may in turn lead to a subsidiary restructuring of the subsidiary subject. For example, in the case of the *kiddush* ceremony, once the experience of God has been restructured, so that he is experienced as time bound, evocable, immanent, and so on, the experience of the *kiddush* ceremony may be restructured as well, so that the ceremony itself is experienced as an evoker of God's hiddeness and immanence. The *kiddush* cup may come to be experienced as holding not only the wine, but also the immanence of God, hidden therein. The ritual dynamic is thus even more complex and subtle: it travels in multiple directions.

6

In this section I apply the *mitzvah*-as-metaphor theory in detail to the performance of another *mitzvah,* that of *teki'at shofar.* My aim is to provide further evidence for the way in which the theory illuminates the performance of *mitzvot,* to show how it accords with traditional interpretations of *mitzvot,* and, through its application, to consider other aspects of the theory itself.

In order to begin the analysis, it is important to note that reflection about ritual *mitzvot* generally suggests that they may be divided into three classes: theistic, historical, and humanistic.

> A ritual *mitzvah* is *theistic* if its principal subject is the nature of God and/or his relation to individual persons, mankind as a whole, or nature and natural processes.
>
> A ritual *mitzvah* is *historical* if its principal subject is some period, past, present, or future, in the history of the Jewish people, where the ritualist's experience of such stands in a causal relation with his experience of God.
>
> A ritual *mitzvah* is *humanistic* if its principal subject is the nature of man or the nature of human relationships, where the ritualist's experience of such stands in a causal relation with his experience of God.

Theistic ritual *mitzvot* are, I think, self-explanatory, and it is not difficult to think of many examples of *mitzvot* that fall into these categories. A word should be said, however, about the historical and humanistic categories. If a ritual's principal subject is *only* the nature of mankind, human relationships, or the Jewish people, then in what way is it unique to the religious life-plan? Secularists need to get the nature of mankind or of the Jewish people right as well. And if it is not unique to the religious life-plan, then it fails to satisfy the "purely religious end" standard. It is for this reason that I added the condition that the ritualist's experience of the humanistic and historical principal subjects must stand in a causal relation to the ritualist's experience of God. This condition excludes the humanistic and historical principal subjects from the secularist's life-plan and connects it intimately with the highest ends of the religionist. The uniqueness condition would thus be satisfied.

Another consequence of this system of classification emerges if we take it to be a necessary condition for the metaphoricality of ritual *mitzvot* that the principal subject of the ritual be theistic, historical, or humanistic. Suppose, for example, that the *kiddush* ceremony gives rise in me to an experience of the party I recently attended at which a toast was given to my friend using the same brand of wine, and that this then restructures my experience of the party along metaphoric lines. While here the ritual behavior functioned metaphorically, it is hardly a characteristic of ritual *mitzvah*-metaphoric function. What makes for characteristically *mitzvah*-metaphoric function is precisely the nature of the principal subject that is restructured.

While this system of classification does pick out this characteristic *mitzvah*-metaphoric restructuring and will prove useful for an analysis of ritual *mitzvot,* as we shall soon see, it does have a certain limitation. This arises from the complexity of the phenomenon it purports to classify, since any individual ritual may be theistic *and* historical *and* humanistic at different stages of its performance, and even simultaneously. A complex ritual, rich in traditions, may indeed have many subjects, and which one will predominate for the ritualist depends upon the ritualist's sensitivities, background beliefs, and knowledge. I shall call this complexity the *multimetaphoricality* of ritual. Nevertheless, by applying this triadic model to the analysis of ritual, we can at least isolate and classify its various dimensions.

Shofar is an excellent example of this multimetaphoricality, for it has been interpreted by the classical sources as having principal subjects in each of these classes. I shall in fact organize my discussion of the metaphoricality of shofar around this classification, selecting only a limited number of examples from the immensely rich explanatory literature which has arisen around shofar, to show how it can function metaphorically in each of the three categories for the religiously sensitive ritualist. First I shall consider the relevant *physical* properties of the ritual object and performance itself, considering how they interact with some metaphorically related principal subject. Then I will look at the *literary* or *historical* allusions attached to the performance, which the sensitive ritualist brings with him or her to the experience of the ritual, since these too will be interacted with the ritual's (multiple) principal subjects. I shall use the noncommunicative model of ritual as metaphor, since this is somewhat less complicated than the communicative model, although it should be apparent that the analysis will work for both.

Theistic

Consider first the shape of the shofar. It is bent, with the narrow mouthpiece inserted into the mouth and its body projecting outward and upward, growing wider the farther it gets from the mouth. Sound is experienced as entering its narrowest and lowest level and rising to its highest and widest point. Consider too an important aspect of Rosh Hashana, which is traditionally experienced as *yom ha-din,* a day of cosmic trial. In this context it is most natural that the shofar, the ritual object most closely associated with Rosh Hashana, would interact with the ritualist's experience of God as judge; the ritualist would thus experience himself as dependent upon God's goodwill and grace for life and happiness. Just as the sound of the shofar rises from the mouth upward to the heavens, just as the sound of the *teki'ah* rises from the lower to the higher note, so, too, in the experience of the ritualist, the Jew's thoughts and deeds rise upward to God. The ritualist's experience of this rising property, as shared by the shofar (and its sound) and his thoughts and deeds which face God in judgment, causes the experience of God to be restructured, so that God is experienced as judge, weighing and evaluating all that the Jew places before him.[20] Then the shofar itself, through the bilateral interaction phenomenon, is experienced no longer as a mere instrument, but as that which helps to create the judge-defendant relation between God and the Jew.

God too has, as it were, various attitudes towards man. He can closely examine the minutiae of man's sins and, of course, find man wanting, or he can overlook and transcend those narrow shortcomings, examine him less exactingly, with generosity and mercy. The shofar starts narrow and low. God as judge can be experienced as sharing that very property: God can decide on narrow and exacting grounds. The shofar and its sound elevates and expands. God as judge can be experienced as sharing that very property: He can transcend those narrow and exacting grounds and judge munificently and bountifully. Thus the ritualist experiences these properties as shared by the shofar and by God, and, as a result, experiences God as a judge who can transcend the confines of strict justice, who can bestow mercy even when strictly undeserved. The rising sound and shape of the shofar interacts with the experience of God and restructures it. The experience of the shofar too is restructured bilaterally, as a purveyor of this message of God and redemption. Even the ascent of the blower of the shofar onto the *bima* is a metaphor for the ascent of man's deeds before God and the ascent of God himself.[21]

There is more. If the Jew experiences God as judge, then he experiences himself as a supplicant on trial before him. As a supplicant, he cries out. But in what language and with what words? An inarticulate cry of despair as well as hope: the broken sound of the *teru'ah* blast, which rises from the shofar's lowest point, the mouth of the blower, up to the heights of the shofar's peak and beyond, to God himself. The shofar causes the ritualist to experience God as object of supplication, and it causes the ritualist to experience the relation between man and God as supplicant to listener and bestower. The broken and soaring sound of the shofar interacts with the experience of the relation between God and man in the context of the Day of Judgment, and it also interacts with the experience of prayers of supplication. The shofar in turn is experienced as the purveyor of inarticulate cries and hopes.[22] Further, the tenuous bond between God and man is experienced as supported by the secret language of the shofar, as ineffable as the shofar cry itself.[23]

The shofar is bowed and bent. This property is experienced as shared with the human relationship to God; the interaction causes the ritualist to experience himself as bowed, bent in supplication, broken before God, just as the shofar is bowed and bent, just as the *teru'ah* sound breaks and wavers. The shofar itself is then experienced as the Jew's agent, his bowed and bent representative and mouthpiece before God.[24]

The sensitive and informed ritualist would be steeped in the literature and traditions associated with shofar, and so the shofar would give rise to other theistic principal subjects as well. To mention just one among many examples, the shofar used by Ashkenazi Jews is typically a ram's horn. The ram is a principal figure in one of the great biblical stories, *akedat Yitzhak*. At the very last moment, before Abraham sacrifices Isaac, God intervenes, Abraham sees a ram whose horns are entangled in a nearby thicket, and he takes the ram and slaughters it in lieu of his son Isaac. To the sensitive ritualist, the ram's horn of the shofar may give rise to an experience of the primordial biblical ram, which replaced the threatened Isaac. That experience would likely give rise to others with which his experience of the shofar would interact. Thus, for example, he may come to experience himself in relation to God as entangled and immobilized too, in the thickets of anxiety and wrongdoing, as prevented from achieving his highest ends.[25] He experiences too the glory of God's presence and his consequent readiness to sacrifice himself for it, as Isaac did before him. He experiences the highest ends of his life as so valuable that the means he chooses to achieve those ends include self-denial as well.[26]

Historical

The historical subjects of shofar as metaphor largely depend for their role in the ritualist's experience of shofar upon their inclusion in Jewish history, especially as told in the Bible. First, there is the revelation at Sinai, a central event in Jewish history. The shofar, which was sounded at Sinai according to the Bible, may be experienced by the knowledgable ritualist as interacting with the experience of sounding the shofar on Rosh Hashana. The sound of the shofar gives rise to an experience of that people/nation-making event; the shofar is sounded before the entire congregation, standing in awed silence. The revelation at Sinai also took place before the congregation of Israel standing in awe before God and the unceasing blast of the shofar. These shared properties restructure his experience of his lonely self (there are humanistic dimensions of this as well); he now experiences himself as bound horizontally, across to all Jews in his congregation, even to all Jews around the world, as they too on the very same day listen to the shofar. He experiences himself as bound vertically as well, back into the time of his ancestors, who throughout the ages listened as he does to the voice of the shofar, all the way back to his ancestors, who stood at Sinai before God and the sound of his shofar, who bore witness to God's presence in the world, who undertook to live according to the obligations demanded by his presence, and who became one people in obligation and witness before God. The shofar ritualist thus experiences himself as heir to the theistically grounded obligations, to the national unity and purpose of the past. He then experiences the blast of the shofar not merely as the sound of the ram's horn, but as a call to intensify his experience of that community, to act upon it, with all the heirs of that shofar blast of the past.[27]

The shofar in biblical literature marks not only a transforming event in the past, but also a transforming event in the future. In Isa. 27.13 the shofar blast ushers in the messianic era. The experience of the shofar on Rosh Hashana interacts with the experience of the long-hoped for shofar blast of the messianic era, and the ritualist's experience of the present splintered state of his people is restructured according to the heartening and challenging vision of a common and transformed destiny. The shofar, in turn, is experienced as a call to the ritualist to help realize that destiny and as a broken supplication before God to speed the process towards its realization.[28]

Humanistic

The thoroughgoing restructuring of the shofar ritualist's experience of God and his relation to man, as well as the ritualist's experience of his people and his relation to them, is bound to have a profound impact upon his experience of himself. If he experiences himself as on trial, if he experiences his fate as tenuous and riding upon the ultimately unpredictable decision of another, then he experiences the vulnerability of life itself. The experience of the vulnerability of life, in turn, gives rise to a sense of urgency in life's missions, an experience of the significance of each moment. It gives rise to the urge to evaluate the lives we lead, to engage in self-criticism, to feel anxious about the value of our accomplishments. The experience of birth, and according to tradition Rosh Hashana is the birthday of the world, gives rise in the sensitive ritualist to the experience of death, for all that is born will die. Thus this experience of being on trial for life itself, this experience of impending death, structures our experience of ourselves and our past in very significant ways, much as the existentialist writers have long stressed. The straight *teki'ah* sound is experienced as sharing certain properties with the blast that traditionally marked the start of a great trial, and the interaction results in the experiential restructuring described above. The wavering *teru'ah* or *shevarim* sound is experienced as sharing properties with expressions of incertitude, anxiety, and self-doubt. Each staccato sound lasts but a short moment; life too lasts but a short moment over the long stretch of God's eternal time. The *teru'ah* stops and starts; it is experienced as sharing properties with hesitant, anxious self-questioning. It interacts with the experience of life itself: each moment is experienced as taking on its own urgency, as sharp and demanding as the short cry of each staccato note. The ritualist introspects, bends into himself, much as the shofar is bent. The ascent of the shofar, the ascent onto the *bima* by the shofar blower, interact metaphorically with the ritualist's own personal growth, as he recognizes the inherent limitations of life and his own personal limitations. His experience of himself, his potential and his mission, is restructured. And he feels an urgency to act forcefully upon these new experiences, a feeling as forceful and urgent as the *teki'ah* blast itself.

7

We have seen how the *mitzvah*-as-metaphor theory provides an explanatory framework and a theoretical underpinning for the rich array of classical interpretations that have grown around the shofar ritual, as well as for new ways of seeing it too. The account not only allows for this richness, but also encourages it. Unlike the symbolist school, which tends to look for fixed referential relations between a ritual and its subject, the metaphor approach personalizes ritual, making it radically context-dependent. The maximally sensitive ritualist will experience many things when he performs ritual, and all these experiences contribute to the metaphoricality of ritual, provided they are theistic, historical, or humanistic. There is no one set of "correct" referents to ritual; ritual is what the ritualist makes of it. But what the typical sensitive and knowledgable ritualist makes of it metaphorically does indeed contribute to the highest ends of the religious life, as I believe the shofar example makes clear.

Ritual has often been criticized on pragmatic or existentialist religious grounds. Ritual is repetitive, runs the argument, which renders it inherently unable to enrich the religious experience of the ritualist; it encourages rote, mindless, and inauthentic behavior. In practice, of course, this occurs. Ritual is indeed performed in precisely this way by at least some ritualists at least some of the time. Nevertheless, ritual, properly understood, *need not* function in this way. Even the most striking of metaphors, paintings or sculptures, can be lost on the insensitive reader. Similarly, ritual may be lost on the insensitive performer. Nevertheless, accounting for ritual as metaphor unleashes an immensely rich set of categories for responding creatively to ritual performance. Much as great myth retains the power to fascinate children, or adults, upon rereading, so too ritual retains this power as well. The vast multimetaphoricality of shofar reflects the myriad ways in which the imaginative, knowledgable, and sensitive ritualist can interact with ritual. The power of ritual echoes the power of metaphor, poetry, great art, and music. Just as great art long retains the capacity to stimulate fresh ways of looking, so too ritual long retains the power to stimulate new experiences, new principal subjects, new interactions, and new restructurings.

Finally, it is worth adding that the intricate details of ritual performance contribute substantially to its metaphorical riches. As the analysis of shofar as metaphor shows, the numerous details of the shofar performance give rise to varied principal subjects and varied interactions. The idea is not to explain why some originator may have instituted one particular detail over another; this leads to artificiality and, as Maimonides maintains in the *Guide* (3.26), is in any case unknowable, at least when God is the ritual's originator. Explaining the details of the *mitzvot* in terms of the ritual-as-metaphor theory amounts to explaining the ways in which the religiously knowledgable and sensitive performer is likely to respond metaphorically to the detail in question. Is it likely to help give rise to the experience of one rather than another principal subject? Is it likely to call attention to one rather than another property of the principal subject? Is it likely to result in one rather than another sort of restructuring? Answers to these questions depend upon the mindset of the sensitive and knowledgable ritual performer. Are there any allusions within the classical literature relevant to the detail that he is likely to bring to his experience of the ritual? Does the context of the ritual make it likely that the detail will generate a particular wish, desire, or attitude, which in turn will contribute to the experiential restructuring that is the task of the ritual?

No doubt many of these questions may be asked in the usual symbolist interpretation. Nevertheless, the key difference is that for the ritual-as-metaphor theory, no claim is made that the answer to these questions will reveal some objectively existent referential relation or "deep meaning" to the ritual. The existence of these is not required at all (although, of course, their existence is not denied either). Rather, the assumption is that there may be many different correct answers to these questions, since, as has been maintained throughout this essay, the metaphoricality of any ritual performance depends entirely upon the particular experiential set of the performer.[29]

NOTES

1. For the classic and exhaustive treatment of the history of the inquiry, see Heinemann 1949.

2. Heinemann 1949, vol. 2, pp. 240ff. Heinemann does not, but probably should, add a fifth category drawn from the mystical tradition, according to which the value of certain rituals is to restore the Godhead itself to its ideal state. In general, Heinemann's study pays insufficient attention to the Jewish mystical tradition.

3. Halevi, *The Kuzari* 3.13 (Hirschfeld).

4. For a discussion of Luzzatto's views, see Heinemann 1949, vol. 2, chap. 3.

5. See Heinemann 1949, vol. 2, pp. 56–60.

6. "A Basic Outline of Jewish Symbolism"; partial translation in Hirsch 1957, pp. 303–420. See also Hirsch 1962, pp. 54–214; 1969, pp. 83–87; 1963.

7. Geertz 1973, p. 90.

8. Geertz 1973, p. 127.

9. Geertz 1973, p. 112.

10. See also the works of Mary Douglas, especially her *Purity and Danger* (1966).

11. Given the limitations of this essay, I cannot spell out in detail how the theory I propose answers all these questions. Nevertheless, I hope the reader will get some sense of my approach to these problems from the discussion that follows. For a somewhat similar view of metaphor, although quite different in a number of important respects, see Davidson 1984, pp. 245–64.

12. See Boorse 1976.

13. Black 1962, p. 44. See Goodman 1976 for a nominalistic construal of Black's basic approach to metaphor. Black expanded on his basic thesis about metaphor in Black 1977.

14. Wittgenstein 1968, part II, xi.

15. Gregory 1973, pp. 7–12.

16. Arnheim 1969, p. 61.

17. Thinking of metaphor as an interaction has its roots in Richards 1936, p. 93, and was picked up and developed by Black 1962 and 1977.

My interpretation of the interaction is different from theirs, in that I stress the interaction of experiential sets, an outgrowth of the functional theory of metaphor summarized above.

18. Josef Stern has brilliantly analyzed the complexities of these relations in Stern 1987, pp. 109–128.

19. Mendelssohn stresses this as well. See Eisen 1990, p. 258 for a discussion of this point.

20. Finesinger 1931, p. 218.

21. Finesinger 1931, pp. 215–16.

22. Agnon 1967, p. 75.

23. Agnon 1967, p. 74.

24. Agnon 1967, p. 68.

25. Agnon 1967, p. 66.

26. Agnon 1967, p. 72.

27. Agnon 1967, pp. 65–70.

28. Agnon 1967, pp. 64, 67, 71–72.

29. This paper is drawn from a larger work, entitled *Ritual as Metaphor*. I am grateful to participants of the 1991 meeting of the Academy for Jewish Philosophy, especially to Josef Stern, for comments made on an earlier version of the paper.

REFERENCES

Agnon, S. Y. 1967. *Days of Awe*. Edited by Nahum Glatzer. New York: Schocken Books.

Arnheim, R. 1969. *Visual Thinking*. Berkeley and Los Angeles: University of California Press.

Black, M. 1962. *Models and Metaphors*. Ithaca: Cornell University Press.

———. 1977. "More about Metaphor." *Dialectica* 31:431–57.

Boorse, C. 1976. "Wright on Functions." *The Philosophical Review* 85:29–45.

Davidson, D. 1984. *Inquiries into Truth and Interpretation*. Oxford: Clarendon Press.

Douglas, M. 1966. *Purity and Danger*. London: Routledge & Kegan Paul.

Eisen, A. 1990. "Mendelssohn on the Commandments." *AJS Review* 15:239–67.

Finesinger, S. 1931. "The Shofar." *Hebrew Union College Annual* 9:212–26.

Geertz, C. 1973. *The Interpretation of Cultures*. New York: Basic Books.

Goodman, N. 1976. *Languages of Art*. Indianapolis: Hackett Publishing Company.

Gregory, R. L. 1973. *Eye and Brain*. New York: McGraw-Hill.

Halevi, Y. 1968. *The Kuzari.* Translated by H. Hirschfeld. New York: Schocken Books.

Heinemann, I. 1949. *Ta'amei ha-Mitzvot be-Sifrut Yisrael.* 2 vols. Jerusalem: The Jewish Agency.

Hirsch, S. R. 1957. *The Timeless Torah.* Edited by J. Breuer. New York: Feldheim.

————. 1962. *Horeb.* Translated by I. Grunfeld. 2 vols. London: Feldheim.

————. 1963. *Commentary on the Pentateuch.* Translated by I. Levy. 6 vols. London: I. Levy.

————. 1969. *The Nineteen Letters.* Translated by B. Drachman. New York: Feldheim.

Richards, I. A. 1936. *The Philosophy of Rhetoric.* Oxford: Oxford University Press.

Stern, J. 1987. "Modes of Reference in the Rituals of Judaism." *Religious Studies* 23:109–28.

Wittgenstein, L. 1968. *Philosophical Investigations.* Translated by G. E. M. Anscombe. New York: Macmillan.

CHAPTER 6

Jewish Ritual and the Experience of "Rootedness"

Joshua L. Golding

1

A good deal of recent philosophical literature on the nature and significance of ordinary (as opposed to mystical) religious experience focuses on the "presence of God" experience, that is, the type of experience in which it appears to an ordinary religious person that God is present in some way. One issue hotly debated is whether this sort of experience provides any rational support for the belief in God's existence. While this is certainly an important area of discussion, other aspects of religious experience also deserve philosophical reflection. Although I am not a sociologist of religion, it seems to me that quite a number of ordinary religious persons do not regularly have the "presence of God" experience, and so, if there is something regular in their religious experience that rationally supports their belief in God's existence, it must be something else. Moreover, religious life involves a lot more than the belief in God's existence, and there may be elements of religious experience that do not rationally support a belief in God's existence, but still play an important role in the religious life. To investigate the rationality of the religious life, we must philosophically attend to these other elements of religious experience as well.

One sort of experience that is not uncommon and that seems to play an important role in the religious life is what may be called the experience or the sense of "rootedness." I myself know a number

of religious people who report having this experience while participating in religious rituals, and it seems to function as a *reason* for
their continuing to observe those rituals. It also seems to play an
important role for some *ba'alei teshuvah*—those who were raised
in nonobservant homes and become observant. Many such people
"experiment" with a ritual, like putting on *tefillin* or making *kiddush* on Shabbat, and find that it gives them a sense of rootedness.
They then take this as a reason for continuing to observe that ritual
and perhaps even for observing other Jewish rituals as well. The
aim of this paper is to explore the experience of rootedness in the
context of Jewish ritual.

2

I have already claimed that it is not uncommon for religious persons to experience rootedness during their participation in religious rituals. What is this experience? In this section, I aim at a
rough characterization that is, admittedly, loose and metaphorical;
I attempt a more precise description in the next section. By the
term *religious ritual,* I mean any religious act that is *not* also a
moral or ethical act. In this sense, all *mitzvot* are Jewish rituals,
except for those that are matters of *mishpat* or *gemilut chasadim*
or *derekh eretz*. However, no claim in this chapter requires that
there be a sharp boundary between those religious acts that are
rituals and those that are not.

The best way to begin to describe the experience of rootedness
is by conjuring up a specific example from the realm of Judaism.
Consider a Jew who is sitting at the Passover *seder* during the
reading of the *Haggadah*. During the course of the evening, he may
find himself experiencing a certain sense of fit, appropriateness, or,
as I call it, rootedness. This experience is not merely an aesthetic
sense of balance or propriety, nor is it merely the sense of a certain
tastefulness or charming quality about the ritual. Rather, the experience of rootedness runs more deeply; it carries with it the sense
that there is something right or valid about one's being engaged or
involved in the ritual of the *seder,* the sense that somehow, in some
deep way, this is one's proper place, this is where one belongs. Thus
I call it the experience of rootedness—as in the expression "being
rooted in place."

The experience may be more or less intense at certain moments during the ritual. Or the experience may come and then disappear, lasting only for a short while. And it may happen that the person becomes self-reflectively aware of the experience only after it has happened, perhaps even after the ritual is over.

Of course, this experience does not necessarily occur for every religious Jew at every *seder,* much less every ritual. My claim is only that this experience is not an uncommon occurrence during religious ritual. And for some, this experience occurs not only during one ritual, but also during the performance of other rituals as well. For instance, it may occur while a person is praying or dipping in a *mikvah* or sitting in a *sukkah* or learning Torah or lighting candles on Shabbat or visiting the *Kotel.* Perhaps different people respond in this way to different rituals, and perhaps there are some rituals to which almost no one responds in this way.

A significant fact about the experience of rootedness is that it does *not* occur only in religious contexts. It can happen in non-religious contexts and to nonreligious persons as well. For example, a person may experience rootedness in the context of some interpersonal relationship; while in the presence of a loved one, one may have the experience or sense that this is where one belongs, this is one's proper place. Moreover, sometimes religious persons experience rootedness while performing religious acts (such as giving charity) that are *not* rituals in the sense I have defined above. Nevertheless, I submit that for many religious persons, rootedness is most strongly felt in religious contexts, particularly during participation in ritual.

I have used a number of terms to characterize the experience: *rootedness, fit, appropriateness, valid, right,* a sense that one *belongs,* or has *found one's place.* It may be objected that there is not one unitary experience here but rather a number of experiences that I have lumped together. In the next section, by showing how these dimensions revolve around a single point, I shall try to defend my claim that there is basically one experience here with several dimensions. But I will myself claim that, in any given case, one or more of these different dimensions may be more or less pronounced.

Also, I admit that even my very rough characterization of the experience is already laden with my own interpretation of it. I plead that there is no sharp distinction between description and interpretation. Now this in itself does not allow me to describe the experience in any terms I please. At this initial stage, the crucial question is whether, as I claim, many religious persons can honestly and sincerely subscribe to having this experience and would be willing to describe it in the same way as I have. There are then the questions of how to carry the interpretation of the experience further, what significance and implications it has, and whether it is rational to base any beliefs on that experience. These are issues I shall take up in the remaining sections.

3

In this section I aim at a more precise description of the experience of rootedness, by attempting to delineate its various dimensions. In doing so, I both commit myself to a more substantial position and open myself more to the criticism that I am misdescribing the experience in question, or perhaps even inventing an experience that nobody really ever has. My topic is the experience of rootedness as such, whether in the religious or nonreligious sphere, but my focus is on the religious case and, in particular, the case of Judaism. Again, my claim will be that many religious persons can honestly and sincerely subscribe to having this experience and would be willing to describe it in the same precise way as I shall. One preliminary remark is necessary. Although I shall describe various dimensions of the experience of rootedness, I make no claim that these dimensions are *sharply* distinguishable.

The Practical Context

The experience of rootedness generally occurs in the context of some physical activity, where the term *physical activity* is taken widely enough to include not only eating in a *sukkah* or shaking a *lulav*, but also uttering prayers, studying a text, sitting silently in meditation, or even just being in someone else's presence. We may refer to this physical activity as the "practical" context in which the experience of rootedness may occur.

The Conceptual Context

The experience of rootedness generally has some conceptual framework in which it occurs. That is to say there is generally some theme or themes—in the religious case, tenets or doctrines—

that in some way form the context in which the experience of rootedness occurs. Moreover, generally speaking, the person undergoing the experience has at least some understanding of those themes. Consider again the religious Jew participating in the *seder,* who finds himself experiencing rootedness. Here, the experience of rootedness occurs in the context of a cognitive apprehension of certain themes in the *seder,* such as the salvation and exodus from Egypt, the smiting of the first-born Egyptians, and so forth. These themes may be articulated in propositional form as tenets, for example, God took Israel from Egypt, God smote the Egyptians, God commanded Israel to eat matzah, and so on. Generally speaking, a person who experiences rootedness at the *seder* will have at least some intellectual grasp of some of these tenets.

It seems to me that the conceptual context plays a stronger role in the experience of rootedness in some cases than it does in others. Indeed, for some religious persons, the experience of rootedness may arise more through the apprehension of the themes in the conceptual context than through the performance of the religious deed itself, that is, the practical context. However, it seems generally true that both contexts are significant for the experience of rootedness. Having noted these two contexts of the experience of rootedness, we can now turn to a closer examination of the experience itself and its various aspects.

The Emotional Dimension

The experience of rootedness has an emotional dimension. In general, the experience carries with it a "positive" or desirable feeling or mood of some sort. Now it does not necessarily involve a "fun" or even joyous feeling. The experience of rootedness may occur concurrently with joy or solemnity, depending on the occasion. During a celebratory occasion such as the *seder,* joy is more likely, whereas during services on the Day of Judgment, Yom Kippur, solemnity is more likely. So, what then is the positive or desirable feeling associated with the experience of rootedness itself? Perhaps it is instructive here to reflect upon a rootedness experience from the nonreligious sphere. When a person experiences rootedness in the presence of a loved one, he feels a kind of serenity or calmness, a stillness within. The opposite emotion is that of root*less*ness, that is, a feeling of nervousness or anxiety. I suggest that in the religious case, too, the experience of rootedness carries with it a feeling of serenity or calmness.

The Normative Dimension

The experience of rootedness involves not merely an emotion or feeling of serenity, but also a normative or valuational dimension. What I mean by this is that, quite apart from what one feels at a subjective level, one has the sense that there is something objectively right or valid or about what one is doing. By "objectively right" I mean not morally right, but something akin to it. Perhaps I can best explain this by again resorting to a rootedness experience from the nonreligious sphere. When a person experiences rootedness in the presence of a loved one, he not only feels at a subjective level an emotion of serenity, but also senses that, in some objective way, there is "something right" about his being with that other person. This is not a matter of it being "morally right" to be there, but then again, this is not merely a positive or desirable feeling either.

The Existential Dimension

The experience of rootedness not only has an emotional and normative character, but also involves what may be called the "personal" or "existential" dimension. By the "existential" dimension of the experience I mean the aspect of the experience that has to do with one's very self or person, the core of one's being or existence. This is importantly related to the emotional and normative dimensions but is not identical with either. Let me explain.

In my earlier, informal description of the experience of rootedness I suggested that it involves the sense of having found where one belongs, or of having found one's place. Let us pursue this analogy a bit further. Suppose a person wanders from his home through the city until he is lost. After some time he finds his way back. Upon finding his home he can be said to have the experience of finding his place, finding where he belongs. Surely upon having this experience he may have an emotion or a feeling of serenity or calmness. This is the emotional dimension of the experience. Moreover, he may have the sense that, quite apart from this feeling, there is something objectively right or at least proper in his being at home, in what is, objectively speaking, his own place. This is, so to speak, the normative dimension of his experience. But the experience of finding his place is itself surely not *identical* with its emotional or normative aspects. It has an aspect that concerns the status of the person himself, namely, his being in his own place.

The same holds for the experience of rootedness during religious ritual. This experience involves more than an emotion or feeling of serenity. And it involves more than the sense that there is something objectively right or valid about what one is doing. The experience also concerns the status of one's very self or person, namely, that of being "in place"—not, of course, in a physical sense, but in an existential sense, having to do with one's very self or person, the core of one's being or existence. This is the existential dimension of the experience of rootedness.

Thus far, there is no view dictated here about the precise relations between the emotional, normative, and existential dimensions of the experience of rootedness. Nor have I claimed that the boundaries between these dimensions are hard and fast. In fact, at this stage I am willing to leave open the question of whether one dimension is, in its deep structure, derivative from the others. For example, some philosopher might claim that what I have called the "normative" dimension of the experience is really some complex sort of emotion or that it is reducible to some facet of the existential dimension. My claim here is that, at the prima facie level of description, these three dimensions are involved in the experience of rootedness.

Of course, one wants further account and explanation of the experience of rootedness. In particular, the existential dimension requires more illumination. What does it really mean to say that one has "found one's place" in an existential sense? But we have gone about as far as we can go in the attempt at precise description without getting into an interpretation or theoretical explanation of the experience. That is the business of the remaining sections.

4

For those who agree with what has been said so far, namely, that there is such a thing as the experience of rootedness as I have described it, and that it is not an uncommon occurrence among religious persons, the question arises as to how to interpret and explain this experience further. What does this experience really signify? What explains its occurrence? In this section I shall try to work out one way of interpreting and explaining this experience from a traditional Torah perspective. My aim in this section is to state this explanation in a intelligible way. It is not my aim in this section to consider whether or not this explanation is justifiable from an objective or external point of view, that is, from a point of view that is not already committed to a Torah perspective. I shall consider this critical question only in the next section.

I propose that from a Torah perspective, the experience of rootedness can be interpreted in light of the doctrine that, through the fulfillment of the rituals and *mitzvot* of the Torah, the Jew engages in his own "self-realization" or "completion" or *hashlamah*. This doctrine may be labeled the "doctrine of Jewish Teleology," and it requires some exposition and documentation from traditional sources.

First a brief exposition. The doctrine of Jewish Teleology says that man in general—and the Jew in particular—has a certain nature and that embedded in that nature is a certain potential for self-development. Moreover, the doctrine says that the actions which constitute this development are the *mitzvot* of the Torah. Accordingly, the fulfillment of the *mitzvot* is *fitting* or *suitable* to the nature of man and, in particular, to the Jew's nature. Now it is not causally predetermined that this development occur; it is not dictated by the constitution of the psyche or personality or by biology. Whether or not this development occurs depends partly on external circumstances, most importantly on the agency of God, of the individual himself, and of the community or society at large.

Now for some documentation. It is easy to find this doctrine in the writings of both Jewish philosophers and kabbalists. For example, in classical Jewish philosophy, we find the doctrine discussed by Saadiah Gaon[1] and Maimonides.[2] In a later period, the Maharal[3] and R. Moshe Chaim Luzzatto[4] discuss and develop the doctrine at length. It is also found in the *Zohar* and in writings of the Lurianic school.[5] Needless to say, these sources differ from one another on many issues, but they all affirm the doctrine of Jewish Teleology as I have defined it.

Is the doctrine of Jewish Teleology present in Scripture and in rabbinic literature? Certainly, the more general doctrine that man was created in order to serve his maker and that the people of

Israel, in particular, has been fashioned in order to carry out this mission, is a teaching that is found throughout Scripture and in rabbinic literature.[6] But this general doctrine does not itself imply that man has a "nature" and that keeping the Torah is fitting or suitable to man's nature. One might even be tempted to think that Jewish Teleology, as I have defined it, is not originally a Jewish teaching and that the philosophers and kabbalists mentioned above derived it by fusing the scriptural tradition together with a doctrine of classical Greek philosophy.

However, it can be argued that the doctrine is present, albeit if only implicitly, both in early rabbinic literature and in the Scriptures. To begin with, it is said in *Bereshit* that man is created in God's image, and, whatever this means, it implies that man has a certain nature and that it is similar to God's nature. Insofar as God's commands, the *mitzvot*, are expressions of God himself— "God's way"—it is implied that the *mitzvot* are fitting or suitable to man's nature. This "fittingness" of God's Torah to man is described in the opening chapters of *Mishlei*, several verses of which are summed up in *Mishnah Avot* (6.7):

> Great is Torah, for it gives life to those who fulfill it in this world and in the world to come, as it is said: "For they are life to those who find them, health to all their flesh." "It shall be health to your body, marrow to your bones." "It is a tree of life to those who take hold of it; happy are those who support it." "They shall be a graceful garland for your head, a necklace around your neck." "It shall place on your head a graceful garland; a crown of glory shall it bestow upon you."[7]

While the focus of this *mishnah* is the claim that keeping the Torah gives or enhances life, these same verses also imply that keeping the Torah befits man's nature.

A related doctrine found in rabbinic literature is the notion that the Torah is, so to speak, the "blueprint" of creation. The very first *midrash* in *Bereshit Rabbah* says that "the Holy One, Blessed Be He, looked into the Torah and created the world." Another *midrash* states that "the Torah was created before the world,"[8] and yet another states that "the Torah is the instrument through which the world was created."[9] These passages may plausibly be taken to mean that the creation is a *cosmos,* a structured order, whose pattern resembles that of the Torah. In some sense, then, the Torah is embedded into the structure of the world. If we combine this with another *midrash,* which expounds the notion that man is "a world in miniature," a "microcosmos,"[10] the result is that the Torah is embedded into the structure of man.

Yet another *mishnah* in *Avot* (3.18) states as follows:

> He [R. Akiva] used to say, Beloved is man, who was created in the image [of God]. . . . Beloved are Israel, who have been called children unto God. . . . Beloved are Israel, who have been given a precious instrument [i.e., the Torah] through which the world was created. . . . An additional act of love [unto Israel] is that it was made known to them that they had been given a precious instrument, as it says [Proverbs 4.2] "For I have given you a good thing to take, do not forsake my Torah."[11]

Here R. Akiva juxtaposes the notion that man was created in God's image, together with the notion that the Torah is the blueprint of creation and the notion that Israel plays a special role in the cosmic drama, since they are God's "children" and have been given the Torah, which is a "good thing to take." These are the essential elements in Jewish Teleology: man has a divine nature, Israel is especially divine, the Torah is the blueprint of creation, and the Torah befits the nature of Israel.

So much by way of documentation of the doctrine of Jewish Teleology. Before moving further, two points are necessary. First, it is important to distinguish two varieties of teleology, which differ over the role of rationality. The view we might label Aristotelian or *Rationalistic Teleology* holds that the actions that befit man's nature are rationally comprehensible. That is, one can rationally figure out both what man's nature is and what actions befit man's nature (although there may not be an algorithmic method to decide the right action in each case). On the other hand, *Nonrationalistic Teleology* affirms that while man has a nature and that certain actions befit man's nature, man's nature is *not* entirely rationally comprehensible, and one *cannot* always rationally figure out which actions befit man's nature. That is, what makes certain actions rather than others befitting to man's nature is not always rationally comprehensible. Now *Jewish Teleology* affirms that man—and in particular the Jew—has a nature and that the actions that befit that nature are prescribed by the Torah. As such, Jewish Teleology could be rationalistic or nonrationalistic. But the question of whether Jewish Teleology is best viewed as rationalistic or nonrationalistic goes beyond the bounds of this paper.

Secondly, it is crucial to note that although the doctrine of Jewish Teleology, as I have described it, is espoused by the Torah, it does *not* explicitly mention God or God's existence, nor does it entail it, at least not without further argument. One might try to argue that if any form of teleology is true, there must be an intelligent designer of nature. However, apparently Aristotle believed that at least his brand of teleology does not require that nature have an intelligent designer.[12] I myself am not sure this is a coherent position; perhaps it depends on what variety of teleology one holds. But if Aristotle was right about this, then it is conceivable that Jewish Teleology could be true even though God does not exist. That is, it is conceivable that performing the *mitzvot* constitutes the Jew's self-realization or completion even though God does not exist. Of course, if one believes this, one has to have some rather nontraditional way of looking at man's natural end, since if there is no intelligent designer such as a traditional God, then presumably there is no God to relate to, presumably no afterlife, and so forth. And it goes without saying that someone who believes this would have a radically unorthodox view of the Torah. In any case, my point here is simply that Jewish Teleology does not, without further argument, entail the existence of an intelligent designer of nature, or that God gave the Torah to Israel.

So much for explication and documentation of the doctrine of Jewish Teleology. It is easy to see how the experience of rootedness may be interpreted and explained in light of that doctrine. In the previous section I suggested that a main component of the experience of rootedness is that of "finding one's place" in an existential sense. It is worth dwelling on the metaphor of finding one's place. To find one's place is to find where one belongs, that is, where there is a matching or fitting between oneself and the place in question. A fish out of water, for example, is not "in place" because it is not suited naturally to live out of water. To find one's place then is to find where one is naturally suited to be. From the perspective of Jewish Teleology, the explanation for why a religious person may undergo this experience during participation in a ritual or *mitzvah* is simple: he is engaging in a bit of self-realization, completion, or *hashlamah* by performing the ritual, and he is also *aware* of this event or condition within himself. To find one's place existentially during a religious ritual is to find that the ritual suits one's nature or self. The normative and emotional dimensions of the experience of rootedness can also be explained on this basis. Since the person is aware of engaging in an activity that befits his nature, he has the sense that there is something objectively right about what he is doing. Also, because of the fit between one's nature and one's activity—between, so to speak, one's internal state and one's external environment—one feels a kind of calmness or serenity.

It is also worth dwelling on the metaphor of rootedness itself. To be rooted is to be grounded or located firmly in place. The root of a plant is what gives it life, what makes its existence possible. To develop roots is to develop one's basic life sources. For the root of a plant is in some sense its basic self. In undergoing the experience of rootedness, one has the experience not only of developing oneself, but also of disclosing oneself to oneself. Thus, during an experience of rootedness, one sometimes has that uncanny sense that "this is me," or "this is who I really am." From the perspective of Jewish Teleology, the explanation of this is straightforward. The Jew who experiences rootedness during religious ritual does so because the ritual befits his nature. In the process, he also becomes more deeply aware of his own nature and therefore has the sense that "this is me," "this is who I really am."

Incidentally, it is worth remarking that, according to Nonrationalistic Jewish Teleology, we can in some fashion explain why the Jew may experience rootedness even during those rituals or *mitzvot* that are not rationally understood by him or that are not even rationally comprehensible in principle (assuming, *pace* Maimonides, that there are such cases). For according to this version of the doctrine, all the *mitzvot* befit man's nature, even though there is no rational explanation for how every *mitzvah* does this. Thus, it is possible for a person to be aware that certain *mitzvot* or rituals befit his nature, even though there is no rational explanation for how they do so.

Before closing this section, I must mention one further subtlety in the present explanation of the experience of rootedness. The doctrine of Jewish Teleology says that *all mitzvot,* both ritual and nonritual, befit man's nature. Hence, given Jewish Teleology, one would expect the experience of rootedness to occur as often during the performance of ritual *mitzvot* as it occurs during the performance of nonritual *mitzvot*. But earlier, I myself made the empirical claim that although this experience occurs sometimes during the performance of nonritual *mitzvot*, it occurs most commonly during ritual rather than nonritual *mitzvot*. How can this be explained from the perspective of Jewish Teleology? One possible answer is that in fact the experience of rootedness does occur equally often in both cases, but it has a special character that makes it stand out in the case of ritual. The nonritual *mitzvot* (those falling into the realm of morality) befit the nature of man in general, whereas the ritual *mitzvot* befit the Jew in particular. Thus, if and when the Jew experiences rootedness during nonritual *mitzvot*, he does so in a rather general way. He may have the experience of "finding his place" during, say, giving charity, insofar as he is a human being. But when he experiences "finding his place" during, say, sitting in the *sukkah*, it is more intensely and uniquely *his* place in which he finds himself, since it is insofar as he is a Jew that sitting in the *sukkah* befits his nature. This would explain why it is during ritual rather than nonritual *mitzvot* that the Jew most strongly and most characteristically experiences rootedness.

5

In the previous section I suggested how the experience of rootedness during Jewish ritual can be interpreted and explained from a traditional Torah perspective, in light of Jewish Teleology. I did not consider whether this is the only, or the best, explanation of the experience. In this section I shall briefly address the following critical question: Does the experience of rootedness during Jewish ritual provide some *rational support* for belief in the doctrine of Jewish Teleology and for the belief that one ought to observe the rituals and *mitzvot* of the Torah? A full answer to this question goes well beyond the compass of this paper; I shall limit myself here to some brief remarks and a rather moderate conclusion.

Consider the following, rather hasty, sketch of an argument. The experience of rootedness is not an uncommon occurrence, and like any other event it requires an explanation. Now we have already seen how the experience of rootedness can be explained by postulating the doctrine of Jewish Teleology. Hence, the experience does indeed provide some rational support for believing the doctrine. Furthermore, Jewish Teleology says that, by performing the *mitzvot* and rituals, a Jew completes or realizes his nature. Thus, as a corollary, the experience of rootedness also provides some rational support for the belief that the Jew ought—in some not insubstantial sense of "ought"—to observe the rituals and *mitzvot* of the Torah.

As I said, this argument is hasty, and it faces several potential criticisms. I shall describe four separate criticisms.

1. Perhaps the experience of rootedness can be explained in other ways than by postulating Jewish Teleology. For example, it could be argued that the experience of rootedness during some religious ritual is psycho-generated by such religious beliefs as the beliefs that God exists, that God has commanded the ritual to be performed, and perhaps even the belief in the doctrine of Jewish Teleology itself. Thus, returning to a previous example, it may be claimed that the Jew experiences rootedness during the *seder* precisely because he believes (whether truly or falsely) that God exists, that the Torah is divinely given, and that by performing the *seder* he is fulfilling a divine purpose. Perhaps other such psycho-genetic accounts of the experience of rootedness are also possible.

2. Members of other religions also experience rootedness during their rituals, some of which are incompatible or at least at odds with Jewish ritual. Moreover, an argument parallel to the one sketched above would say that Christian experiences of rootedness support Christian Teleology, Muslim experiences of rootedness support Muslim Teleology, and so forth. Yet these seem to conflict with one another and with Jewish Teleology. Hence, none of these arguments should be given any weight at all; they are all equally inconclusive.

3. Some Jews do not experience rootedness at all during religious ritual. If Jewish Teleology is true, why don't they? Moreover, some Jews convert to other religions, and they seem to experience rootedness during non-Jewish rituals. How can this happen if Jewish Teleology is true? Moreover, even those Jews who do experience rootedness during Jewish ritual do not experience it during all rituals, only during some. If Jewish Teleology is true, why don't they?

4. Since most Jews experience rootedness only during some, not all, Jewish rituals, Jewish Teleology is not required in order to

explain the phenomenon in question. That is, one needs to explain why rootedness occurs for those rituals in which it does occur; there is no need to postulate that *all* Jewish rituals befit the Jew's nature. Postulating Jewish Teleology goes beyond what the evidence supports.

These criticisms are of varying merit. But clearly, the argument sketched at the outset of this section is too simplistic and needs revision. Instead of attempting to do that here, I shall close with a more moderate conclusion. A person who experiences rootedness during some Jewish ritual has at least *some* rational support for believing that *that particular* ritual befits *his* nature and, therefore, for believing that he ought (in some not insubstantial sense of "ought") to observe that ritual. Of course, rival alternative explanations of this experience are possible, but, unless some rival explanation is clearly and compellingly convincing, this would not detract from the present claim that the experience provides *some* rational support for this minimal belief. Moreover, the more often he experiences rootedness during that same ritual, the more rational support he has for the belief that that ritual befits his nature and that he ought to observe that ritual.

Many questions still remain, even if this modest conclusion is accepted. Does the experience of rootedness during Jewish ritual provide *any* rational support for belief in the *doctrines* that form the conceptual context for that ritual? (For example, does the experience of rootedness during the *seder* provide any rational support for believing that God took Israel from Egypt?) If the answer to this question is positive, does the experience of rootedness during *one* Jewish ritual provide any rational support for believing that other *thematically related* rituals also befit one's nature? (For example, does the experience of rootedness during the *seder* provide any rational support for believing that observing the ritual of *sukkah* also befits one's nature?) Does the experience of rootedness provide any rational support for the belief in the divine origin of the Torah or for belief in the existence of an intelligent designer, that is, God?

Finally, questions arise concerning the doctrine of Jewish Teleology. In what way are the *mitzvot* and rituals supposed to befit the nature of man and in particular the Jew? Which version makes more philosophical sense—Rationalistic or Nonrationalistic Teleology? Which version is more authentic to traditional Jewish sources? These are some of the questions to which we have been led by philosophical reflection on the experience of rootedness in the context of Jewish ritual.

NOTES

1. See *Emunot ve-Deot* 3, Exordium; 5.1; 6.4.
2. See *Moreh Nevukhim* 3.27.
3. See *Tiferet Israel* chaps. 1–13.
4. See *Derekh ha-Shem* 1.2–4.
5. See G. Scholem's summary of kabbalistic views in "Man and His Soul," in *Kabbalah* (New York: Dorset Press, 1963), pp. 152–65.
6. See the verse toward the end of *Kohelet* ". . . Fear God, and keep his commandments, for this is all of man." Tractate *Shabbat* 30a reports the following commentary on this passage: "R. Simon b. Azai (some say b. Zoma) said, "The entire world has not been created except in order to command man" (my translation). According to this, the very purpose of creation is to command man.
7. The translation is from *The Daily Prayer Book* by David Birnbaum (New York: Hebrew Publishing Company, 1977, p. 530). The verses are from *Mishlei* 4.22, 3.8, 3.18, 1.9, 4.9.
8. *Bereshit Rabbah* 1.4.
9. *Sifrei Devarim* chap. 48.
10. See *Tanchuma Pikudei* 3; *Avot de-Rabbi Natan* chap. 31.
11. The text that includes the phrase "through which the world was created" is a variant reading. The translation and insertions are mine.
12. See Aristotle, *Physics* 199b.

CHAPTER 7

The Concept of Worship in Judaism

Norbert M. Samuelson

DEFINITIONS

Hebrew Scriptures

The most appropriate Hebrew nouns corresponding to the English word *worship* are *avodah* and *tefilah*. The root of the first is *ayin, bet, daled*. In the simple active conjugation (*qal*) it means to work, labor, toil, till (soil), worship (a deity), and/or serve (a person). In the reflexive conjugation (*hitpael*) it means to be worked, be adapted, and/or be enslaved. Another noun constructed from the same root is *eved*. It can mean a slave, a servant, and/or a worshipper.

The noun *avodah* itself means work, labor, service, employment, worship, and/or liturgy. It is most commonly associated with the ritual in the Jerusalem Temple.[1] The English term that preserves the appropriate ambiguity of the noun as both liturgy and labor is *service*. A "worshipper" is someone who serves God. As such, we can distinguish two kinds of worship. In both cases, what the worshippers do is the same, namely, they serve their deity. The difference is whom or what they serve. One slaves either in the service of "the creator" or in the service of someone "strange/foreign." The former case, *avodat ha-boreh* (the service of the creator), is of ultimate positive value. The latter case, *avodah zarah* (strange service), is idolatry, and it is of ultimate negative value.

The root of *tefilah* (most commonly translated as "prayer") is *pe, lamed, lamed*. It appears in the Hebrew Scriptures in two conjugations. In its intensive active form (*piel*) it means to think, en-

245

treat, supplicate, plead, judge, decide, and/or punish. In its reflexive form (*hitpael*) it means to do by (to, for, and/or with) oneself whatever it means to do in the first conjugation. It is in the reflexive form that the verb most commonly is translated as "to pray."[2]

Most instances of prayer in the Hebrew Scriptures involve directing a petition to God. In almost every case the prayer is a supplication on behalf of the nation in which the actor is a political leader. The clearest examples involve the kings Hezekiah (2 Kings 19.15, 20; Isa. 37.15, 21; 2 Chron. 30.18; 32.20) and Manasseh (2 Chron. 33.13), the High Priest Ezra (Ezra 10.1), the governor Nehemiah (Neh. 1.4, 6; 2.4; 4.3), and the prophets Moses (Num. 11.2; 21.7), Samuel (1 Sam. 7.5; 8.6; 12.19, 23), Elisha (2 Kings 6.17, 18), Jeremiah (Jer. 42.2, 4), and Daniel (Dan. 9.4, 20). Less clear examples are the following: Abraham prays for a foreign king, namely, Abimelech (Gen. 20.7, 17), an unnamed "man of God" prays for King Jeroboam (1 Kings 13.6), Isaiah prays for King Hezekiah to recover from illness (2 Kings 20.2; Isa. 38.2), King Manasseh prays for himself as well as for his nation (2 Chron. 33.13), and King Hezekiah prays solely for himself (2 Chron. 32.24). Furthermore, both King David (2 Sam. 7.27; 1 Chron. 17.25) and King Solomon (1 Kings 8.28–30, 33, 35, 44, 48; 2 Chron. 6.19–21; 7.1) pray to give thanks for their "house." All of these cases still suggest that prayer may be restricted to petitions for matters of at least national significance. However, there are a number of instances where the object of supplication is less political; for example, Jonah prays to the Lord for his own safety (Jon. 2.2) as well as against Tarshish (Jon. 4.2), and the prophet Elisha prays for the health of a child (2 Kings 4.33). The instances of biblical prayer that, at least on the surface, seem to have the least to do with politics are the following: Hannah prays for a child (1 Sam. 1.10, 12, 26, 27; 2.1),[3] Jeremiah prays for guidance in a land purchase (Jer. 32.16), and Job is instructed to pray for the welfare of his "friends" (Job 42.8, 10).

In all of these examples God answers the petitions. However, there are a number of cases of prayer where God does not respond. The most numerous instances are those where Jeremiah refuses the request of the leaders to pray on behalf of the nation, because the petitioners are unworthy of divine favor (Jer. 7.16; 11.14; 14.11; 37.3). In this context two instructions about prayer are worth noting. First, the priest Eli says that no one can pray for someone who sins against the Lord (1 Sam. 2.25). Second, the *"chasid"* is instructed to pray to God "at a time when He can be found" (Ps. 32.6). Presumably there are times when even the prayers of the most righteous, irrespective of the significance of the petition, will not be answered.

English Usage

The English term *worship* is used as (1) a synonym for prayer and/or (2) a general term for a set of communal rites most commonly (but not exclusively) associated with organized religions and/or (3) a word for an attitude of extreme devotion to, love of, and/or veneration of something and/or someone who most commonly (but not exclusively) is identified as a deity. The critical terms here are *prayer, rites,* and *devotion.*

"Prayer" sometimes indicates a religious rite, but usually it is understood to be (1a) a request by a subject (singular or plural, i.e., by an individual or a community) of another who most commonly (but not exclusively) is identified as a deity and/or (1b) any form of direct relationship between a subject (singular or plural) and another, identified as a deity. That relationship most often (but not exclusively) is understood to be a form of communication between the relata.

A "rite" is a "ceremony." It is an act or a set of acts by an individual or a community that follows a prescribed set of rules by some communal authority. It often has, but often does not have, a religious connotation.

"Devotion" is the quality or state of someone who is devoted to someone or something. People are devoted to (3a) what they consecrate or (3b) what they "give themselves up to," that is, to what they are willing to give an excessive amount of their time and energy.

What all of these different uses of the term *worship,* in Hebrew and in English, share in common is that they always express a relationship between two otherwise distinguishable entities, that at least one of the relata (viz., the worshipper) is an actor, and that the form of behavior identified is to some extent "extreme." In one and only one understanding of worship must the other relatum (viz., the object of worship) also be an actor, namely, in the sense of worship as prayer, where "prayer" is understood to be a form of communication. In every other sense this may, but need not, be the case. The sense of worship as a rite always has a communal connotation, even when the actor/worshipper is an individual, since how that individual ought to act is determined by communal norms. In contrast, the sense of worship as devotion always has an individual connotation, even when the actor/worshipper is a community, since a community can give itself over to someone and/or something only if the individual members of that community are willing to behave in this way. The term that bridges the separation in meaning of worship as rite and as devotion is *prayer,* which always may or may not have, depending on context, the meanings associated with rite and devotion.

The worshipper in prayer is always a person or persons. However, whether or not prayer itself is a personal relation depends on the character/nature of the object of worship. Prayer will/can be personal only if its object is personal. Consequently, prayer to a deity will be a personal form of relationship, that is, a form of communication, if and only if the object of worship is a person.[4]

The term *worship* plays a critical role in determining what is or is not idolatry. We have already seen that, in specifically Jewish terms, if the object of a worshipper's worship is not the God of Israel and the form of behavior is extreme, then, depending on how extreme it is, the object of worship is a false deity and the worshipper is an idolator. In the case of prayer, worship is idolatrous when worshippers entreat of the object what ought only be entreated of the God of Israel. Similarly, a rite is idolatrous if it is a ritual that ought only be directed towards this same deity. In the case of devotion, the critical question is: How "extreme" does the "giving up of oneself" have to be before it becomes idolatrous?

A common answer to this question is tied to treating the object of worship as something of ultimate value, which means that the worshippers are willing to give more of their time and/or energy to this object than to the God of Israel, no matter who or what that object may be. (In this sense, unselfish, unrelenting devotion to family, people, and/or nation are all idolatrous.) It is of interest to note that in this context extremely unselfish behavior is morally less worthy than selfish behavior, since it is Israel's deity and only Israel's deity who qualifies morally for such excess. Consequently, worship has moral value. The critical issue in assessing that value is determining who and/or what is the object of the worship.

GOD[5]

To determine the nature of the object of worship is as critical in judging the utensil value of a form of worship as it is in reckoning its moral value. Worship is a relation between a worshipper and an object of worship. What forms of relation are and are not appropriate for a worshipper largely depend on who or what the intended deity is. Throughout the history of the religion of the Jewish people, a number of different understandings of who its deity is have emerged, not all of which are compatible. These different understandings of the nature of God entail a number of different determinations of modes of worship, not all of which may be compatible.[6]

The Deity of the Hebrew Scriptures

Deities in the Hebrew Scriptures are living things (*chayot*), whose existence is associated more with the element and/or spatial region of primordial fire than with other primordial elements/spaces such as earth and water. The only deity worthy of worship is an entity who makes (*oseh*) the universe through speech and breathes other spatial/material things either into or out of life. The universe is brought into existence to serve him, which, in general, involves preparing proper forms of sacrifices at the proper place, at proper times, and in the proper manner. In general, "the proper manner" is the context through which what we call "ethics" enters biblical Judaism. The deity of Israel, unlike most other deities, desires that his worshippers create a just society as much as he cares about the quality of the creatures sacrificed, and both kinds of concerns are treated qualitatively in the same way, namely, as determinations of the conditions under which sacrifices are or are not acceptable.

To worship this deity is to obey his commands. Hence, worship is ultimately and primarily a political/legal matter. There is no qualitative difference between sacrificing an unblemished bullock with a meal offering of fine flour (e.g., Num. 19.1–3) or fasting (e.g., Num. 19.7) or refraining from acts of murder, adultery, and theft (e.g., Exod. 20.13). These are all understood as acts of obedience to a deity whose will, expressed through acts of speech, is the sole reason for the existence of all creation. In other words, God, the creator, relates to his creations as a ruler relates to those whom he rules, namely, through law. To worship the Lord is to obey him. Whether or not obedience entails any other form of relationship (e.g., communication) is (at most) of secondary importance.

The Deity of Classical Jewish Philosophy

By the twelfth century C.E. (at the latest) there is a consensus among most educated Jews that statements about God in the Hebrew Scriptures cannot be understood in their most literal sense. How they are to be understood, however, remained problematic. While Maimonides' philosophical/theological judgments had an authority among subsequent generations of rabbinic thinkers equalled by no other rabbi, his radical version of negative theology was the single most unrepresentative expression of how classical Jewish philosophers interpreted biblical statements about God. Far more representative of a mainstream in Jewish theology was Gersonides' account of positive statements about God in terms of Aristotle's category of *pros hen* equivocation (*meshutefet im . . . beqodem veichur*). Attributes predicated of God and of anything else are related as their subjects are related. As God is the first cause in relationship to which everything else is an effect, so all attributes have a form of cause-effect relationship as those entities are predicated of their respective subjects.

There is, as Maimonides insisted, a radical separation, in both existence and thought, between God and everything else. The Bible's insistence that only God is the creator while everything else is a creature was interpreted by the Jewish Aristotelians as a distinction between a first mover and more remote movers and by Spinoza as a distinction between substance and modes. In both cases, the model most appropriate for expressing the extent to which this relationship is intelligible is that of the asymptote. A function that infinitely approaches but never realizes a limit is defined by its limit. Our universe is a world of flux, but that flux has direction. Its end is God. While God is infinitely distant in every respect from his creatures, he nonetheless stands in his static perfection as the end toward which all behavior, human and nonhuman, organic and inorganic, terrestrial and celestial, is directed.

For these philosophers, the prime example of creator-creature relationship was knowledge. For humans to know something is for them to know its intelligibility (*seder*), which is identical with its definitive form (*tzurah*), which is identical with its final end (*takh-lit*). As individuals are defined by their distinct degrees of success in approximating their species-ideal, so each species itself is intelligible in terms of its unique location/rank within a formal hierarchy defined by proximity to God. Hence, by knowing anything, the knower enters into relationship with God. All knowledge ultimately expresses relation to God.

The deity whom Jewish philosophy identified with Aristotle's Prime Mover or middle Plato's the One or later Plato's Demiurge was related to all human knowledge in describing the act, as well as the object, of knowledge. Objects of knowledge come into material existence when God informs them. Without form, matter is nothing, and the form that makes matter something comes from God. Similarly, it is this same deity who actualizes the mental forms that human beings call "concepts" (*muskalot*). The intelligibility of the universe is identical with the forms of everything in the universe. Those forms exist absolutely in God, materially in physical objects, and mentally in those who know those objects. While the forms differ in their mode of existence in these three ways, in themselves (*beatzmam*) they are a single thing (*davar echad*).

A specific form that exists absolutely, mentally, and materially is the same form in all three modes. In its absolute mode it is in the mind of God, or, to speak more accurately, is God, since a consequence of God's unity is that God and each of his attributes are a single thing. Hence, to the extent that all knowers know anything, they know God. Furthermore, it is God's unity with this form that both brings its material expression into existence and actualizes our concepts of it. Hence, the more we know about anything, the more we learn that there is no ultimate difference between God, the world, and our knowledge of God. What is ideally the same differs only in modal perspective. What God knows he knows in a single act, where the knower, the known, and the act of knowledge are a single thing. For us to know what God knows would be expressed as a single conjunction whose simple elements are infinite in number. It is this modification of the "infinite" that both separates us from and unites us with God. The single proposition that is God and, as such, is known only to God is, from the perspective of human knowledge, an asymptote that both directs and limits the multiplicity of all human intellectual endeavor.

To worship this deity is to seek to discover the order inherent in his universe. Hence, worship is ultimately and primarily a scientific pursuit. To discover the laws of chemistry is qualitatively no different than determining the laws of political science. Both intellectual discoveries ultimately express states of being in which the worshippers ever slowly climb an infinite ladder that brings them closer to their own unity with the deity, who is ultimately the only proper object of study. In other words, to worship God is to study him through his manifestation in the order of nature. Whether or not such study entails any other form of relation (e.g., performing public rituals) is (at most) of secondary importance. For example, scholars attended daily worship services in their communities because they knew it was the right thing to do. "Right" here is purposely ambiguous; it could mean "what is morally obligatory" or "what is politically expedient." In fact, for most Jewish Aristotelians, these two expressions are only different perspectives on what is a single value judgment.

The Deity of Modern Jewish Philosophy

While Maimonides' radical expression of negative theology is not representative of classical Jewish theology, it becomes normative in modern Jewish philosophy. From at least Hermann Cohen on, it is an understanding of Maimonides' account of God-talk that most characterizes the way that Jews are to relate to God. The God of Judaism is defined in Anselm's terms as "something no greater than which can be conceived." Whatever those words mean to Christian theologians, modern Jewish philosophy interprets them to mean that, by definition, whatever can be conceived is not God, and God is the only entity of whom this can be said.

For example, Rosenzweig asserts that the element world originates an infinite number of nothings, all of which strive to become something. The "something" (*Etwas*) at which they all aim is God. This striving (again, best modeled on the mathematical metaphor of the asymptote) defines both God and the world. The element world becomes the set of these endless nothings that never become the something toward which they are directed. Furthermore, God is defined by this vanity. In Kantian terms, insofar as what God is, is expressible in discursive language, its form of judgment is infinite. God is the negation of each of the unlimited number of members of the class of possible (past, present, and future) things. As they come to be, God becomes not them.[7]

As interpreted by Cohen's disciples, Emmanuel Levinas and Steven Schwarzschild, what can be expressed only paradoxically in discursive language appear as imperatives in the richer language of ethics. Reality in God is ideal. It is not actual. Everything that is, is not what ought to be. As such, everything that we see to be is known to not be what it ought to be. As such, the "is," is properly understood as a divine call to action. Jewish reason interprets the "This is" of Christian reason to mean "Seek God, not this."

The deity of modern Jewish philosophy is a moral ideal. To worship this God requires both study and obedience. The command is, "Do that which is not, not this that is." The content of the command—the specifics that fill in the place holders "that which" and "this that"—is provided by study. Here worship involves the emphasis on scriptural law as politics as well as the classical rabbinic emphasis on rational study. However, the biblical ideal of sanctified, static space becomes an asymptotic model of sanctified, dynamic time; similarly, the classical ideal of a sedate academy of scholars is replaced by the model of students who learn about reality through political action. The affirmation of whatever is, is idolatry; hence, Jewish theology is inherently revolutionary. To do good is to imitate God; to imitate God is to transform the nothing of what is into the ideal something of what ought to be. Whether or not the good is pursued in God's name is irrelevant. The proper worship of God is characterized, not by propositions, but by an uncompromising commitment to the ideal in social action.

Here thought of success is not merely of secondary importance; it is the essence of idolatry. To think that you may succeed entails that you think that what ought to be (the divine) can actually be in the domain of time and space (the is). Such thought in itself affirms the contrary of what God is. It is, to paraphrase Rosenzweig, the faith of the fanatic, whose efforts to speed the redemption of the world only delays it.

Divine worship takes place primarily within the social/political sphere; but it is action that must be pure. The worshippers give their lives up to it without thought of success—if anything, in expectation of failure—solely because they know it to be what is right. It is Jewish philosophy, not the worshipper, that affirms that this "right" is the God of our ancestors.

CONCLUSION: APPROPRIATE FORMS OF WORSHIP

Worship as Ritual

To worship the deity of the Hebrew Scriptures is to create a polity whose central act is sacrifice, whose primary rulers are priests, and whose most important institution is a temple. Without such a state there can be no adequate worship. Of course, this was the crisis brought about by each destruction of the Jewish theocracy. Between states, worship becomes primarily remembrance of a past in hope of a better future, that is, repetition of acts without a temple whose value is to keep alive the memory of the temple, so that proper service to the deity may be reestablished when the time comes.[8]

The mode of worship proper to such a deity with such an intent is most appropriately what Roman Catholics call "High Mass." Here the ideal involves individuals who are differentiated into clearly orchestrated roles (e.g., as congregants, choirs, singers [cantors], and readers [rabbis]), where everyone performs their prearranged and rehearsed parts with appropriate emotive enthusiasm, but without innovation, where readers read and singers sing "well" in "beautiful" sanctuary settings. It is worship best understood on analogy with grand theater, where the virtue expressed is associated more with aesthetics than with ethics.

When successful, all of the performers enhance their awareness that the deity whom they worship is the creator of the universe. In such worship the primary feeling shared by and transmitted to the participants is awe/fear/respect (*yireh*). However, what this mode of worship tends to lose (if not inhibit) is a sense that God also is the revealer, that is, that the deity who could speak the entire universe into existence can also address each of us. To have the sense of "being addressed" requires modes of worship less valued for their beauty than their intimacy, and more valued for their spontaneity than their orchestration.

Worship as Study

To worship the deity of classical Jewish philosophy is to enter a community whose saints live more like Albert Einsteins than Levi Yitzhaks of Berdichev. Its central act is study, its guiding spirits are scientists, and its most important institution is the academy. In general, the restrictions on free inquiry that inhibit open research in most Jewish-sponsored educational institutions have made the secular university a more appropriate setting for divine worship. However, such worshippers can be found in synagogues. Where they attend formal prayer services, they are likely to be more interested in sermons or "words of Torah" (*divrei torah*) than in reciting the ritual in the prayerbook; but more often than not they are more likely to be found in synagogue adult education classes. Here the ideal involves individuals, in isolated research, or in collaborative efforts, or in critical dialogue with colleagues or students, who bring all of their conceptual powers to bear on attempting to discover what is true. It is worship best understood as a valuative pursuit, where the values expressed are more 'scientific' than aesthetic.

In this case the primary feeling shared by and transmitted to the participants in worship is the joy of discovery. In this context the worshipper can sense God as revealer as well as creator. However, revelation here is what Rosenzweig discounted as "unspoken speech." The discoverer is not "addressed" in the sense that the theologically orthodox Rosenzweig understood revelation. Rather, the worshipper of the God of classical Jewish philosophy sees the world as a gift from a playful deity. The divine game is called "Mystery." The world becomes a divinely initiated "scavenger hunt" or "crossword puzzle," where no prize is sought other than the discovery of the solution itself. What this mode of worship tends to inhibit in the individual worshipper is a sense that God also is the redeemer. The discovery of the intelligibility and laws of nature as expressions of the will or mind of God promotes a feeling of satisfaction with what is, which, in turn, inhibits a feeling of rage that *this* is, is not what ought to be. Moral judgments dissolve into truth judgments. To sense having personal responsibility, that is, being commanded, requires modes of worship less valued for the use of intellect and more valued for the exercise of conscience.

Worship as Morality

To worship the deity of modern Jewish philosophy is to devote one's life to the seemingly unrealizable ideal of perfecting the world in the concrete. The central act in such worship is political activity, guided by pure moral ideals, on the battlefront of every social institution in which worshippers happen to find themselves, be they states, academies, synagogues, and even families.

The literature most expressive of this kind of Jewish worship is film. It applies to most of the work of the director Sidney Lumet. This world- and life-view also underlies the structure of Woody Allen's most positive statement about Judaism, *Crimes and Misdemeanors*. Two allegedly Jewish views of divine providence dominate the film. One is that of Judah, namely, that the world is moral, the good are rewarded, and the evil punished. The other is that of Cliff, namely, that the world is immoral, the good are punished, and the evil prosper. The story line itself suggests that both are wrong, namely, that at the descriptive level the world is amoral, that is, there is no correlation whatsoever (either direct or indirect) between morality and success.[9] However, that does not mean that morality is futile. On the contrary, morality is something that human beings create, project onto the universe, and, in so doing, create reality. The spokespeople for this view are the Jewish philosopher Professor Levy, Rabbi Ben, and Judah's father.

A sharp contrast is drawn between the amoral world of experience and the divine/human world of morality.[10] The former is a world without love and forgiveness, because these are both part of the God/man cocreation of the moral order.[11] Those who, because they lack both love and forgiveness, have never known either, think that the world of experience is reality.[12] However, those who have had the good fortune to be touched in their youth by moral persons have the strength and "vision" of character to know that the ideal is the real. Cliff thinks that movies are unreal because they reflect morality, but, throughout the film, events from the experienced world are paralleled by movies, that is, by human creations that project order onto the apparently haphazard events of human interaction.[13] The reward for virtue is more virtue, and the punishment for sin is more sin. Hence, the "misdemeanors" of borrowing money illegally and having an affair lead Judah to the "crime" of murder. In Judah's own words, at first he did "a foolish thing, senseless, vain, dumb," and his "one sin leads to a deeper sin." Feeling guilt, Judah tells Ben that "after two years of shameful deceit . . . I awakened as if from a dream." Ben tells him, "It's called wisdom. It comes to some suddenly. We realize the difference between what is real and deep and everlasting, versus the superficial payoff of the moment." Ben loses the ability to see "the superficial" but grows in his ability to see "what is real and deep and everlasting." Judah is blind to this moral reality. He sacrifices long-term gain for short-term advantage. Ben advises Judah to tell Miriam the truth about his affair in the hope that they could move together to a deeper life. Instead, Judah has Dolores murdered and, in so doing, preserves the static (deadly) superficiality of his marriage.

It is Rabbi Ben's form of worship that is most associated with ethics. When sincere, all who worship enhance their awareness that the deity whom they worship is the redeemer of the world. As such, it is what Judaism has professed as the highest form of prayer. In such worship the primary feeling shared by and transmitted to the participants is hope. In its purest form it is what Schwarzschild called "hopeless hope." It affirms that some day the messiah will come, and that day will be the end of days.

NOTES

1. The noun appears in Gen. 26.14; 29.27; 30.26. Exod. 1.14; 2.23; 5.9, 11; 6.6, 9; 12.25, 26; 13.5; 27.19; 30.16; 35.21, 24; 36.1, 3, 5; 38.21; 39.32, 40, 42. Lev. 23.7, 8, 21, 25, 35, 36. Num. 3.26, 31, 36; 4.4, 19, 23, 24, 26–28, 30–33, 35, 39, 43, 47, 49; 7.5, 7–9; 8.11, 19, 21, 22, 24–26; 16.9; 18.4, 6, 7, 21, 23, 31; 28.18, 25, 26; 29.1, 12, 35. Deut. 5.15; 13.7, 14; 15.15; 16.12; 24.18, 22; 26.6. Josh. 22.27. 1 Kings 12.4. Isa. 14.3; 28.21; 32.17. Ezek. 29.18; 44.14. Ps. 104.14, 23. Job 1.3; 34.25. Lam. 1.3. Ezra 8.20; 9.8–9. Neh. 3.5; 5.18; 9.17; 10.33, 38. 1 Chron. 4.21; 6.17, 33; 8.26; 9.13, 19, 28; 23.24, 28; 24.3, 19; 25.1, 6; 26.8, 30; 27.26; 28.13–15, 20–21, 32; 29.7. 2 Chron. 8.14; 10.4; 12.8; 23.2; 24.12; 29.35; 31.2, 16, 21; 34.13; 35.2, 10, 15, 16.

2. The verb appears in this form in Gen. 20.7, 17. Num. 11.2; 21.7. 1 Sam. 1.10, 12, 26, 27; 2.1, 25; 7.5; 8.6; 12.19, 23. 2 Sam. 7.27. 1 Kings 8.28–30, 33, 35, 44, 48; 13.6. 2 Kings 4.33; 6.17, 18; 19.15, 20; 20.2. Isa. 16.12; 37.15, 21; 38.2; 44.17; 45.14, 20. Jer. 7.16; 11.14; 14.11; 29.7, 12; 32.16; 37.3; 42.2, 4, 20. Jon. 2.2; 4.2. Ps. 5.3; 32.6; 72.15. Job 42.8, 10. Dan. 9.4, 20. Ezra 10.1. Neh. 1.4, 6; 2.4; 4.3. 1 Chron. 17.25. 2 Chron. 6.19–21, 24, 26, 32, 34, 38; 7.1, 14; 30.18; 32.20, 24; 33.13.

3. Since the child to be born turns out to be Samuel, it could be argued that this prayer also is political. However, within the context of the prayer itself, Hannah is a commoner praying for something that has no significance beyond her own family circle.

4.   Concerning what I mean by the term "person," see Samuelson 1972.

5.   What follows in this section of the paper is generalization—first from the data of the Hebrew Scriptures, second from the standard corpus of texts in medieval Jewish philosophy (from Saadiah through Albo), and third from the corpus of texts in that tradition of modern Jewish philosophy that develops from Spinoza and Mendelssohn through Kant and Hegel to Cohen, Buber, Rosenzweig, and Levinas. I do not intend in this paper either to justify the legitimacy of generalization or to explain the methodology employed in forming my generalizations. However, a brief word, at least, is called for on the kind of thought or analysis that lies behind the statements in this section. The model for generalization used here is more akin to the formation of laws in the physical sciences than it is to the inference of general conclusions in the social sciences. When I say that one of the three text collections mentioned above says P, I am not claiming that every document D in the collection, C, either explicitly says P or that every scholar agrees that it says P. Rather, I am claiming that what P expresses captures the primary direction in C, a direction from which all exceptions are to be understood as deviations. I have no doubt that many scholars will point to some D in some C that calls P into question. In some of these cases I would argue that the scholar has misinterpreted D, but I expect that there are in fact many instances of D that do in fact falsify P. These proposed falsification instances in isolation may in fact be falsifications of the generalization or they may only be exceptions (i.e., deviations). I would be interested in hearing such cases (I can think of many candidates); I would want to deal with each of them individually, in terms of their place within the overall corpus of texts in C. What I am trying to do in this section of the paper is to walk a fine line between being unable to "see the forest for the trees," that is, focusing so exclusively on single texts that they cease to be relevant to anything other than themselves, and being unable to "see the trees for the forest," that is, forming generalizations that are so innocuous that, while they are not falsified by any relevant data, they say nothing substantive whatsoever. Again, I do not intend here to justify the enterprise, and, given its validity, I hope that scholars who know the collections in question will agree with my judgments.

6.   There are at least two senses in which the modes of worship described below may not be compatible. The first has to do with time. Given that to worship is to act in a particular way that is judged to be more valuable than to act in any other way, to participate in the performance of rituals and to study and to be engaged in political causes impose mutually exclusive demands. The demands of the finite amount of time available to human beings requires that priorities must be assigned to

participation, and these priorities are determined by which modes of worship are most expressive of the demands that arise in the relationship between God and the worshippers. The second has to do with the God worshipped. I have argued elsewhere (in Samuelson 1972) that the deity of the Hebrew Scriptures cannot be the deity of the classical Jewish philosophers. The question remains open whether or not the God of classical Jewish philosophy is the deity of modern Jewish philosophy. I discussed this question in a paper at the Academy for Jewish Philosophy's 1987 meeting on idolatry. In brief, the issue turns on whether or not the conception of divine attributes in Gersonides' case and/or the Cohen-Diesendruck interpretation of Maimonides' position is correct. If it is, then classical and modern Jewish theology are compatible. If it is not, then these two traditions are incompatible, since medieval theology would entail that, in some significant sense, being is good.

    7.   E.g., Rosenzweig 1985, pp. 27–28.

    8.   It is somewhat ironic that the form of modern Judaism that had the greatest intellectual opposition to understanding the communal Jewish prayer service in terms of the biblical sacrificial cult developed what in practise is the most "priestly" form of Jewish worship.

    9.   It is not at all clear that Lester is as shallow as Cliff believes him to be. Near the end of the film we see signs that he is more generous, and less self-serving, than we had formerly thought. (For example, he pays for Ben's daughter's wedding.) Furthermore, there is no reason to believe that Holly is a fool to choose to marry Lester. She tells Cliff that Lester is "not what you think. . . He is warm, caring, romantic," and she implores Cliff to give her "a little credit" for good judgment. The point is not that the good are rewarded. Rather, the point is that to believe that the wicked are rewarded is equally foolish. There is no logical correlation between happiness in the phenomenal world and morality in the ideal world.

    10.   Even Jack Rosenthal has a moral code. For example, he tells his brother, "You've staked me many times; I don't forget my obligations." Only Judah seems unwilling to risk his success and happiness for moral duty. He believes both that the world has no value and "without God the world is a cesspool," i.e., his world is a cesspool that he himself creates. Similarly, Professor Levy states that the world is a cold place and that under certain conditions you cannot stand it anymore. Surviving coldness depends on the love experienced as a child. Levy, the concentration camp survivor, lacks this experience, and, consequently, jumps out of a window. What matters is the human-created experience of love, not philosophy. Any metaphysical system is incomplete. What it lacks is the experience of love. In Levy's words, "We define ourselves by the choices we have made. . . It is only we with our capacity to love who give meaning to the indifferent universe. Yet . . . we go on in hope that future generations will

understand more." Levy's death is due to bad fortune, viz., he was born into the world of the Holocaust. In contrast, Judah has no excuse; he had a loving father, from whom he inherited a "spark" of morality. But he squandered his inheritance. He tells Cliff, "In reality, we rationalize, we deny; or we couldn't go on living." He declares that this is reality in contrast to fiction. (Lester also associates lack of standards [this time in making movies] with being realistic.) However, from Ben's example we learn, in Levy's words, that this reality is merely the reality that Judah's "choices" define.

11. Ben says, "If there is true love, there is forgiveness. I couldn't go on living if there isn't a moral structure . . . [or] forgiveness." It is the search for love that leads Cliff's sister, Barbara, to allow herself to be abused by men. She says that she is so alone because "I don't have anyone to love." Cliff also, even though he is married, has no one to love. Cliff thinks his failure is that he lacks Lester's success, when his real failure is his pursuit of love (with his wife Wendy and with Holly). In this sense he has no more moral vision than Judah.

12. The "real" is constantly invoked to justify immoral decisions. Judah thinks that Jack lives "in the real world" and Ben "in the kingdom of heaven." Until the end, Judah resides between the two. He must decide where he is going to live, and when he agrees to have Dolores killed, he opts for Jack's reality. In Judah's words to Cliff in the film's penultimate scene (when Judah tells Cliff what he did as if it were a movie plot), this is the "tragedy" in Allen's "fiction." Cliff (speaking more like Allen the director than his assumed film persona) suggests that the hero of this story should assume moral responsibility for what he did and, in so doing, become like God, viz., the source of moral order. Judah dismisses this courageous suggestion contemptuously as "fantasy."

13. Cliff's four-month wait for Holly to return from London is compared to Edward G. Robinson's imprisonment in *The Last Gangster*, and Cliff's marriage to Wendy is compared to the marital relation of Robert Cummings and Constance Bennett in *Happy Go Lucky*. Similarly, Detective O'Donnell's investigation of the murder of Dolores is coupled with Betty Hutton singing "He says murder he says, . . . [and it is] nobody's murder but his own," i.e., by murdering Dolores, Judah murders his own chance for a "real" life, i.e., a life of depth and quality.

REFERENCES

Rosenzweig, F. 1985. *The Star of Redemption*. Translated by W. W. Hallo. Notre Dame: University of Notre Dame Press.

Samuelson, N. 1972. "That the God of the Philosophers is not the God of Abraham, Isaac and Jacob." *Harvard Theological Review* 65:1–27.

CONTRIBUTORS

Joshua L. Golding is Assistant Professor of Philosophy at Bellarmine College. His publications include "Toward a Pragmatic Conception of Religious Faith" (*Faith and Philosophy*, 1990) and "On the Rationality of Being Religious" (*Logos*, 1992). His current interests are in philosophy of religion, epistemology, and ancient philosophy.

L. E. Goodman is Professor of Philosophy at the University of Hawaii. A specialist in medieval Islamic and Jewish philosophy, he has published studies of most of the major Muslim philosophers as well as of such Jewish thinkers as Maimonides and Saadiah. Among his recent books are a translation with philosophic commentary of Saadiah Gaon's *Book of Theodicy* (1988) and a philosophic study, *On Justice* (1991).

Menachem Kellner is the Sir Isaac and Lady Edith Wolfson Professor of Jewish Thought at the University of Haifa. The author of many articles in Jewish philosophy, his most recent books are *Dogma in Medieval Jewish Thought* (1986), *Maimonides on Human Perfection* (1991), and *Maimonides on Judaism and the Jewish People* (1991). He is currently preparing a critical edition, with a translation and an interpretive essay, of Gersonides' *Commentary on Song of Songs*.

Ze'ev Levy is Professor Emeritus of Jewish Thought at the University of Haifa. He is the author of numerous articles and of eight books, among which are *Between Yafeth and Shem: On the Relationship between Jewish and General Philosophy* (1982) and *Baruch or Benedict: On Some Jewish Aspects of Spinoza's Philosophy* (1989).

David Novak is the Edgar M. Bronfman Professor of Modern Judaic Studies at the University of Virginia. He has written numerous articles in Jewish philosophy and theology and is the author of seven books, among which are *The Image of the Non-Jew in Judaism* (1983), *Jewish-Christian Dialogue: A Jewish Justification* (1989), and *Jewish Social Ethics* (1992).

Norbert M. Samuelson is Professor of Religion at Temple University. The author of many articles in Jewish philosophy, both medieval and modern, among his recent books are a translation and commentary of Abraham ibn Daud's *The Exalted Faith* (1986) and *The First Seven Days: A Philosophical Commentary on the Creation of Genesis* (1992).

263

Moshe Sokol is Associate Professor and Chair of the Department of Philosophy at Touro College. His articles have appeared in *Religious Studies, AJS Review, Modern Judaism, Jewish Law Annual,* and in other scholarly publications. He has recently edited a volume of essays, *Rabbinic Authority and Personal Autonomy* (1992).

INDEX